Islamic Women : Then and Now

Islamic Women : Then and Now

M.Z. Ansari

Prashant Publishing House
DELHI - 110094 (INDIA)

PRASHANT PUBLISHING HOUSE
C-34, 28 Foota Road, Gali No. 3
West Karawal Nagar, Delhi-110094
Phone : 9810396373, 22963970

Islamic Women : Then and Now

First Published : 2008

ISBN : 978-81-906344-4-1

PRINTED IN INDIA

Published by Mr. R. K. Jha M/s. Prashant Publishing House, Delhi and Printed at H.S. Offset Press, Delhi.

PREFACE

The development of mechanization and the ever-increasing growth in production at a rate greater than the level of the actual needs of people, the necessity of persuading consumers through thousands of deceptions and frauds, the urgency with which all auditory usual, psychological, sensory, aesthetic, artistic and venal means to transform man into an involuntary agent of consumption, further required that the capitalist should take advantage of woman's existence; not of woman's physical strength or her work power as a simple worker sharing with man in production, but rather of her power to attract with her beauty, by trading in her honour and respect, through her power to entice, to captivate minds and wills and to transform them, to impose consumption on consumers. It is clear that all this was done in the name of her 'liberty' and her becoming 'equal' with man.

Politics also did not lag behind in making use of this factor; one can read the circumstances of this regularly in newspapers and magazines. In all these things, the existence of woman is exploited and woman is used as a means for accomplishing the aims of man: and all this under the cover of 'liberty' and 'equality'.

—Author

Contents

1

HISTORY AND CULTURE

First of all, prior to studying about the status of women in Islamic society and before dealing with the position of women under Islam, it would be well to examine how the question of women's rights and their claim for complete equality with men came to the forefront in modern times and what the underlying causes were which added strength to women's claim for freedom and equality. Such an analysis is called for in order to ascertain how far women's movement in modern history flourished out of a scientific and rational understanding of their powers, faculties and social functions and how far it represented merely a blind revolt against tradition, custom and artificial social restrictions and was prompted by desires untinged with altruism. It is necessary to make a dispassionate search for rational as well as non-rational factors in the modern women's movement, because otherwise our conclusions are likely to reflect the partisan spirit of one or the other side in the bitter controversy that has raged over women's demands.

An American writer, Mary R. Beard, sums up three divergent viewpoints on the subject of women's place in society in her book, *Woman as Force in History*. She says:

> *One is the view that 'the women's problem,' a definition inspecting woman's place in society satisfactory to herself, can only be solved by complete equality with men, and that this equality can only be established under Communism. A second view is that woman must find her greatest happiness and contribute most to the state by limiting her ambitions to domesticity and still more narrowly to child-bearing, in order that the population*

rate may be high enough to keep a given nation secure against crowded societies on its borders, and strong enough within for aggressive action when desired against neighbours or more distant communities; this is the ideology of Fascism. The third view is that woman must have the right to choose her way of life even to the point of self centered interests; this is one among the ideologies of democracy.

Let us now see the actual historical circumstances which gave birth to these three viewpoints on the subject of women's place in society. We shall first deal with the democratic viewpoint which is historically prior to the ideology of fascism and communism.

The eighteenth century was a period of great social and intellectual unrest in Europe. The rising intelligentsia, and the middle classes of Western countries found themselves encumbered with a host of social barriers, economic restrictions and intellectual fetters which were blocking the path of progress in every direction. They were legacies of an age of feudalism which was already past. The feudal landlords, the Catholic Church with its vast power over men's bodies and souls and the Pope, headed the Church organisation, had a vested interest in perpetuating age-old customs and artificial social restrictions which the new spirit was seeking to break through. In these circumstances, it was not unnatural that, for the rising bourgeoisie of European countries, freedom and liberty should acquire a sanctity out of all proportion to their importance in the total scheme of human values. Thus, in the eighteenth and nineteenth-century Europe, liberty and freedom became exclusive sovereign values.

The importance of all other ideals was lost sight of and the complementary values of order, discipline and responsibility, without which there could be no real liberty, were ignored and brushed aside as of no moment in the lives of-nations. History bears witness to the fact that when some powerful idea takes root in a civilisation, it permeates every sphere of human life and activity. The same thing happened with the notion of liberty which, extending from the domain of politics, invaded the social sphere and expressed itself in a demand for the readjustment of sex relations. Powerful voices were raised on behalf of the rights of the female sex which had long suffered from innumerable legal and social disabilities. Freedom and equality of, the sexes became accepted principles with the new social reformers.

In France, which was the centre of all revolutionary ideas, the Romantic school of literature and poetry first made an organised drive to popularise the ideal of sex equality. George Sand, who headed this school, was a woman of loose sexual morality. She proved unfaithful to her husband Who was driven to separation. Thereafter she led the life of a libertine forming promiscuous sexual relations with a number of men, among whom was Alfred Musse, a French poet of some renown. In her novels, *Lelia and Jacques*, she severely criticised the institution of marriage and advocated free love. George Sand was followed by another group of poets, novelists and dramatists among whom Alexander Dumas and Alfred Naquet stand out as the most prominent.

These writers laid emphasis on the natural birthright of men and women to indulge in free sexual relations without the encumbrances of marriage. Mention must also be made of Mary Wollstencraft who wrote her book, *A Vindication of the Rights of Women*, in 1702. She reflected a more rational outlook which was coloured more, by the altruistic desire to serve the cause of women than open the floodgates of license. In this pioneer work she protested against the unjust and unequal treatment of women and condemned the whole system of law and custom that governed the relations of men and women. Her influence on the-women's movement in France was deep and widespread. These tendencies were reinforced by the Neo-Malthusian movement in England and France which sought to limit the growth of population by popularising the use of contraceptives.

The Industrial Revolution in England, by throwing upon the crowded cities a vast army of peasants and rural craftsmen, unable to support their families, further accentuated this process and brought women into the economic field for the first time in history. The radicals and philanthropists of the 'fifties and 'sixties like Robert Owen, Ruskin, Bentham, and John Stuart Mill gave further impetus to the women's movement. In 1861 Mill wrote his famous book *Subjection of Women* in which he argued, with great precision and logic that the subjection of women was the product of age-long custom and did not testify to any inherent inferiority in the female sex.

Mill contended that the distinctions between men and women which went to show the inferiority of women in the domains of mental and intellectual productions; were not natural but artificial, that is, a product of subjecting environment. The education and external circumstances in which women were being brought up were, according to him, responsible for their seeming inferiority; all other talk of her innate inferiority, he pointed out, was logical perversion and psychological misunderstanding. Under the stress of these social changes and intellectual movements, family ties loosened and domesticity lost its importance for women who were forced into the economic field by circumstances beyond their control. The ideal of sex equality came nearer, fulfilment than ever, though in ways which boded ill for the happiness, of individuals and the moral health of the community. In the Great War of 1914, a vast majority of the male population in European countries had to join the war services and many of non-military occupations, hitherto regarded as the closed preserve of the male sex, were thrown open to women who became more and more convinced of their ability to compete, with men on equal terms in all fields of life.

In 1941 when America entered the Second World War, millions of American women were taken into the armed forces, placed in uniform, disciplined by officers of their own sex working under naval and military authorities, accorded official ranking and honoured with decorations for bravery under fire; to relieve men for fighting, thousands of uniformed women worked as secretaries, clerks and officials. With skill and courage, women served as doctors and nurses in the battle areas and in war hospitals at home; and many were killed at the fronts while working near or under fire. In all the drives to raise money in aid of the armed services, American women assumed leadership and served in the ranks. They laboured to uphold the morale of the services at home and abroad. They toured the war areas and fronts as entertainers of the men under arms. They entered the war-production plants by millions and made possible the output of munitions and other war supplies on a scale that astounded the whole industrial world.

At the end of the war, American men and women alike in general hoped for a return to civilian life, and this meant a heated debate over public policies to be adopted with regard to 'equality of rights' in the distribution of employments, in the competition for places and rewards in economy and society. The old debate over women's place in society was reopened with added intensity. When in 1944 the War Department of United States issued its booklets for the education of soldiers at round table forums, it included one manual to invite a pointed argument: 'Do you want your wife to work after the war?' In this discussion one side argued that times have changed, that it is good and fitting for women to work that they are competent in any kind of job, hanker after economic independence, and are likely to hang on to a cash nexus for dear life. On the other side were those who argued that woman's place is in the home that her function is child-bearing and rearing and that men will not stand her competition with returned veterans.

So far we have examined the circumstances in which the democratic ideal of equality of sexes arose and gathered strength. Now let us turn to the Communist ideal. The leader of Communism in Russia, V.I. Lenin was ably supported and encouraged throughout his period of struggle by his wife, Krupskaya. When Lenin climbed to power in Russia, Krupskaya who had been a zealous champion of sex equality, helped to drive home, the issue of women's rights as one of the basic issues of the, revolution.

Lenin and his wife both knew very well that the Communist movement could have little prospect of success without the active support of women. And to win their full support, recognition of their right to full participation in the Communist regime was immediately given. In a speech delivered in September 1919 at the Fourth Moscow City Conference, Lenin declared: 'The Soviet Government has applied democracy to a greater extent than any other country, by the fact that in its laws not the slightest hint for any inferiority of women is left. I repeat, not a single state and no democratic legislation has done even half of what the Soviet Government did for women in the very first months of its existence.' In a conversation with Klara Zelkin, a prominent German socialist, Lenin elaborated the doctrine that 'real freedom for women is possible only through Communism.' Women must appreciate this and throw their energy into the Bolshevik Revolution,' he insisted.

'The Communist women's movement must itself be a mass movement, a part of the general mass movement. There can be no real mass movement without women. Unless millions of women are with us we cannot exercise the proletarian dictatorship, cannot construct on Communist lines. We must find out our way to them, we must study and try to find that way.' In Krupskaya's introduction to a Pamphlet by Lenin on Women and Society, the double power of women's revolutionary agitation and the Communist theory of its underlying importance were brought out. Krupskaya wrote, 'Ever since the beginning, of the Soviet rule, equal rights for women have been an object of interest, not only for women but for men as well.'

As a result of these ideas, which impressed themselves on youthful minds, Russian women in great numbers agitated and organised at home and abroad for the realisation of their objects. They secured positions in Russia with the secret police and both judged and punished opponents of the Communist Party. After German troops invaded Russia, women who were not members of the Communist Party rushed like members of the party to defend their country. The Russian women, Communists as well as non-Communists, engaged in all phases of armed combat with the foe.

Like the Russian Soviet Revolution, the Fascist Revolution in Italy, Germany and Spain was also confronted with the necessity of winning women's support and their active cooperation in the struggle for Fascist ascendancy. The Fascist attitude to women was explained by Professor Maria Castellani in a volume on Italian Women, *Past and Present,* in which she said, 'Fascism recognises women as a part of the life-force of the country, laying down a division of duties between the two sexes, without putting obstacles in the way of those women who by their intellectual gifts can reach the highest positions.' Adolf Hitler, leader of the German Nazis, formulated the attitude of his movement towards women in a speech at Nuremburg on 15 September 1934, when he said, 'Woman has her battlefield. With each child that she brings to the nations, she fights her fights for the nation.' Such women as Sophic Rogge-Boemer, who called for the military training of women, were suppressed by Hitler and Goebbels in favour of women who devoted their strength and interest to child-bearing. Young women in large numbers responded enthusiastically to indoctrination on this point and entered the numerous maternity homes founded by the Nazis.

We have seen how the Democratic, Communist and Fascist viewpoints about the rights of women and their place in society were in part moulded by certain historical conditions and in part by political expediency designed to secure a larger following by enlisting the support of women. As far as the democratic viewpoint is concerned, it was free from the taint of political expediency but there was present in it from the very beginning a negative urge to sweep away age-long restrictions. Democracy failed, as in other fields, to develop a positive doctrine of women's rights and duties and continued itself to the removal of old abuses.

In contrast with the above-mentioned attitudes towards the problem of sex relations, Islamic teachings in regard to the position of women can be traced to neither of the sources. There was no political necessity for the Prophet of Islam to gain the favour of the fair sex, because the social conditions of Arabia were such that women's influence on the larger affairs of life was bound to be negligible. Nor was the Prophet of Islam confronted by the necessity of enlisting women for fighting a national war of defence or aggression against foreign countries. Therefore unlike Hitler and Mussolini, he had no motive to define women's rights and duties with an eye on the requirements of military defence or aggression.

Again, in contrast to democracy, which was the outcome of a negative urge, to sweep away old restrictions that blocked the way to progress, Islam was more concerned with bringing some sort of discipline to a race of wild, freedom-loving Arabs who knew no respect for law and order and obeyed no central authority. The problem, therefore, for Islam was not so much the loosening of artificial bonds, as creating law, order and discipline among a people steeped in license and unacquainted with healthy social or moral restrictions. For all these reasons, Islam treated the question of sex equality and women's rights on its own merits and defined its attitude to sex relations on the basis of human nature rightly interpreted. Islamic teachings on this subject, therefore, spring from the ultimate facts of human nature in its social context. Military necessity, political expediency or merely blind revolt against the past did not in any way affect Islam's solution of the sex problem.

The question of the relationship between man and woman and their respective rights and duties is really a part of the larger socio-economic problem of man. Its solution depends on the way in which this larger problem is dealt with by a civilisation. It is wrong, therefore, to study the question of woman's rights and her place in society in isolation from the total context of human relationships in all their aspects. Before we pass any judgment on the particular way in which a civilisation deals with the sex problem, we should consider its total approach to human existence, so as, to, enable us to view its specific solution in their larger and total setting. But for this, we shall have to define the basic attitude of a civilisation towards life in general. In the next chapter, therefore, we shall attempt to define the basic approach of Islam towards human existence, in contrast with that of the Western civilisation, because this approach has decisive bearing on the way in which Islam grappled with the problem of sex equality and the rights of women.

Because of the pressure of many forces every country of the Moslem East, as we have seen, shows some trend of change in the relationship between religion and life. The control of Islam as an iron clad system of rules and traditions is giving way to a more individual interpretation of religion. Since this new spirit of religious liberalism deeply affects the life of women, one constantly feels the desire to know the personal attitude of Moslem women toward their religion, and their share in determining the new religious thought in Islam.

The older generation as a whole in every country tends to be conservative in all religions but this is especially true of Islam. This unquestioning adherence to the literal interpretation of the teaching of their religion is especially characteristic of women in the middle and lower levels of society, regardless of age, and also of the village women of Asia. This great majority of Moslem women, who have remained untouched by Western influence, have been little conscious of any changes in Islam, and have themselves undergone no change in their religious outlook. In fact, they constitute very often a distinct deterrent to change, opposing any deviation from established social customs, which are in their minds identified with religious sanctions. It is very often the orthodox wife or mother who maintains the rigid conservatism of the home, however lax men may become in their observance of religious customs outside the home.

The full meaning of Islam for the devoted Moslem woman is difficult for a mere outsider to understand. This is one veil of Moslem life which the Western observer cannot lift. Accustomed to a different form of religious experience, one from the West may easily draw a false conclusion regarding the relationship of Moslem women to their religion. The small number of women in the mosques in most countries — Turkey is an exception-which offers a striking contrast to the usual predominance of women in churches in the West, might be interpreted as a lack of worship of Moslem women, if one did not know that it is not the public prayers in the mosque but her private prayers at home which have primary significance for the Moslem woman. In her home the orthodox woman will pray, with her face turned towards Mecca, five times daily in the name of the Prophet to the one God, and will cherish the devout hope as a constant follower of Muhammad, that she may make the pilgrimage to the Holy City.

The keynote of the Moslem woman's religion is complete acquiescence to fate; to protest against a lack of privileges is quite foreign to her nature. Islam may have deprived her of privileges but not of responsibilities. Her primary obligation is to accept as the will of Allah, whatever is written on her forehead as her fate. This spirit of fatalism has insured the undisturbed control of Islam over the destiny of Moslem women through the centuries. Today, although the great majority of Moslem women have remained unchanged in their personal attitude toward their religion, a small minority of women has begun to question the relationship between the accepted teaching of Islam and the demands of their modern world. Education inevitably is undermining the characteristic attitude of fatalism toward religion and life. One begins to find in the different parts of the Islamic world Moslem women expressing an independent opinion of the interpretation of Islam, in order to bring religion into accord with modern needs.

Speaking on purdah in a public address, Lady Abdul Qadir, one of the outstanding Moslem leaders of India, said: "Purdah, as observed among certain classes of Indian Mohammedans, is far beyond anything enjoined by Islam and requires modification according to the needs of the day and the rapidly changing times." Another interesting illustration of the modern approach to Islam by a Moslem woman in India is the aggressive challenge to the Ulamas, the authorities of Islam, made by Begum Habibullah, an enlightened Moslem leader in Lucknow in a newspaper article, in which she showed that the Koran does not teach educational inequality and segregation of women.

Indian women are deeply imbued with religion, but their religious devotion today does not cloud the vision of the educated minority, nor even of a larger number, so that they cannot discriminate between religious and social questions. The widespread testimony against child-marriage gathered from Indian women of all classes *by the Age of ass came as a great surprise Consent Commission,* doubtless to many in India and elsewhere who had not realized that there is a Growing spirit of religious freedom among Indian women. The All-India Women's Conference, representing as it does the inter-communal effort of women leaders to release social reform from the bonds of religious tradition, has repeatedly given utterance to the new religious liberalism. In India, more than in any other country of the East, women have been impelled to protest individually and collectively against social handicaps. The active promotion and support of the Child Marriage Act, and the repeated resolutions against polygamy passed by the All-India Women's Conference, are exerting a powerful force toward the freedom of Hindu and Moslem women from these and other social customs, hitherto regarded as determined by religious sanctions.

The fact that women have challenged the inviolability of these sanctions is perhaps no less important than the social reforms themselves. Some Indian leaders are especially concerned to keep their endorsement of social advance in harmony with religious teaching. In the discussion on polygamy at a recent All-India Conference, one of the Moslem delegates explained that she favoured the abolition of polygamy, but she wished to call attention to the fact that "it was permitted by their religion only in case of strictest necessity arising, as for example, in the event of there being no issue from the first marriage."

Syria offers an interesting example of an interpretation of the social teachings of the Koran, made by a young Druse girl Nazira Zainud-Din, in her book, *As-Sufur-Weel-Hijab* (Unveiling and Veiling), which evoked much comment. This book was translated into several languages, widely circulated, and brought the author a trunkful of clippings from all over the world. The Islamic teaching concerning the veil was discussed also in an oratorical contest at the American University of Beirut by Madame Ihsan Shakir El-Kousy, to whom reference has already been made. In her address, which received the second prize, she showed that the Koran does not prescribe the veil. Thus, incidentally she justified her own presence unveiled in a large university.

These two examples, however, are not typical of the .women of either Syria or Egypt as a whole but less so of Syria. There is very little evidence of any analysis of Islam and very little articulate expression on religion by women in Syria: a very small minority of Egyptian women is actively interested in the relation of religion to reform. The attitude of Madame Sharawi Pasha, to whom reference has already been made as the outstanding Moslem woman leader in Egypt, shows general conformity to the prevailing policy in Egypt as regards the promotion of social advance. She has carefully based her demands for social reform on the spirit of the Koran and has not promoted reforms which do not have Islamic sanction. For example, her claims for equality of education for girls have been based on the teaching of the Koran. She has urged a law prohibiting polygamy. Reference has been made to her very effective protest against polygamy in a public lecture at the American University in Cairo last year. But while protesting against polygamy she recognizes the exceptions for polygamy which are granted by the Koran (adultery, childlessness and incompatibility). One has the feeling that this policy of maintaining a careful balance between Islamic teaching and social reform, which is followed by Madame Sharawi and the Feminist Union, is dictated more by political expediency than by religious conservatism.

Among the women of Palestine no deviation from the conventional attitude toward Islam is evident. Moslem women simply reflect the prevailing religious conservatism. However, the interesting feature in the situation, to which reference has already been made in another connection, is that Moslem women pay the price for this conservatism, of which the veil is the symbol, willingly and with a sense of pride; since by retaining the characteristic Islamic customs they feel that they have a certain distinction in contrast to the Zionist community. It is worth recalling the incident showing the counter-influence of Arab national feeling in reference to the veil, when the, group of Arab women unveiled made a protest against Zionism. But as already explained, the veils were later resumed when the habitual spirit of conservatism reasserted itself. The great majority of Moslem women in Palestine, as elsewhere, are not aware of the new conflicting currents of thought.

The attitude of women in Iran and Iraq toward religion, as toward social advance, is one of passive acquiescence. Changes in Turkey have aroused much interest in both countries, and the Turkish method of drastic social and religious reforms has been little questioned in reference to its having an adverse effect on religion. The women of Iraq and Iran have been primarily interested in the achievement of Turkey. Very often in Iraq I heard the statement: "We need a Kamal Ataturk." In Iran the hope was frequently expressed at the time of my visit several years ago, that the Shah would follow Kamal Ataturk's example and issue an order to remove the *chaddur*. In Iran as elsewhere it was erroneously believed that unveiling in Turkey had been made compulsory. This hope has now been realized and, it is interesting to note, that the definite regulations against the chaddur have not apparently caused a widespread religious shock among the women of Iran. Even the conservatives are accepting the new freedom as they accepted the former social restrictions, in an attitude of acquiescence.

In marked contrast to the attitude of women in Iraq and Iran toward Turkey, Moslem women in India have repeatedly asked me with deep solicitude whether Turkey had cast aside Islam. "Have Turkish women lost their religion?" was the question that came alike from the student group and from conservative older women. The new freedom of Turkish women, if secured at the sacrifice of religion, would seem to Moslem women in India to have cost too high a price.

In Turkey women have regarded religious changes together with all other changes, as merely a natural part of the general transformation taking place in Turkish life. There has been remarkably little analysis of the new situation in reference to the effect on religion. During the first crucial years of change the conservatives retained the veil, which older women doubtless associated with religion. But by this time the veil has, I believe, for the great majority lost any religious significance it may have had. However, recent municipal legislation of Adana and some other cities, has doubtless brought a shock to those who still have the feeling of the relationship between the veil and Islam. But they will probably accept the enforced change philosophically, as did a conservative Turkish woman in Adana, whose comment on the new regulation was: "Well, the sin will be charged against those who issued such an order and not against us, because they are forcing us to do this against our wills." This idea that unveiling is an actual sin, is probably held by very few Turkish women today.

The viewpoint of these orthodox Turkish women can scarcely fail to be affected unconsciously by the modern atmosphere, which has become steadily more natural, even in the smaller towns of the Interior. The new type of preaching of the *hodjah* has also had its effect. As a simple Turkish woman in Talas told me several years ago, "They tell us different things about religion today. The hodjahs formerly taught that women must always be veiled and their voice never heard in public. But they say now that these things are not religion." Thus, the most orthodox women have been steadily exposed to the new idea, that social customs are not necessarily, identified with religion.

The educated Turkish woman has adopted such new ideas as a logical part of the modernization of Turkish life. Before the recent period of reform this educated minority was already progressive in religious thinking for, as has already been mentioned in the discussion of Turkish education, the social- religious revolution in Turkey was preceded by a gradual period of preparation. Today due to many forces there is said to be a decline in the formal practices of Islam. "Many people no longer pray five times a day. Everyone is too busy," was the comment of a young Turkish business woman. A young teacher explained why comparatively few young people go to the mosques. "We must make our worship more modern to suit our modern clothes and customs. Praying without shoes and with many genuflections was a good thing in the Prophet's day but does not suit our present kind of life."

Although the private prayers of the formal type are still continued by many Moslem women in the homes and to a lesser extent in the mosque, as has always been the case among women, the turning away from the ritualistic worship by the younger generation is undoubtedly a marked present-day tendency. However, this should not, as has been said before, be interpreted merely as a trend toward irreligion, but perhaps it may indicate the genuine urge for a reform in worship, so that it may be something more than a prescribed ceremonial. "We are beginning to recognize the difference between essentials and nonessentials," a thoughtful Turkish woman said. "The religious forms and social restrictions are not suitable today. These can be changed without destroying our fundamental belief".

Another Turkish leader, talking with a Moslem woman from Jerusalem, who had expressed the belief that Turkey had sacrificed Islam, said, "We have separated religion from externals and made it personal. Religion is not a matter of clothes-the veil and the *fez*. It is not based on form but feeling. The repudiation of Islamic formalism therefore does not mean giving up Islam. The women of Palestine may be more outwardly religious in the orthodox sense of Islam but not necessarily more truly religious in the inner meaning of the term than are the women of Turkey." In regard to this transfer of emphasis from the external to the more individual idea of religion, a young Turkish woman student in Istanbul University expressed the opinion that there is need now for a more positive interpretation of religion. "Most of the younger Turkish girls will grow up with very little idea of Islam," she said, "since nothing positive has taken the place of the old forms, which have lost their appeal, and since very little attention these days is paid to religion." The need for a more definite constructive idea of religion is probably not as yet generally recognized by the younger generation in Turkey, which associates religion merely with a peaceful existence of quiet contemplation in the shade of mosque walls and not with an intensely active modern life.

However, a number of thoughtful Turkish leaders, both men and women, but perhaps especially women, are beginning to realize the need of a new relationship between religion and life. It is, I believe, not too much to expect that Turkish women, who have gained so much from the social and religious reforms in Turkey, may now make some special contribution to the rethinking of religious values. Their voice, and the voice of Moslem women in other countries, which have been so little heard in shaping religious thought in the past, may help to answer the crucial question in the East today, as to whether the present spirit of religious liberalism in the Moslem world will mean the disintegration of Islam or the beginning of a new era of more vital faith.

FUNDAMENTAL APPROACH

Life, for the individual, according to the above verses is an opportunity, provided by nature, to bring out the best and most spiritual in him by being placed within a network of human relationships which constantly put him on trial in respect of his social sympathies and sense of justice towards his fellow-men. The purpose of life, therefore, is the spiritual betterment of man. Nature secures this cud by placing individuals in a social situation where they may develop their altruistic self and restrain their egoistic desires. The response of the individual to the requirements of this situation is a measure of his spiritual progress and an index of his success or failure in the trial spoken of by the Holy

Quran. A society may achieve phenomenal success in any or all of these aspects and still remain spiritually bankrupt, if in the distribution of material wealth and the products of technical development, it betrays an insufficient regard for social justice and human equality. On the other hand, there may be civilisations lacking in material productivity, yet marked by a high sense of fellow-feeling and greater regard for human values. The test of a civilisation, from the Quranic viewpoint, lies in the harmony of relations between its component parts, whether horizontally as affecting the different national groups which inhabit its sphere of influence or vertically as, reflected in the mutual attitude of the different economic classes whose total productive efforts sustain its material existence. That is the meaning of the Quranic statement that 'God created Death and Life in order to try which, of you is best in conduct.' The primary value of civilisation, according to this attitude, lies in the moral conduct of its individuals as reflected in their beliefs, institutions and class and sex relations, etc. Here, and not in its mechanical development and technical efficiency, should be sought the criterion of its success or failure.

In passing judgment on Islamic teachings with regard to sex relations and the ideal of sex equality, it is necessary to keep in mind this aspect of the matter. As against Western civilisation which regards the abundance of material wealth, technical skill and mechanical efficiency as of primary importance and which subordinates, as of instrumental value and secondary importance, the ideal of social justice and other spiritual values.

Islam puts primary emphasis on just those qualities of the soul which lead to greater social harmony and prevent class conflicts. Material wealth and the human qualities which tend to increase it are not belittled by Islam. They are allowed only a rank of secondary importance. This difference in the two systems of values alters the perspective in which human and social problems are tackled respectively by Islam and Western civilisation. Islamic civilisation stands midway between ancient ascetic cultures, which negated life and matter and looked upon the things of this world as having a soul-degrading effect, and the materialistic culture of the modern West, which has turned material wealth and economic prosperity into objects of idolatrous worship. From the Islamic viewpoint, economic wealth and the qualities which help its furtherance are good only in so far as they subserve spiritual interests and make for greater social harmony. When raised to the level of primary importance, they become the agents of the devil.

PRIOR TO ISLAM

Man is a combination of contradictions. He is an embodiment of virtue and evil, love and hatred, good and bad. He is, on the one hand, the best of the creation, the vicegerent of Allah on earth, the most exalted-personages, called prophets (peace be upon them), belonged to the human race. On the other hand, tyrants, like Haman, Shaddad, Pharaoh and Namrud, whose atrocities send a shiver through our bodies even today, were also born into this race. But The Almighty in His Infinite Mercy made the arrangement to reform humanity and eradicate sin and vice, and sent Prophet Muhammad (peace and blessings of Allah be upon him), the last of the Prophets, the mercy for the worlds among mankind and vouchsafed him the Holy Quran; the complete code and constitution for our guidance. It embraces all aspects of human life.

Almighty, the Exalted. has made sexual intercourse as a means of protection and perpetuation of the human race. He has created two sexes called man and woman having irresistible charm and attraction for one another. One sex is badly in need of the other and is a source of satisfaction for the other and vice versa. The life of one without the other is incomplete and devoid of any purpose and meaning.

This is the reason why a man as a complete man cannot do without a woman and likewise a woman, as a woman, cannot lead a peaceful and comfortable life without a man. But man is by nature rash and hasty. He has proved to be extravagant even in this respect and has transgressed the lawful limits in the satisfaction of his sexual desires. This trend is fatal for humanity and the human race.

Just as Islam does not permit man to transgress the lawful limits in other spheres, it does not allow him to deviate from a natural, balanced course in the matter of sex. A permanent moral code has, therefore, been given to us so that we may mould our lives according to it. Those who fear Allah and the Hereafter and have love and respect for His Messenger (peace and blessings of Allah be upon him) will be able to reform themselves by reading this book.

Status of Women and their Degeneration : There is no denying the fact that when Islam promulgated the rules and regulations concerning moral conduct and behaviour, people had forgotten the real purpose and significance of marriage. The peace and happiness which conjugal life gives to the husband and wife were not enjoyed by them. The mutual love and affection which brings the two souls and their two families so near and inculcates mutual love and cooperation between them, no longer existed, nor did there remain any good and wholesome influence from such marriages. Even modesty and chastity, which are the essence of marriage, were cast to the winds. Only the custom existed, but the real spirit and purpose of marriage did not exist.

In every part of the world woman was subjected to unbearable tortures by man, who treated this weak and delicate creature like a beast of the jungle. Women were purchased and sold like cattle and household goods. Men did not hesitate to beat women to satisfy their lust. They were even compelled to prostitution. So these wretched creatures not only satisfied the lust of their husbands, but earned for their husbands through nefarious trafficking. Before the advent of Islam woman was considered a creature between human and beast whose main function was to bear children and to serve man. Due to this very reason, the birth of female babies was considered to be disgraceful and to bury them alive at their very birth was taken as a laudable action. The information which is gleaned from the pages of the Holy Quran about this evil practice of the days of Ignorance is pathetic and heart-rending.

Besides other things this also alludes to the fact that in the birth of man, woman has her share. When man is not born of his own accord, what right does he possess to treat man with honour and respect and degrade woman? The human body is a compound of both man and woman; but according to medical research, it is woman who creates the major part of the human structure. It is woman who bears the burden of a child during pregnancy, then delivers, suckles and rears the child. Just think, what does man do for his child? Is it not a sheer folly on our part that we should hate the existence of a woman who gives us shape and form during pregnancy and is responsible for our existence? It is woman who reared us, trained us, enabled us to walk and speak and provided our needs at the time when we could not express. It is she who served us till the age of competency. And in spite of all this sacrifice we treat her with hatred and contempt. Woe be upon the people who entertain and express such ideas concerning woman.

There is no reason to be wroth and to feel annoyance at the birth of a female, it is sheer folly on the part of man that he considers a blessing a curse. If these female babies should not grow up and become women and you do not marry them off, wherefrom will you get hale and hearty soldiers?

The mankind began its journey with the union of man and woman. It also spread the human race and evolved science and art, trade and industry and civilization and culture. All other relations amongst mankind are either the outcome of the union of man and woman or are the result of external causes and circumstances in the absence of which no such relations could be evolved. A neighbour loves another neighbour, a companion embraces another companion, a traveller joins another traveller; similarly a student associates with another student and a trader cooperates with another trader, because they have mutual interest. But as soon as their interests cease, they fall apart and become strangers to each other. But this is not the case with the union of man and woman. Their union is based on the natural feeling and attraction which keep them united in spite of their range of action and interest being quite separate.

A woman, no doubt, nurtures the human race with her blood and looks after the affairs of her home, but she finds it difficult to work in the field and defend herself against the enemies, for, she has no sufficient strength to do so. Her heart is the abode of only love, sympathy and sacrifice; whereas man is hard and sturdy, therefore, his duties include hunting, farming, trade and defence. This difference of strength between man and woman has been the matter of grace and disgrace in periods of history. Man has physical power and strength; what he can do, a woman cannot do because of natural weakness, so man was considered superior and woman inferior. Hence, the countries which were well-known for their justice, character-building and grant of human rights, considered man as superior to woman.

Woman was victimised for a long time. When her agony reached its climax, the situation became very serious. The modern age brought revolution in every aspect of life and changed the status of woman. Formerly she was slave but now she is 'free'. The Industrial Revolution in Europe helped woman achieve her 'Freedom'. She broke the chain of 'slavery', and came in the open field. The doors of employment were opened for her which helped her to revolt against man.

Woman desired freedom not for the betterment of her lot but for vengeance. She went to such an extent in this process that she herself took the place of man. She forgot the fundamental principle that woman can't take the place of man. Both are quite different in their capabilities and characteristics. Man and woman are physically and psychologically quite different from each other.

The main difference between man and woman is of sex and this difference cannot be removed by means of education, training or environment. They differ in their very nature. What a man can do, a woman cannot do it; and what a woman can do, a man cannot do. But the West accepted the equality of man and woman not because it has proved their natural differences wrong but simply because it found it the only solution for the freedom of woman from 'man's tyranny'.

It is explicitly clear that the West has created its own standard of respectability. According to this criteria, only the characteristics and strength of man have been taken into consideration and the nature of woman has been neglected. She has been invited to bring herself to that standard if she wants to be honourable in the society. In fact, she ought to have been assigned the task according to her nature and capabilities. Then, she would have not resorted to the artificial means to acquire dignified position in the society.

The Western thinkers maintain that present concept of the nature of woman is nothing but an artificial state created by man's constant tyranny. Her talents have been suppressed. Had she been free to act, she would have achieved better position even in the fields reserved for man. As far as intellect and reasoning are concerned, it is wrong to say that man and woman are equal in these respects. They think woman would have performed her duty better if she had been free to act. But it is also possible that she would have remained at the same position where she was before, despite her freedom to act. Hence it is false to say that she can also fulfil the responsibilities of man.

The history shows that woman had opportunities, in different periods, to struggle along with man, but she failed to achieve the status of man owing to her natural weaknesses. Besides, the modern world has provided her freedom along with man for over the last one century, but her freedom has brought no change of any sort in her feminine nature.

Another stand that Western thinkers take, is that if woman is removed from civil and social work, the advancement in the field of modernization would be reduced to fifty percent and the progress of fifty years will take one full century. This argument is absolutely false and baseless, as society is not a technical institution for the progress of one particular technique. On the contrary, it came into existence due to the association of various departments of human life. Some of these departments belong to woman also. If these departments are abolished, the whole society will suffer. Hence, evolution of society means progress of every department to achieve overall higher standard of life.

Despite all facilities, woman has not been proved as useful as expected in the assigned fields. A less qualified man has been proved more useful than a highly qualified woman. The reason is that woman wants to do the work of man but her nature does not allow her to succeed in her efforts. Her natural characteristics forbid her to follow the modern trend, This struggle has put her in such a condition that worries even the West. Now, it is a proven fact that Western way of living has failed to provide a dignified status to woman in the society, while all talk of women lib remains mere sloganeering.

2

Social Status

Experience shows that women are generally hardworking and self-contented. They love their husbands from the core of their hearts, bring up their children with the utmost care and are the best household managers. They are sincere and loyal. There are more virtues and less weaknesses in them.

The laborious and hardworking nature of a woman can be judged at the time of difficulty. Modern research has proved this fact. The great scholar Lumbrose has written: Just imagine the hardships and tribulations a woman has to go through during pregnancy and at the time of delivery, otherwise the accomplishment of this delicate and difficult task of multiplication of the human race would not be possible.

No doubt woman is a delicate creature. She has a weak and delicate heart. Coquettishness is in her nature. She is of buoyant and jovial nature. She is also easily annoyed and flares up at trifling matters. A man should adopt some reasonable attitude taking into consideration all these things. In the verses pertaining to divorce, men have been admonished not to commit tyranny and aggression.

In order to ensure discipline and stability in domestic life men have been given power over women. If both were vested with equal power, it would have ruined the peace and harmony of the domes tic life as two kings cannot rule over one state. Secondly, men have been given permission to rebuke or to avoid sexual intercourse or to beat, not causing any serious injury, if the woman is found guilty of manifest immodesty. Then the rights of husbands against their wives and those of wives against their husbands have been explained. The husband has been instructed to feed and clothe his wife with fairness. He must not take undue advantage of the power vested in him and do what he wishes; but it is his duty to fulfil the needs tastes and interests of his wife as she is dependent on him. Experience shows that if any person is dependent on the other in a certain sphere of life and the latter does not care for his sentiments and tastes, the former's feelings are injured and he feels disgusted.

Before the advent of Islam there was no restriction on the Arab men and women meeting and talking with each other just like the modern western people of today.

Islam put an end to these practices of the Days of Ignorance. The second duty of women is that they should ask the permission of their husbands before they allow any man (Mahram or Ghair Mahram) to enter their houses and should not let such men enter their houses whom their husbands do not like.

Holy Prophet's Treatment with His Wives : The Holy Prophet (peace and blessings of Allah be upon him) has taught that a Mumin should be an embodiment of virtues and of excellent moral conduct and behaviour and that the best of you in this respect are the kindest of you to their wives. The Messenger of Allah (peace and blessings of Allah be upon him) has observed:

> *The most perfect of the believers in faith is the best of them in moral excellence, and the best of you are the kindest of you to their wives.* *(Tirmidhi)*

According to the above Hadith, the sign of the most perfect and best believer in faith is that he is the kindest to his wife. The husbands should, therefore, be kind and benevolent to their wives and should always try to fulfil their lawful needs and desires to please them. He whose treatment with his wife is the best possesses the most excellent virtues among us. During a short meeting, a person may pose excellent behaviour and manners; but the permanent and lasting company of his wife exposes his real character and temperament. The wife is the real test of his natural and inherent qualities.

Once the Messenger of Allah (peace and blessing of Allah be upon him) said: Avoid beating the living creatures of Allah. In

Arabia the women were treated no better than animals. They were entirely at the mercy of men. Men had the right to take the life of a woman or to beat her as an ordinary thing. But with the advent of Islam, the persecution of women ended and they heaved a sigh of relief.

The result of the emancipation of this downtrodden humanity began to be felt in society as is evident from this Hadith. One day Hadrat Umar (Allah be pleased with him) came to the Messenger of Allah (peace and blessings of Allah be upon him) and said: Women have become daring to their husbands. Hearing this the Messenger of Allah (peace and blessings of Allah be upon him) said that the above instructions may not be observed strictly; but the husbands took an undue advantage of the 'relaxation' and complaints began to pour in. Thereupon the Messenger of Allah (peace and blessings of Allah be upon him) said: Many a woman surrounded the family of Muhammad and complained that their husbands were not good people. (Riyad Al-Salihin)

Sympathizing with Woman

It is the moral responsibility of the husband to be good and kind to his wife. If any misfortune befalls her, he should not withdraw his love and favour; but in the difficult time his treatment should be more kind and sympathetic. If she happens to fall ill, he should take her to the doctor. If she is in difficulty, an attempt should be made to solve her problem. If her face becomes uglier due to illness, indifferent and harsh treatment should not be adopted with her; but every effort should be made to console her. If he would not sympathise with her, her feelings would be injured and her jovial and buoyant face would become dejected. The indifferent attitude of her husband would rend her heart with frustration.

Just imagine, you bring a beautiful, fascinating lady and are ready to sacrifice everything for her. You have purchased the best wedding dress and ornaments just to please her. But by chance she falls ill, and smallpox makes her face ugly or snatches away the light of her eyes. When she looks into the mirror, her eyes become wet with tears or if she becomes blind, the whole world plunges into darkness for her. She weeps bitterly day and night. To add to her calamities, you threaten to turn her out. She is tortured for no fault of her own. Where has her husband's love gone? How has spring turned into winter? All these are the vicissitudes of fortune. Just think, is it proper or human? Is this not a disgrace to love and sheer injustice? It must also be kept in mind that the painful sighs and tears of a helpless and downtrodden woman do not go waste. Islam does not permit this terrible attitude and hard-heartedness. The Prophet (peace and blessings of Allah be upon him) said: He who does not make mercy, Allah will not make mercy on him. (Riyad Al-Salihin)

What has been said above is only to give an understanding of the problem. It is the duty of the husband to try his utmost to win the heart of his wife. He must have full regard for her feelings and sentiments.

There is a well known story that one night while Hadrat Umar (Allah be pleased with him) was on patrol, he heard the voice of painful songs from a house. Hadrat Umar (Allah be pleased with him) asked the reason for this. He was told that the husband of this woman had proceeded on Jihad. He was deeply moved at her sincere love for her husband and asked Hadrat Hafsa (Allah be pleased with her) how long a woman can bear her husband's separation. Her answer was: For four months. Thereupon he issued the following order to his Commanders: A married person should not remain away from his wife for more than four months. (Durr-e-Mukhtar)

It is evident from the above historical incident that it is also among the duties of the husband that he should not be indifferent to the feelings, sentiments and the natural sexual urge of the wife. If he was to stay in a foreign country for long, he should keep his wife and children with him. This fact has also been explained by the Holy Quran in a verse regarding Ila. If a person resorts to *Ila* (a vow of temporary cessation of marital relations) without naming a period, he is bound either to re-establish the normal relations after four months or to divorce his wife. After the lapse of this period, the husband has no right to keep his wife and she is free to marry any man.

Expenses for Wife

Among the great responsibilities which Islam has put on the husband, his duty is also to provide necessary expenses for the maintenance of the house such as food, clothing, lodging, etc. So that his wife can rear her children without much worry.

It has been mentioned in the Holy Quran:

Let him who hath abundance spend of his abundance, and he whose provision is measured, let him spend of that what Allah hath given him. Allah asketh not of any soul save that which He hath given it. *(65:7)*

None has to bear more burden than he can bear, but the responsibilities placed on him are proportionate to his power and ability. It has been mentioned in another verse of the Holy Quran:

The duty of providing food and clothes to nursing mothers in a seemly manner is upon the father of the child. No one should be charged beyond his capacity. *(2:233)*

The responsibility for providing the means of sustenance has been put on the husband so that the woman can bear and rear her children with full concentration of mind. This helps in the proper development of the personality of the child. We have already quoted a Hadith that among the duties which a husband owes to his wife, one duty is: You should be fair to them in feeding and clothing them. *(Tirmidhi)*

Other Liberties

Another right of a wife over her husband is that the latter should allow her to see her parents and her near relatives i.e. Mahrams. The Messenger of Allah (peace and blessings of Allah be upon him) used to see his affectionate daughter and Hadrat Abu Bakr and Hadrat Umar (Allah be pleased with them) also used to go to the Prophet's house to see their daughters. A large number of such instances have been mentioned in the Ahadith. The Jurists are of the view that if the wife goes to see her parents once in a week, the husband should not object to it. But this is permissible if the parents are unable to see her for some genuine reason, otherwise, they should themselves go to see her. If there is a dispute between husband and wife and there is a danger that it would take a serious turn, the husband has been instructed not to take a hasty step. If the situation is not improved even by beating, a judge should be appointed from each side to resolve the dispute. The Holy Quran says:

> *And if ye fear a breach between them twain (the man and wife), appoint an arbiter from his folk and an arbiter from her folk.* (4:35)

But it must be kept in mind that the judges should be honest and sincere. It is then that they would be able to resolve the dispute, otherwise they would further aggravate the situation. The Holy Quran testifies to this fact:

> *If they desire amendment Allah will make them of one mind. Allah is ever Knower, Aware.* (4:35)

Rights and Duties of Wife

We have so far discussed in detail the rights of the wife against her husband. Now let us see what instructions have been given to the wife concerning her husband. We can judge from the rights and duties of both what strenuous efforts have been made by Islam to guard modesty and chastity and to ensure stability, love and harmony in conjugal relations.

Any rule or law which holds one party responsible, leaving the other free to do as it likes may be apparently nice but it cannot be called perfect or good. Only such rules and laws are complete as are applicable to all and guard the rights of one against the other. There is no denying the fact that woman is a weak and sentimental creature and because of this very reason she deserves our favour, love and regard and it is our duty to overlook her shortcomings. But this does not mean that she is absolved of her duties. Had it been so, the life of both husband and wife would be devoid of any purpose and charm.

Priority of Husband

Islam has kept in view the inherent weaknesses of woman. Due to this reason man has priority over woman. He has been appointed as the leader or president insofar as the family life is concerned, as he has the ability to solve the difficult matters. Allah the Exalted has said in the Holy Quran:

> *Men are in charge of women, because Allah hath made the one of them to excel the other, and because they spend of their property.* (4:34)

It means men have been given priority and eminence over women in the matter of knowledge and action. They are responsible for supporting them and providing food, clothing and lodging to his family. Hence he is the leader or president of the house.

There is no denying the fact that man is superior to woman due to his God sent virtues and capabilities. A woman has to go through certain periods in which she is rendered almost unable to do anything and she has to depend upon others, for instance, during pregnancy, suckling, rearing of children, menstruation and during the period of discharge of blood after childbirth. Hadrat Shah Wali Ullah has written:

> *It is necessary and akin to nature that man should have authority over woman as man possesses perfect intellect, he is an expert politician. He defends vehemently and guards respect and honour. He has priority over woman as he provides food, clothing and lodging.*

The modern research has proved that the brain of man is stronger than that of woman. He is more intelligent and wise. His mind is more mature. He possesses a strong body and muscles. We have already quoted the views of some writers. We give below some excerpts from modern research scholars: The famous rationalist scholar and philosopher, Dr. Proudon writes in his book:

> *"The perception and intuition of woman is as weak as is her intellect in comparison to man. Her character is also different. Her nature is also different. That is why her criteria of judgement of merits and demerits of a thing also vary. This difference between man and woman is lasting and abiding. It is her inherent nature."*

That is to say, modern research has proved beyond doubt that men have more capabilities than women in every respect.

Equal Rights

From the authority given to man it should not be construed that in Islam, a wife is the maidservant of the husband. This view is incorrect. Only a person who is ignorant of Islamic knowledge can hold this view. Sometimes it happens that a husband and wife have different opinions on certain matters. If there is any such dispute between them, the opinion of the husband should be given precedence over the opinion of the wife as he is the head of the family because of his special knowledge and capabilities.

Islam desires that all matters may be settled amiably with mutual consent of both husband and wife. There is equality between the two and both husband and wife have rights against each other and they also owe duties to each other. The Holy Quran has mentioned:

> *And they have rights similar to those (of men) over them in kindness, and men are a degree over them. (2:228)*

This brief verse contains a fundamental principle that men and women are equal in all respects and their rights and duties are also equal except that, as explained above, men have power over women. In all other matters concerning conduct and behaviour and 'Ibadat and social dealings they are equal and there is no reason for holding them in contempt. Islam has for the first time given such prestige and honour to womenfolk.

A philosopher has rightly observed:

> *"If Allah wanted to make a woman the head of the family, she would have been born from the portion of the body where the head is set and if He wanted to make the woman a maid-servant, He would have created her from the lowest portion of the body having feet. As it was not Allah's will and He wanted equality, mutual love, harmony and respect and honour for each other, He created her from the side of man."*

Despite the fact that man is the head of the family, he has been asked to consult his wife and settle all matters by mutual consent of each other. Where the Holy Quran has ordained that the mother should suckle her baby for a full two years and the duty of providing food and clothing, etc., to the woman who suckles rests with the father, it has also been ordained that if the woman desires to wean the child, it should be done by mutual consent of the husband and wife. It has been mentioned in the Holy Quran:

> *If they desire to wean the child by mutual consent and consultation, it is no sin for them.* *(2:233)*

It is obvious that mutual consultation is necessary in all matters. The gist of what we have said above is that Islam has framed rules and regulations for the married couple which if acted upon, would bring mutual love and harmony between them and protect their modesty and chastity.

In these hard times, we came across instances of rifts between husbands and wives of rich families over triflings. Their relations are strained. Both begin to live separately. Years pass on and both persist in their behaviour just to keep their false prestige. This period of separation is full of great hazards for both as no one is without sexual desire. Islam condemns such a way of life, there is no room for it in Islam. We shall discuss this point in detail in the next pages.

A Pious Woman

If the husband and wife had acted upon the excellent principles of Islam, the matter would not have gone from bad to worse. On such a critical occasion, if the husband's view-point, his being the head, were to be accepted, the dispute would surely have come to an end. The Holy Quran says:

> *"So good women are the obedient, guarding in secret that which Allah has made them guard."* *(4:34)*

In the above verse the virtue of a pious woman has been explained and she has been instructed to be loyal to her husband so that if there is any difference of opinion between them, it should not cause separation between them. The Messenger of Allah (peace and blessings of Allah be upon him) has further instructed the women to live amiably with their husbands: 'A woman who asks for divorce from her husband on triflings, is forbidden the smell of paradise.'

In the above Hadith women have been admonished that if any unagreeable thing occurs between the husband and wife, she should not demand divorce from her husband, as such, things do happen in married life due to difference in temperaments.

It is, however, the duty of a pious lady that in the event of a clash with her husband, she should overcome her anger considering her husband to be the head of the family. She should keep in mind that it is her duty to obey him. If she is sure that her husband has given her unjust treatment, she should try to convince him that he is wrong. She should however, be careful and cautious and present her viewpoint in a civilized manner.

God forbid, when any woman takes the law in her hand, the married life is bound to be disturbed and this small kingdom of the husband and wife will be ruined. The one inevitable result of this quarrel would be that both husband and wife would lose their honour and prestige when the people would come to know that they are unable to manage their household affairs.

Due to the husband's love for his wife, the latter must also please him, be solicitous for his ease and comfort and have respect for and honour him. She should always keep in mind that he is the head of the family and it is her duty to pay due respect to him. The Messenger of Allah (peace and blessings of Allah be upon him) has observed:

> *"If I had ordained any individual to prostrate before the other individual I would have ordained the wife to prostrate before her husband."* *(Mishkat)*

A husband who showers all his love and affection on his wife and spends his hard earned money to provide her comforts and amenities, taking her to be the centre of his devotions must be respected and honoured by his wife. A mere show of respect and honour is not sufficient; but there must be sincerity in these sentiments so that she may win his heart. For the wife the necessity for seeking her husband's pleasure exists in this world and also in the Hereafter.

> *"When a woman whose husband is pleased with her dies, she would enter Paradise."* *(Mishkat)*

A wife can win the heart of her husband through love and

sacrifice. If the wife obeys him and fulfils his genuine demands, he will sacrifice all for her sake and do all that is in his power to please her. Loyalty and obedience in lawful matters are among the excellent virtues of a wife. The Messenger of Allah (peace and blessings of Allah be upon him) has observed:

> *"A woman who had offered five times prayers and kept the fasts for the month (of Ramadan), and guarded her modesty and was obedient to her husband would be allowed to enter any of the gates of Paradise."*
>
> *(Mishkat)*

Along with the duties like prayer, fasting and the guarding of modesty, it is also the duty of a woman to obey her husband. It is evident from the above Hadith that whereas it is necessary to fulfil the rights of Allah it is also the bounden duty of a wife to obey her husband. A woman who fails to fulfil the duties she owes to her husband cannot succeed. Once the Messenger of Allah (peace and blessings of Allah be upon him) was questioned as to who is the best woman, he answered:

> *"The woman who pleases her husband when he sees her, obeys him when he orders and does not have any bad intention in her heart against his person nor against her husband's wealth."* *(Mishkat)*

What more stress can be laid on woman obeying their husband? A woman who is not obedient to her husband is surely not a good woman in the sight of the Messenger of Allah (peace and blessings of Allah be upon him). She may be possessing an exalted worldly position and wealth and riches, but she is unfortunate and wretched, if she is not a good woman in the sight of the Messenger of Allah (peace and blessings of Allah be upon him).

The wife should fulfil her husband's lawful demands only. If he transgresses the limits prescribed by Allah and asks her to commit acts against the Shariah, she is allowed to refuse her husband. An incident has been narrated in the Hadith: Once a woman of Ansar came to the Messenger of Allah (peace and blessings of Allah be upon him) and said: I have got my daughter married. Perchance, the hair of my daughter have fallen down. Now my son-in-law demands that the hair of some other woman should be added to her hair so that she may look beautiful. Thereupon the Messenger of Allah (peace and blessings of Allah be upon him) observed: Curse be upon the woman who adds other's hair to her hair.

The wife must, however, obey her husband in permissible things. An obedient wife has been called the greatest of Allah's favours in Ahadith. The status given by Islam to the obedient wife can be judged from the following Hadith:

> *The best of the things from which a believer can benefit next to the fear of Allah is a pious wife. If he orders her, she obeys and if he sees her, she pleases him. If she takes a vow before him, she fulfils and if her husband is away she has good intention against her person and property.*
>
> *(Ibn Majah)*

It is evident from the above Hadith that the best of Allah's favours, next to fear of Him, is a pious and obedient wife who loves her husband dearly, has a smiling and cheerful fascinating face and amiable disposition. She guards her modesty and chastity. The Messenger of Allah (peace and blessings of Allah be upon him) has said: If the husband asks his wife to go from one mountain to the other and from there to the third, the true wife is one who obeys this command.

Islam wants that the relations between husband and wife should be stable and abiding. It has framed rules and regulations keeping in view the nature and temperaments of both. The duties which the wife owes to her husband must be fulfilled by her wholeheartedly. Once the Messenger of Allah (peace and blessings of Allah be upon him) said: A woman must fulfil the lawful demands of her husband and a woman cannot relish the sweetness of faith unless she fulfils the lawful rights of her husband.

We have already mentioned a Hadith that the husband is the head of the whole family including the wife, then how far is it correct on her part to disobey her husband? As she is the better half of her husband and his friend and life companion, it is the duty of a friend to give sacrifice for a friend. She should do everything cheerfully and of her own accord. She should never consider that she is a maid servant or a captive.

Sexual gratification is apparently a worldly act; but in this matter, too, if the husband calls his wife for sexual intercourse, she should obey him out of love for him. The Messenger of Allah (peace and blessings of Allah be upon him) has observed: "If a person calls his wife for his need, she must go to him at once, although she may be standing near the oven (for baking breads)."

There is an explicit hint in the Hadith that if she fails to comply with the husband's above order, she is guilty of sin. The Messenger of Allah (peace and blessings of Allah be upon him) has further observed:

> *"If a husband calls his wife to his bed and she refuses to come, the angels hurl curses on her till morning."*
>
> *(Bukhari)*

The women of the Prophet's and Caliphs' times tried their utmost to please their husbands. An expression of slight anger by their husbands disturbed their peace of mind. They obeyed their husbands even when they held indifferent and discourteous attitude.

> *Hadrat Aishah (Allah be pleased with her) was once wearing silver rings in her hands. The Messenger of Allah (peace and blessings of Allah be upon him) seeing these rings in her hands asked: What are these, O' Aishah! She said: I have worn these to please you.*
>
> *(Uswa Sahaba)*

Due to these excellent rules of social conduct and behaviour, both husband and wife had great love and affection for each other. How much love and devotion had Hadrat Khadijah (Allah be pleased with her) for the Messenger of Allah (peace and blessings of Allah be upon him). As you know, Hadrat Khadijah (Allah be pleased with her) was a rich lady. When she was married to the Messenger of Allah (peace and blessings of Allah be upon him) she sacrificed all her wealth for her husband's sake. Whenever he was in difficulty, Hadrat Khadijah (Allah be pleased with her) helped him and consoled him.

> *Hadrat Aishah (Allah be pleased with her) is also well known for her love and devotion for the Messenger of Allah (peace and blessings of Allah be upon him). She*

washed his clothes with her hands, applied perfume, crushed miswak *(tooth stick) for him and kept it with care. She wove the rope for the sacrificial animal with her hand. Once the Messenger of Allah (peace and blessings of Allah be upon him) covered himself with a blanket and went to the mosque. The Companions pointed out that there was a spot on the blanket. He took off the blanket and sent it into the house. Hadrat Aishah (Allah be pleased with her) took a pot of water and washed the blanket with her own hands. She got it dried and sent it to the Holy Prophet (peace and blessings of Allah be upon him).* *(Uswa Sahaba)*

The wives of the Companions also possessed the same sentiments of love and devotion for their husbands. They did their utmost to please their husbands. Hadrat Zainab, the loving daughter of the Holy Prophet (peace and blessings of Allah be upon him) was married to Abu Aas. The latter had not yet embraced Islam when the battle of Badr began. In this battle between the infidels and the Muslims, Abul Aas fought from the side of the infidels. The Muslims won the battle by Allah's infinite mercy and grace and a large number of Quraish were made captive by them. Abul Aas was also one among them. When the Holy Prophet (peace and blessings of Allah be upon him) declared that the captives should be set free on payment of ransom, Hadrat Zainab, the Holy Prophet's daughter and the wife of Abul Aas, sent her precious necklace as ransom for Abdul Aas. This necklace belonged to Hadrat Khadijah (Allah be pleased with her) her mother and she had kept it with her in her memory.

The wife should not hesitate to serve her husband. The Prophet's wives served him. Hadrat Fatima, the Holy Prophet's daughter used to look to the needs of her husband and did all the household work. In Bukhari there is a separate chapter under the heading: 'The work of a woman in her husband's house' wherein it has been mentioned that blisters were caused on Hadrat Fatima's hands by working the hand-mill.

The Muhaddithin have drawn the conclusion from the above incident that women should themselves do ordinary household work. If Hadrat Fatima (Allah be pleased with her) could work the hand-mill she must also be kneading the flour and baking the bread herself. According to Imam Malik, it is the duty of the wife to do the household work herself if her husband cannot afford a servant, even if she belongs to a rich and wealthy family.

Among the three persons who did not participate in the battle of Tabuk and were boycotted by the people at the Holy Prophet's command, was Hilal bin Umayyah (Allah be pleased with him). After a few days the Holy Prophet (peace and blessings of Allah be upon him) commanded their wives to boycott them till the decision about them was revealed. Thereupon Hilal bin Umayyah's wife went to the Holy Prophet (peace and blessings of Allah be upon him) and reported: My husband is an old man. There is no servant to serve him. Therefore, I may be permitted to serve him. The Holy Prophet (peace and blessings of Allah be upon him) granted permission to Hilal's wife to serve her husband.

Hafiz Ibn Qayyim has narrated the incident of Hadrat Asma, the wife of Hadrat Zubayr. How solicitous was she for the needs of her husband and how hard did she work for him.

A great shortcoming of woman is that they are stubborn and persistent. They must shun from this habit. It is a common experience that whenever anything goes against their whim and desire, they fly into rage and begin to exchange hot words. Thus the relations of husband and wife are strained and the husband is fed up with his wife.

If there is something reasonable, the wife should try to convince her husband. It is not proper to quarrel and wear an angry look. If the husband is in angry mood, she should become polite. If it is quite necessary to express her displeasure, she should do so; but care should be taken that their relations do not become bitter.

If the husband is aggressive and rude, she should show wisdom and not do anything in a hurry. It is better that she should reconcile with him even if it is against her wishes.

A careful study of what we have said above makes it amply clear that the rules and regulations promulgated by Islam foster the sentiments of love and harmony among husband and wife so that the real aims and objects of marriage are fulfilled to their fullest possible extent and the people lead a peaceful and comfortable life. By living amicably they can protect their modesty and chastity in the most excellent manner.

Due to this reason, the rights and duties of both against each other have been explicitly determined. If both of them fulfil their rights and duties they owe to each other, there remains no cause of complaint or rancour against anyone.

It is a great sin to cause rift between husband and wife. A person who is guilty of this act would be deprived of the bounties and rewards of the Paradise. The Allah's Messenger (peace and blessings of Allah be upon him) mentioning the evil tactics of the devil and his team said: The devil sits on his royal throne and sends his disciples among the people for mischief making. He who commits the greatest evil receives the greatest reward. When these mischief mongers come back, they submit their reports to their leader regarding their evil exploits and wrong doings.

Islam is a religion of peace and harmony. It puts an end to hatred and enemity among the people and exhorts its followers to live amicably. A person who tries to create hatred and discord among the people by instigating one against the other cannot be called the real follower of Islam. It is a heinous sin to cause hatred between husband and wife due to which the house is turned into a veritable hell. The clash between husband and wife might lead them to evil way of life and moral delinquency which do not behove a true follower of Islam.

THEIR DIGNITY

The sum total of Islamic teachings is to raise human dignity and honour. It relieves mankind from disgrace and provides higher and honourable place in human society. It imparts the lesson of human dignity. Islam directs humanity to prostrate before Allah alone for the achievement of—superiority over other creations. Mankind is the masterpiece creation of Allah.

In Islam the welfare of mankind depends upon right thinking and right practice. It is sheer ignorance to degrade woman simply because she happens to be a woman, and man is considered a heavenly creature simply because he happens to be a man. Islam has explained it in very clear words that human dignity rests upon piety and virtue. Hence, who is more honourable, man or woman?

Before the advent of Islam, the world had degraded the woman and had almost outcast her. She was thrown in such deep abyss that there seemed no hope of her redemption. Islam boldly remonstrated against this injustice and emphasised that life needed both man and woman. Woman is not created to be derided and cast aside. Like man, woman also has her purpose and right to exist. And the Nature is achieving its aim with the help of man and woman both.

Whereas, all other religions deprived woman of right even to live.' Islam granted her rights almost on a par with man. It also warned that all those who strive to snatch her rights away, will surely be, accountable to Allah on the Day of Judgement.

And when the girl-child that was buried alive, is asked
For what sin she was slain? *(19 : 8-9)*

PRECAUTIONARY MEASURES

Allah Has endowed mankind with charm and beauty. Mankind is also fond of beautiful things. Therefore, man seeks beauty in every thing of the world. He despises ugly and awkward things and he is never tired of seeking beauty in the Nature.

Indeed, it is natural urge of mankind, hence it is essential to fulfil it. But this admiration of beauty is worthwhile so long it is within the limits of Shariah. If it crosses the limits then it opens the door to evil practices which spoil the society. Therefore, Islam restricts the observation of the opposite sex, because, if the sight is not controlled, then it will be difficult to control the sexual desire.

Hearing also leaves profound impression on human feelings and emotions. This impression can be harmful or beneficial. It is the aim of the good law to clarify the lines of loss and gain. Hence, Islam lays down the rule that a Muslim can hear any beautiful song for the satisfaction of his interest. However, it prohibits the kind of hearing which leads to sexual incitement and immorality, because Islam wants a man to be of finest character. There is nothing wrong in listening to sweet melody but it is a sin to listen to anything that is morally harmful. Therefore, music or musical instruments are not allowed in Islam.

The man has been proved very careless in respect of the use of his tongue. Whatever a man utters, it effects the people and the environment. The effects of the tongue are stronger than those of seeing and hearing. The tongue is the means of expression of human thoughts which may be good or bad and accordingly these thoughts leave their impression on the people around. The speaker tries to influence the listener with his power of the tongue. If his speech is liked and appreciated by the listeners then his thoughts grow stronger and this process leads to collective listening and thus his influence grows stronger day by day.

Today the greatest evil of the world is the, nudism, which has greatly influenced the human mind and provided the unlimited means of sensuality. The fair sex is already attractive and charming in appearance and if nudity is added, the mischief is greater, making it difficult for the man to control his passions. Therefore, Islam condemns all means and sources of evil which lead to immorality and destroy the human society. The purpose of clothing is to ward off the evil consequences of nudity and maintain decency in the society.

It is the sign of utter ignorance to think that nudity is the call of modernization. In fact, the nudism is the imitation of Western culture. It has nothing to do with the term, 'Modern.' Islam is the most modern 'Deen'. It, not only allows the advancement in modern science and technology but also encourages all efforts intended to attain knowledge from any part of the world.

The concept of dress in Islam is to cover the-body, specially those parts, which must not be exposed to others. It also emphasises decency in dressing. Therefore, Islam has given certain guidelines for the dresses of the man and the woman and both have to follow these instructions strictly.

It is a very dangerous idea for a woman to meet a stranger in loneliness. Logically speaking there is no sense in meeting a stranger when a woman has no relation with a man. In such circumstances she cannot be sure of protecting her chastity from the attack of the stranger. Therefore '. Islam strictly prohibits woman from meeting a stranger in loneliness. This is done for her own safety and protection of her honour.

GENDER EQUALITY

Equality is a term which is hard to define. There is a sense in which all human beings are equal, but in actual life, we find that no two human beings are really equal in all respects. There are differences of tastes, temperaments, faculties, powers and outlook, all of which cannot be traced to differences of environment or upbringing. It is apparent that the rights and duties of men and their social position flow from these inborn differences. In spite of the fundamental and essential unity of all human beings, it is impossible in practice to level down all differences and inequalities, because some of them are the outcome of native differences. Inequality leads to injustice and oppression only where artificial impediments, whether in the shape of laws and customs or traditions, are super-added to natural inequalities so as to prevent men and women from developing their native capacities to the full. It is the task of religion, state and law to remove all hindrances to human development and create an environment where only natural inborn differences and inequalities may fix a man's station in life.

The ideal of sex equality should also be studied from, the same angle. If by sex equality is meant that artificial customs, traditions and laws which prevent the female sex from playing its full part in collective life and developing its inherent capacities to the maximum extent should be removed out of the way, there is hardly any individual of sound understanding who would disagree. But if sex equality means that the type of mental and bodily faculties, psychological make-up and temperamental equipment possessed by the two sexes is identically the same and that men and women exist and have their, being not as complements to each other but as competitors and rivals in a common sphere of action, then it is an ideal about which most people would disagree. As we shall discuss later, even modern writers and specialists on sex are not agreed on this point.

As far as the Holy Quran is concerned, it promulgated the doctrine of human equality, including sex equality, in a comprehensive verse which negates all inequalities due to sex, race, colour, nationality, caste or tribe.

This is a declaration in plain terms that, in essential human dignity and fundamental rights, all human beings of whatever sex or race or nationality stand on a footing of equality, because they all ultimately spring from a single source.

When Islam appeared in Arabia, women held a very low position in society. They were treated not only as social inferiors but like slaves and chattel. When a man having many wives died, the latter were inherited by his sons like movable property. It was a mark of dishonour for any man to have a daughter, and many preferred to bury alive their female children rather than face social opprobrium. It was Islam and the teachings of the Holy Prophet which dispelled the prevailing idea that women were inferior to men or that female children deserved any treatment different from that meted out to male issues.

Here, again, the Quran lent support to the basic equality of women and men by declaring that each sex complements the other, and neither is inferior in status and dignity. The word 'apparel' may be interpreted to mean either 'protection' or 'dignity and beauty'. The verse would mean, therefore, that men and women protect each other from sin and dishonour or it may mean that woman lends dignity and adds beauty to the existence of man, as, man does to that of woman.

In consonance with this spirit of equality the Prophet of Islam constantly reminded his followers that female children should be treated exactly in the same manner as male issues. Prior to Islam, daughters were looked upon with disfavour and as a kind or economic and social burden. The result was that male members of the family enjoyed a respect which was denied to those of the fair sex. There were marked differences, in the treatment and upbringing of sons and daughters. All this was discouraged by the Holy Prophet (peace be on him) who upheld the rights of female children and insisted on their being treated on a footing of equality. For example, according to a report of Ibn Abbas, the Prophet's cousin, he is said to have declared: 'If a daughter is born to a man and he brings her up affectionately, shows her no disrespect and treats her in the same manner as he treats his sons, the Lord will reward him with paradise' (Kanz ul Amal, p. 277). According to another report from Anas b. Malik, the Prophet said: 'Girls are models of affection and sympathy and a blessing to the family. If a person has one daughter, God will screen him from the fire of the hell owing to his daughter; if he has two daughters, God will admit him to paradise, if he has three, God will exempt him from the obligations of charity and Jihad (ibid). Abu Hurrayrah, a revered companion of the Prophet, says: 'The Prophet of God said that if a person has three daughters whom he provides for and, brings up, God will surely reward him with paradise.' According to Abdullah ibn Masud, the Prophet is reported to have said: 'If a daughter is born to a person and he brings her up, gives her a good education and trains her in the arts of life, I shall myself stand between him and hell-fire' (ibid.). Not content with moral exhortations intended to assert the equal rights of free women, the Prophet went so far as to declare. 'A person who has a female slave in his charge and takes steps to give her a sound education and trains her in arts and, culture, and then frees her and marries her, he will be doubly rewarded' (Sahi Bukhari, Kitab al-Nikah).

It follows that if men and women have equal, duties in regard to prayers, the payment of Poor-tax and, most of all, in the enjoining of good and the forbidding of evil in all their social, economic and political forms, it is necessary that they should have equal educational opportunities. How can a woman enjoin the good in politics or forbid men from bad politics, how can she raise her voice against ruinous economic policies or advocate, beneficial economic reforms, if she is not mentally and spiritually well equipped for the supreme religious duty? It should also be remembered that Islam makes no distinction between secular duties and religious duties. According to the teachings of Islam all duties, whether they concern politics, economics or social well-being in general, are religious duties, in no way different from prayers, fasts and the organisation of social charity. It is, therefore, a plain deduction from the above verses that men and women should be regarded as equal in the fields of politics and education, etc., and, consistent with the discharge of their special responsibilities in their particular spheres, they should receive equal rights in all these fields of action.

The, Prophet not only enunciated this general doctrine of sex equality involving equal educational opportunities but also practised it. Innumerable are the traditions of the Prophet which show that women like men, used to come freely in the presence of the Prophet for putting questions and addressing inquiries on all sort of social, religious and economic matters. The Prophet used to answer their queries and enlighten them on all live issues. Arabia, in particular and the world in general, was so backward in those days that there were no organised educational institutions even for boys, not to speak of girls. So the Islamic attitude towards female education can be studied only from the casual remarks of the Prophet and his permission to women to approach him freely for inquiries on matters of religious, economic and social importance. There is no doubt that the Prophet encouraged women in the spirit of understanding and inquiry. His wife, Aishah, was herself a very learned woman, and during the reign of the first four Caliphs her advice, even on political matters, was eagerly sought by the rulers of Islam.

On Islamic jurisprudence she was and is still regarded as a great authority. In his collection of traditions, Muslim reports that Aishah praised the women of Ansar for their spirit of inquiry and learning, saying, 'How praiseworthy are the women of Ansar that their modesty does not prevent them from attempts at learning and the acquisition of knowledge'; (Muslims, Sahih, Kitab al-Taharat). This statement was occasioned by the fact that the women of Ansar were more eager than others to learn from the Prophet and they used to address frequent inquiries to him. Instead of discouraging them, the wife of the Holy Prophet characterises as highly praiseworthy their eagerness for learning and inquiry.

Despite the great stress it has laid on the essential and fundamental equality of men and women and their equal rights in all matters, of vital concern, the Holy Quran does not believe in that conception of sex equality which ignores the natural differences, special aptitudes and specific powers and faculties of men and women with the resulting of men for some kinds of work and the equal fitness, of women for other types of activity. On the whole, the Holy Quran regards men and women as complementary to each other, one sex making up what the other lacked.

The main points to be noted here are, first, that the female sex must be a source of comfort and peace of mind to its male counterpart; secondly, that men and women excel each other or are superior to each other in some respects and that in the general affairs of life men are partially, but not absolutely, superior to women. These general statements involve certain indirect conclusions which are of the greatest importance to social happiness. The Quran, it seems, first sets forth a general doctrine of sex equality and then qualifies and defines it with the assertion that this is not a bald and undifferentiated equality but one involving special rights and duties both for men and women, within the framework of their special responsibilities: both sexes are absolutely equal to each other.

Now, what are the conclusions to be drawn from the qualifications mentioned by the Holy Quran? It is emphasised by the Holy Book that the female sex is a source of comfort and quietness of mind to the male sex. This can happen only if men and women are united in a more or less permanent based of interests which finds expression in a life planned and based on some idea of the future which requires them to cooperate and not to compete, and integrates them as complements in an ordered whole. These considerations involve a pattern of life of which Marriage, Family and Children are the most important factors because there can be no other abiding interest to hold together two individuals of different sexes. A mere community of intellectual interests or identity of special aptitudes is an insufficient bond even for that microscopic minority to whom, these things matter most. For the large majority of men and women these can hardly provide any link unless they are supported and strengthened by the desire for family life and children. It is obvious, therefore, that Islam does not envisage any social pattern from which family and children have been excluded, and since these two factors involve special functions for women and special responsibilities for men, equality of rights in Islam means an equality which is adjusted to and qualified by the special duties and responsibilities of each sex.

Again the Quran recognises the superiority of both sexes over each other in some respects. To the extent that men are superior to women and women to men in certain matters, the doctrine of equality must be, qualified with due regard to natural, facts. About the special position of men, the Quran makes two statements. First that men are the supporters or sustainers of women in a sense. But it must be noted that this implies no natural superiority on the part of men, nor any inherent inferiority of women, because it is a purely, economic arrangement dictated by natural necessities. The Quran, however, accords a slight superiority to men, in general by saying that men are a degree superior to women. This superiority of men relates both to the domestic and political fields. In domestic life, final authority must rest with one sex or the other. There cannot be two co-equal authorities here as elsewhere. Similarly, in the political field also final decisions should rest with men in general, because men are by nature gifted with a wider vision and also because their comparative freedom from certain natural limitations, which absorb a considerable amount of female time and energy, enables them to devote more attention to political affairs.

Having stated the Islamic conception of sex equality, we shall examine whether the qualifications made by Islam to the general doctrine of sex equality find any support from modern writers on the subject of sex. The question ultimately resolves itself into one of differences between men and women in regard to their faculties, powers, aptitudes and temperaments. If there are such differences and dividing lines, then the doctrine of perfect sex equality can be true only with the qualifications set forth by the Holy Quran and to the extent of these qualifications there ought to follow a scheme of life in which men and women, apart from general and equal rights and duties, must be assigned special rights and exclusive responsibilities. Many modern writers on sex, would generally agree with the above proposition. For example, Dr. Alexis Carrel, a French Nobel Prize winner, says in his famous book, *Man, the Unknown:* The differences existing between man and woman are of a mere fundamental nature. They are caused by the very structure of the tissues and by the impregnation of the entire organism with specific chemical substances secreted by the ovary. Ignorance of these fundamental facts has led the promoters of feminism to believe that both sexes should have the same responsibilities. In reality, woman differs profoundly from man. Every one of the cells, of her body bears the mark of her sex. The same is true of her organs and, above all, of her nervous system. Women should develop their aptitudes in males. Their part in the progress of civilization is higher than that of men. They should not abandon their special functions.

There are a large number of equality enthusiasts among us now who are either unwilling to recognise such radical differences between the two sexes or accepting them grudgingly, insist on their removal and obliteration by conscious efforts. What these people fail to note is that the peace of mind and comfort on which the Quran has laid stress in the relation between the two sexes is the outcome of these very differences. If they could possibly be removed, sex life and marriage would lose much of their charm. On this point we would quote the American writer, Margaret Mead, who says in her book, *Male and Female:* Our tendency at present is to minimize all these differences in learning, in rhythm, in type and timing of rewards, and at most to try to obliterate particular differences that are seen as handicap on one sex. If boys are harder to train, train, them harder; if girls grow faster than boys, separate them, so the boys would not be damaged; if women have a little less strength than man invent machines so that they can still do the same work. But every adjustment that minimizes a difference, a vulnerability, in one sex, a differential strength in the other, diminishes their possibility of complementing each other, and corresponds symbolically to sealing off the constructive receptivity of the female and the vigorous outgoing constructive activity of the male, muting them both in the end to the duller version of human life, in which each is denied the fulness of humanity that each might have had. Guard each sex in its vulnerable moments; we must protect and cherish them through the crises that sometimes are harder for one sex than for the other. But as we guard, we may also keep the differences. Simply compensating for differences is in the end a form of denial.

This sound advice of a writer who herself happens to be a woman and belongs to an advanced country of the West must serve as an eye-opener to those extremists who, in their blind enthusiasm for sex equality, are advocating all sorts of ridiculous reforms and denying the beneficial effects of sex differences as well as the complementary position of man and, woman in respect of each other.

This same American writer, commenting on the increasing entry of women in professional field (of course, under a wrong conception of sex equality) further remarks: 'It is of very doubtful value to enlist the gifts of women if bringing women into fields that have been defined as male frightens the men, unsexes the women, muffles and distorts the contribution the women could make, either because their presence excludes men from the occupation or because it changes the quality of the men who enter.'

It would seem, then, that the doctrine of sex equality cannot be pushed to a point where it means that men and women are equally, fit for all fields of employment or that the indiscriminate entry of women in the professional fields would have no undesirable social effects.

In regard to the Quranic statement that men and women excel each other in some respects and are, therefore, unequal to that extent, we shall quote another American woman writer, Mary B. Bread, who gives a very interesting account of the discussions held on this point by American psychologists, in her book, *Woman as Force in History*. She writes: At its ninth spring meet the Eastern branch of the American Psychological Association held-sessions on the attitude of men and women towards men.

The meeting lasted for two days and nearly one thousand persons were reported attending its session. The main discussion revolved round the results of a questionnaire submitted to an equal number of men and women. By means of this survey designed to explore opinions of men and women about women, the conclusions was reached by its promoters, that both sexes were in a remarkable agreement in favour of equal social rights for both sexes and a wide disagreement in evaluating the emotional stability and originality of women.

In the discussion which followed, a statement of the survey's findings, men and women participated and according to newspaper accounts, 'seven out of every ten men, and an equal proportion of women, believed that men were less influenced by emotion than women in their judgements.' To the statement that 'women are more interested in the trivial things of life than men,' 91.7 per cent of the men and 92.1 per cent of the women gave their assent.

The discovery or assumption that women differ from men governed discussions of the subject by members of the Psychological Association which assembled at Palo Alto a, few years ago, and much importance was attached to glandular differentiations.

'What is the psychological difference between a boy and a girl?' was the question on which they attempted to focus their remarks. The question had been put before the members of the Association for meditation in advance of this meeting. Indeed, a report, framed by two men and one woman of Stanford University, was ready for the guidance of the discussion. Its burden was that the 'original constitutional' equipment of girls and boys differs. And in women, it asserted, the whole glandular system is 'more precarious' than in men. But mental balance is 'superior in the male'. Whys and where-fores of the divergence in mental balance were 'probably' traceable to the basic physical differences, some speakers averred. As the discussion was reported in the Press, its upshot was the consensus that 'women in general have made no relative progress against mental irregularities since they began throwing off conventional restraints at high speed.'

Now, if the above conclusions are true, it means that men, being less amenable to emotional influences and possessing a more stable mental balance, are better fitted for political activity which requires calm reasoning and lesser susceptibility to emotional influences. Similarly, these conclusions also establish the fact that, being mentally more stable, men are bound to remain superior in intellectual pursuits which require persistent and continuous work. These facts make it clear that the ideal of sex equality cannot be accepted without important qualifications and reservations based on the ultimate facts of the psychology and nature of the two sexes.

In the sphere of sexual morality, it has been observed by modern protagonists of sex equality that it is unjust to apply two different standards in respect of men and women; that if sexual laxity in men is not regarded as a very serious offence, there is no reason why it should be so regarded in women. This is true up to a certain limit and Islamic teachings have never made any discrimination in this respect between males and females. Thus adultery, according to Warn, in both men and women, is legally an equal offence punishable with equal penalties. But even in this sphere unalterable facts of nature tilt the balance in favour of men. Discussing this question, Dr. Westermarck says in *The Future of Marriage in Western Civilization:* But even if public opinion would, in the future, grant complete sexual freedom to the unmarried of either sex, the indulgence of it by girls would still be attendant with serious disadvantages already pointed out.

There would undoubtedly be exploitation in women by men; girls who remained virgins would still be preferred as wives, and the others would run the risk of being used for temporary purposes. Feminists advocating equal freedom for men and women seem to overlook the benefits that the men would derive from it; they would find it easier to gratify their desires in a more agreeable manner than through intercourse with prostitutes, and at the same time to acquire sexual experience is considered useful for their future marriage. When speaking of the 'injustice' of different moral demands on men and women, those advocates also fail to notice that this difference is ultimately due to a difference in the sexual instincts of the two sexes.

The ideas expressed above are more or less in line with the Islamic conception of sex equality; As we have shown in the beginning of this chapter, Islam upholds the essential human dignity and fundamental equality of the two sexes, but, along with the common rights and duties of men and women in which both are equal, it concedes some separate rights and prescribes some separate duties for men and women, in accordance with its view that each sex has its specific functions in society and is charged with an independent mission for the preservation and advancement of the human race. Within the limits of their special mission and functions in society, both men and women will have different rights and responsibilities and neither sex should feel jealous of the other if this involves lesser rights for one sex against the other in a strictly limited sphere and on easily understandable terms capable of adjudication in law-courts. According to Islam, there is a specific sex individuality in man and woman which they must preserve and cherish, because it is this individuality which gives them honour and dignity and enables them to fulfil in an effective manner their specific role in society. Where this specific sex individuality, instead of being regarded as a source of honour and dignity, is sought to be pulled and effaced, as if it involved an inferiority in men or women, it produces a dead and colourless equality which is, in effect, a denial of real equality, as it makes for less differentiation and, therefore, for less progress. There are clear instructions of the Holy Prophet on this point which stress the need for preserving sex individuality. Thus Abu Daud records it on the authority of Abu Hurrayrah, a companion of the Prophet, that the Prophet uttered a curse on men who imitate women in their dress and manners and similarly on women who abhorred their femininity by trying to dress and act like men. Similarly, at another place, Abu Daud has recorded that the Prophet severely condemned those women who tried to appear and behave in the form and likeness of men.

Consistent with the exercise of their specific individuality and of the special functions flowing therefrom and involving special rights and responsibilities, both sexes have equal rights and are looked upon by Islam as distinct legal personalities. A wife, even after having come in partnership with her husband, is a separate legal person in Islamic law capable of suing and being sued in her own individual capacity and entitled to sue her own husband for any infringement of her just rights. This is a position which was not accorded to the female sex in Europe and America until the nineteenth century and this too after a great deal of agitation against the existing legal disabilities of women. Blackstone, who was the greatest exponent of the English Common Law and has profound influence on legal theory and practice both in England and America, maintained that the legal position of a married woman was one of unity with husband.

This was the position of a married woman in Europe and America until about 150 years ago. She could lose her rights on her own property, if the husband wished to deprive her of them because the law did not recognise her as separate legal personality. Islam, on the other hand, from its very inception, gave the married woman a separate Legal status with full property rights. Little wonder that a wrong conception of sex equality and extremist stand in respect of female freedom resulted from the sense of utter frustration generated by such great social and legal disabilities. But how could the Muslim women be justified in going to the same extreme length and preaching a conception of sex equality which lacks all scientific and natural basis as evidenced by latest researches on sex psychology.

Championing Equality

In the 6th century the greatest event of the history of mankind which shook the very basic ideals and concepts of man and brought about a complete revolution in his thoughts and views and a total change in his character, was the high-spirited and high-hearted proclamation of the Prophethood of Hadrat Muhammad (peace and blessings of Allah be upon him). The result of this revolution was that it not only took a different turn in man's thought, but also gave a new direction to his life. One significant aspect of this new trend of thinking was the 'concept of woman' which underwent a complete change and thereby established the relationship between man and woman on entirely new grounds.

Before the advent of Islam and the arrival of Prophet Muhammad (peace be upon him) and his proclamation of Prophethood, the history of woman was no doubt the history of subjugation and oppression. She was underestimated and condemned as a low and mean creature and was regarded as the root cause of all evils and disasters. Instructions were given to be careful about her and to avoid her like snakes and scorpions. She was bought and sold like animals. She did not enjoy any absolute or independent position in the society and was made subservient to man. She was denied all rights and had to live on the pity and mercy of man. In such a dark period of the history of woman, Islam raised its voice so vehemently that the whole world reverberated with it. Today no one dares say that her previous position was correct and real.

It was declared that the discrimination which the world has made between one man and the other is false, absurd and baseless. The whole mankind is the offspring of the single human soul. Originally all have the same descent. No one is noble or mean, or low or high by birth. All are equal and enjoy equal position. Any kind of distinction between them on the grounds of family status, race, colour, tribe, region, language, occupation or nationality is null and void.

It was thus a repudiation of the age-old differences and discrimination between man and woman. It brought into light the fact that the very companion of the first man was not of some other kind but belonged to the same species. No different kind of creature was taken for his companionship, rather she was taken from him alone. This first pair gave birth to numerous men and women and among them some or the other kind of relationship existed and thus the whole human generation got spread far and wide. Hence to differentiate and discriminate between man and woman is in fact to differentiate and discriminate between one side of mankind and the other and is the division of the two parts of a single whole. There can be no better elucidation than this for the expression of the equality of man and woman and their equal status.

It is also stated that all human beings are the servants of one God and the children of one and the same father and mother. Therefore on the one side they should worship and obey God and lead their life in fear of Him and on the other, give due respect to the relationships which exist between them. Here, with the honour of man, the honour of woman is also emphasised.

Islam totally repudiated the notion that man is dignified and honoured merely because he is a man and woman is low and mean simply because she is a woman. Both man and woman are equal in the eyes of Islam. Neither the inferiority of anyone nor superiority of anybody is written down for eternity.

Generally, two objections are raised against the position of woman in Islam. First, that the great responsibility of household affairs which is imposed upon her, would debar her from participating in the economic and social development. For this reason it is assumed that her position in the society would not be definite, but would be weak and unstable. Regarding this, it needs to be clarified, that Islam has not barred woman from economic activities, rather it has given permission while imposing on her a few appropriate limitations. Although it is doubtless that her involvement in family affairs affects her economic struggle, Islam offers its own solution to it. Islam has held man legally responsible for the maintenance of his wife and children.

The second objection is that since the great responsibility of the house is vested in woman, she is confined to the four walls of the house. It is conceived that since she is completely engrossed in the home affairs, neither the society would be benefited from her abilities nor would she get any opportunity to contribute her potentialities to society.

This objection is also incorrect and without any substance. Islam has not forbidden woman from other activities which stand beyond the household activities. What Islam virtually intends and emphasises in this regard is that a woman is mainly a queen and forerunner of her house. Hence, she should not bear the outward burden of the work at the risk of her indoor work. She is allowed to participate in the economic struggle with man while performing her role in the family affairs. Furthermore, she can take interest and contribute her abilities in different fields of life while keeping into consideration her condition, social environment and her own interest. History bears witness to the fact that the Muslim women have manifested their abilities, skill and talent in different fields of life and have left a tremendous impact on the age.

The most important thing is, Islam has assigned woman a prominent position at social level. Hence, she can lead an honoured and dignified life without becoming a victim of any inferiority complex. She can, in fact, offer her fullest cooperation to man in building up a chaste and virtuous society while contributing her potentialities and abilities which she possesses.

Different Spheres

There are two important reasons for which Islam assigns different spheres of activity to man and woman. First, it helps them guard their chastity. When both of them perform their work in the same sphere, it will become difficult for them to lead a life of chastity and modesty. If man and woman mix with each other in educational institutions to pursue education and participate in sports and games, and other recreations in parks and picnic spots and engage themselves openly in markets and in business centres without any checks and balances and meet each other without any restriction and this process of intermingling continues not for a day or two but for years together and in this way all the stages from childhood to youth and from youth to old age will be crossed, it is certain that their physical urges will get excited and flared up and will become uncontrolled and unchecked and ultimately they will become victims of indecent sexual anarchy.

In the present age, wherever free mixing of man and woman has been granted, it has resulted in a disaster. Chastity and honour are ravaged and modesty and decency are crippled. It gives rise to vulgar and ignoble sexual lapses which like an epidemic disease goes to such an extent that it becomes difficult to cure and correct it. And now it is taken as an inescapable social evil. Also all the evil results of it are willingly or unwillingly tolerated.

Chastity and modesty are apparently moral values, and it is on this basis that the direction of the whole society is determined. In a society where no importance is given to these values, man from every direction is taken to debased and evil acts and adultery. It gives rise to a particular kind of culture, civilisation, association, manners and literature, each element of which ignites fire in the sexual emotions of man. Contrary to it, the society which realises the importance and value of chastity and purity is erected entirely on a different standard. Each act of such a society reflects the purity of character, modesty and decency, and piety and purity fills the whole environment.

Woman passes through such stages of life which restrict her from performing heavy work constantly. Her menstrual period begins from her youth and continues until she steps into the old age. Moreover, she passes through the most difficult and arduous stages like pregnancy and delivery. All these conditions and stages affect her health, strength and manner and stand as obstacles on the way of constant and laborious work. Now, it is the question of justice that she should not be given any tedious and wearisome works. Islam, therefore, assigns the work which requires more strength and valour to man and the work which is not hard and tedious to woman. Islam solves the problem thus that woman should look after the house while man should perform outside duties.

The very nature, interest and the psychology of woman demands the same sort of work. Woman in herself possesses the qualities of grace, love, patience, devotion and sacrifice more than a man. She fills the whole atmosphere of the family with happiness and order, peace and tranquility and love and affection. But to face the hardships and difficulties of life and to march forward firmly on all ups and downs, strong determination, bravery and intrepidity are the qualities which are required. Man possesses all these qualities far more than woman. The home and the family, however, provide a peaceful environment. The abilities of woman distinctively appear more sharply in the house from which full advantage can be derived. Man can face the complications and problems of life. For this reason man should be given such responsibilities as require more courage and valour.

It is no fairness to woman that she should be taken out from her natural field of work and be pushed into an unnatural field of work. It is not advantageous for her, rather a great loss.

The pains of menstrual period, pregnancy and delivery are unavoidable. Man can hardly assist her in all these difficulties and complications. It is, therefore, not a fair play if she is also given the responsibilities of man.

The woman is the queen of the house. She gets all the love and affection from her father, brother and husband and all the members of her family and all her rights are protected in the house. If woman does not bear the responsibility of the house, she cannot claim her rights. Thereafter she will have to work in such a field to pass her life which will not be in fact her own field and where she will have to face such a partner at every step who will be stronger than her. Then, it can be hardly expected that she will surpass man.

The place of honour and dignity of a woman is her own house, not the market. But in the present age, the importance of house and family is not fully recognised. It is the reason that the important role of woman in the house is interpreted as an injustice to her or that it gives her a low and mean position in the society or to deny her rights which she possesses or to condemn her constantly to the lowest position though a family is the basic unit of every society. The importance and significance of the house stands far ahead than of an office or a bazaar. The service which a woman renders in building the inner environment of her house is more important than the service which she can render outside. Here some aspects of her work are mentioned.

Services of Woman

Today, man is engrossed in innumerable political, social, cultural and other problems. Other factors like health, diseases, poverty, difficulties also coincide with these problems. Sometimes for earning and living, man struggles too severely, bears all kinds of pains and faces innumerable difficulties. For maintaining and uplifting his family, he overcomes insurmountable hardships. In such a state of affairs, he deserves mental peace and content. It is the home which can provide him with all this peace and rest. If he does not get peace even at his own home, it becomes too hard for him to live: Islam teaches that a woman should make her home a 'peaceful dwelling' so that man should forget all his tensions and complications after reaching his home and prepare himself for a fresh struggle after breathing an air of gratification.

It has become an established fact that there is no better nourishment for a child than the milk of his mother. If a mother does not stay at home and engages herself in outside activities, she cannot set herself for breast-feeding. In this way the proper nourishment of the child for a considerable period even after the age of breast-feeding depends on mother. For the proper bringing up of the child, it is not just enough to give him proper nourishment but the child abundantly needs the love and affection, sympathy and an earnest devotion of his mother. If he is devoid of love and emotions from his nearest environment, his whole personality gets affected and even if his personality blossoms it will develop in a very wrong direction. It is the heart of mother which is the source of inspiration for the child. Nobody else can take the place of woman for playing a decisive role. If the mother remains outside the home, the child would yearn for the love of his mother and he will not get it.

For the basic education and training of the child, mother is most suitable. For the purpose of education of the child, it is necessary that his teachers should be very loving and devoted to him, and should be acquainted with the nature and psychology of the child, and tolerate all his mischiefs and check him with love and patience. The most important thing is that the child should also love the teacher and consider even the bitterest scolding of the teacher to be good and beneficial for his well-being and tolerate even the harshness of the teacher. These sorts of feelings do not prevail between any two persons other than between mother and child. Let us look at another aspect. From educational point of view, it is extremely important that there should prevail an intimate and cordial relationship between the teacher and the child. The stronger this relationship, the better and beneficial it would be for the child. Perhaps, because of this reason, classes of higher standards are not much liked in schools because there the relationship between the teacher and the child is weaker in most of the cases. Comparatively, the classes of the lower standards are liked much because here this relationship is found to be stronger. In this manner the mother can provide basic education for her children which they cannot possibly acquire even at school.

Most of the children do not obtain proper education because they do not get better tutors at home or their parents are not able to afford tutors for them. Furthermore, most of the parents do not get proper tutors for their daughters. If the mother is capable enough to educate her children and even feel that it is her responsibility to give proper education to her children, the expenditure which is incurred on education will also get curtailed and help solve many other problems.

Here, one important point from the Muslim outlook on education is that today little attention is being paid to religious education. Very few children obtain religious education. Consequently, the child is sent to school when he has reached the age of school going. He does not get any opportunity even the preliminary religious instructions. Therefore, even the children of some good and God-fearing people remain ignorant of the basic religious tenets. The reason behind all this is that the father does not get time to give them religious instructions and the mother either herself lacks such education or does not take interest in education. If the mother is thoughtful enough and also capable of giving education to her children, they will not be ignorant of their religion, even after obtaining education in schools.

Even for training the children, the role of the mother is most important and significant. It is the mother who stands as an ideal for a child. The child observes the morals and etiquette of his mother day and night and moulds his behaviour noting the behaviour of his mother. The child maintains the same sort of relationship between himself and others on the mode of the relationship which his mother maintains between herself and others. Mother is his virtual model in this aspect and plays a decisive role in moulding the character of her child.

The fact is that the construction of a society depends upon the construction of a house. This is the reason that Islam has completely relied upon woman to construct her house. Islam does not wish to thrust on her other burdens along with this responsibility. The woman is freed even from the financial responsibilities. In the light of Islam, the construction of their house is no less important than Jihad. Hadrat Anas related that once a group of women asked Prophet Muhammad (peace be upon him) that men perform some acts and attain the reward of Jihad, what we should do to get such reward which men get through Jihad in the way of God? Prophet Muhammad (peace be upon him) replied that woman who sits at home receives the reward of Jihad in the way of God.

3

Islamic Social System

Political themes, either related to leadership, political parties or social control, are essential aspects at communal rituals in Islamic Iran:, along with ethical themes on justice, equality, power and empowerment. A ritual symbol may stand for many things at the same time. By this he means that one must consider the informant's explanation of the socio-structural implication of the treatment and usage of ritual objects in performance, as well as the spatial and hierarchical positioning of ritual objects independent of exegesis and usage. At the women's Quranic meetings, the female preacher often went into great detail to clarify the complexity of various issues and examples. She played an important role, not only in teaching women the correct performance of prayers and Islamic rules, but also in teaching how to understand surrounding political events.

The degrees of political involvement and political rhetoric of preachers were distinguished both symbolically and through actual request. This can be deduced: from the distinctive personal, social, and, political views expressed in the context of sermons and the participant definition. It was not unusual to find that a ritual was performed and interpreted by different preachers in a slightly different manner, depending on the political' and educational background of the preachers.

A woman volunteer started distributing *mehr* (the clay of Karbala) to each participant, and as the reading approached the verses requiring the performance of the two units of *sajdeh*, we laid our foreheads on the assumed clay of Karbala, and repeated the verse read by the preacher loudly. The preacher asked those who were menstruating to leave the meeting and stay outside where they could not hear the sound of the verses. This created an: unpleasant situation, for those women who were obliged to leave the room, and some preferred to leave the meeting altogether.

There are explicit differences in the flexibility of a preacher's interpretations and views regarding women's act of purity and veiling. First it is a matter of social and ritual obedience, and secondly it is a matter of ritual in its cognitive sense, and not a problem of a social nature. In several meetings it became clear that the Hezbullahi preacher was distinguished by the participants as one who made repetitive: and restrictive references to women's rigid veiling and conventional behaviour. This was contrasted, by the modesty of the politically neutral preacher (*bi-taraf*), who took a more moderate view.

Some meetings were conservative, as judged by factors such as the number of women wearing bead-scarves under their chador, the content of the Quranic commentary given by the female preacher, and the repetitive offering of the blessing (*salvat*) to Imam Khomeini; and his successor, and president Rafsanjani. The negative term monafeqin, which means conspiracy, is a strong multivocal symbol conveying various messages and contrasting attributes concerning a series of illegitimate social and political divisions. Monafeqin may refer not only simply to good and evil, but also to state political norms, such as the Iranian case of women who are poorly veiled, as well as to any act of political resistance.

The preacher Zaki usually stopped reciting after every short verse (*ayat*) to offer a commentary. She was one of the preachers who thought it better not to continue before ensuring that the participants had a proper understanding of what was being read. She translated the Quranic meaning into a daily context, thereby making its realisation more practical for the participants, who were from various social categories (the majority being housewives and young schoolgirls). The preacher maintained that the kind of suppressions one could experience varied, and convincingly demonstrated this point by the use of metaphors. The reality of one's experience of 'suppression' was open to interpretation.

According to the preacher Zaki, Islamic suppression may be related both to the lack of juridical teachings concerning the rights of men and women and to being a good Muslim in practical terms according to legitimate Islamic codes. Public lessons in juridical matters were often brief, and in response to complicated questions the preachers might postpone answering to make further inquiries from a more learned religious person, such as a male or female *mujtahid*. The metaphor of suppression continued on another level in another Quranic meeting a few days later. This time it was raised by the preacher Mostafi, who defined suppression as acts of political tyranny, and as something that could be harmful to the whole Muslim community.

The *rowzeh* participants were familiar with the name of Salman Rushdie 94 and the Islamic state's political fight against him. He was understood to have committed an act of blasphemy by denying the existence of God and the legitimacy of Muhammad as his Prophet. The preacher Mostafi wishing him a misfortune, and punishment by hanging. Some of the attendants supported her statement by saying amen. The metaphorical references of suppression and the model of corrupt leadership were two on-going political themes in mass media. They were phrased according to the Islamic state dominant political view.

However, on one occasion it was clear that the preacher lacked accurate knowledge of the international political situation, but was familiar with the Islamic state's political rhetoric. For example, on one occasion the preacher Mostafi referred to both the CIA (American Intelligence Service) and KGB (Soviet Intelligence Service) as the American secret service without anybody making any attempt to correct her. This did not prevent her from conveying the desired political message to her listeners, as she accused these international agencies of 'suppression', in their attempts to undermine the Iranian Revolution and its Islamic virtue.

A suppressor of poorly-veiled women: The identities of 'poorly-veiled' and 'non-veiled' (*bi-hejab*) despite their wearing Islamic suits (*manto*), have emerged in conservative political slogans, condemning the degree of immodesty among women. Posters covering street walls, with slogans such as 'death to bi-hejab and bad-hejab', attach a negative label to women, who neglect to veil themselves fully.

'Poorly-veiled' is a negative term applied to those whose appearance and social manner may be defined as fashionable, tempting and provocative; i.e. to those wearing colourful scarves, light colours, fashionable styles, make-up, transparent stockings, etc. This is considered a political act of *monafeqin*, and is generally applied on those who are believed to oppose and destroy Islamic values, instead invoking perversion. The negative image of a poorly-veiled woman as a suppressor of the Islamic community has developed through religious speeches. This is further illustrated by the case of a widow who had arranged a meeting to mark the annual remembrance ceremony for her husband. Close and distant relatives, as well as friends and local women, gathered for the meeting.

The female preacher Mostafi frequently paused to interpret Quranic recitations, and whenever she came to the term *monafeqin* (conspirators), she explained it in terms of external and internal enemies of Islam. She also included women who wore thin stockings together with Islamic suits, for being 'provocative' and modern in style. Furthermore, she accused women who failed to dress properly of weakening the ideology of the revolution, and repeatedly saluted the martyrs (*shohada*) and prisoners of war (*asiran*) with the verse of *salvat*. She unexpectedly addressed the married daughter of the house, a university lecturer who was serving tea to the attendants, asking her to stop serving to allow the audience to concentrate on the sermon.

After the ceremony some participants believed the preacher had become cross with her on account of the way she was dressed. The initiator of the *rowzeh* complained that she was very disappointed, and that the memorial ceremony for her husband had been used for political ends, which was an insult to his memory. She regretted not having invited another female preacher whom she knew herself, rather than this one who had been recommended by her religiously 'orthodox' sister.

An another example of being an Islamic conspirator, the preacher Zaki cited shopkeepers, who would hoard goods (*ahtekar*) and sell things at inflated prices. Economic gains at the expense of those Muslim customers who are in a financially difficult situation was considered an unmeritful act during their fife of permanent economic well-being. Such undertakings were categorised as illegitimate (*haram*), because the aim was solely to accumulate capital.

Despite hoarding being described in official terms as acts of immorality and corruption, businessmen increasingly adopted it as a new avenue for economic success. These Islamic lessons not only suggest the moral identity of authority at the level of family, community and state, but the way they can be corrupted and distract communal social order. Disagreement was expressed among attendants in private religious meetings either as defenders or against the preacher. Although women seemed reluctant to counter the Islamic state policy directly, they often did so metaphorically. They often felt more free to express themselves outside the religious meetings when talking to a friend, to me, or to relatives.

Once, in the month of Ramadan in 1989, and during a regular lesson concerning the performance of prayer, an older participant interrupted the preacher Mostafi and asked the following question: 'I wonder how it can be an act of *halal* (permission) to perform the prayers of *namaz* on the floor of a house, which has been a forcefully confiscated, property (*qasbi*)?' This was not simply a ritual question, but had numerous connotations for participants, who could clearly explain the political issue the questioner had in mind. This created a funny situation, and some smiled slightly at the preacher who could not give a proper answer, and thus postponed it in order to make further inquiries. On another occasion, also at a meeting held by preacher Mostafi, and following the month of Ramadan, a participant expressed her disagreement on the ethical lesson concerning a Muslim duty, saying: 'I wonder how it can be a sinful act to ask why the price of potatoes has increased so rapidly?' The preacher had repeatedly said that in order not to disturb the ongoing operation of the Islamic state, we should avoid any kind of criticism.

A politically reserved attitude, and a symbolic mode of expression, are more common than ever before in Iranian everyday culture, due to the social and political burden. Thus, in the meeting of *rowzeh*, some of the preachers, either as a matter of personal loyalty to the state, or as a way of avoiding politically sensitive issues, may fail to answer 'improper' questions, and cut them short with a *salvat*. The contradiction between the actual political economy of Islamic states and Quranic notion of *zulm* gives a false representation of ideal religious values. Some middle-class and educated participants were more sensitive to speaking up, and expressing such a distortion.

The political opposition between questioner and preacher could be stated metaphorically. In response to the direct and critical political questions, which a preacher could accept as reasonable, she may excuse herself from answering by giving the impression of not being bothered with such issues. She might request her listeners to recite a salvat so to avoid answering the question before inviting the participants to continue the ritual of reading the Quranic verse for the day or before resuming her *tafsir*.

The political overtone of the male preacher at the mosque was even more direct, and covered broader political and social matters to a larger audience. Some considered that the political link to rituals would reduce the 'true' value of Islam. For this reason some hosts were reluctant to listen to or invite, any preacher.

The Quranic term of *efrat-o-tafrit* (too much and too little), is often used by disappointed religious participants, such as Narges, about situations where local events overlap political and religious commitments. Political intrusion is frequently given as the reason for the loss of one's former religious belief, and the loss of sacred traditional religious symbols in general. Nuzhat, a regular religious participant at private meetings, felt disturbed by the political overload in everyday religious activities. She found the regular Quranic recording from our neighbouring mosque loudspeaker disturbing and tiresome. She telephoned anonymously, asking the authorities to turn down the volume of the loudspeaker because she had a sick relative at home.

The connection between the ethical conduct of women's daily behaviour and the entire order of nature was often an element in the Islamic speeches of the preacher. The negative publicity given to unveiled women in the religious arena by male and female preachers was often the cause of public ideological conflict.

In an anthropological study of a Muslim community in Tunisia, the rain ritual: at the time of drought is described as an act of penance and a rite of reconciliation by which the members of the community are 'purified' and reincorporated.

In the context of the urban Shirazi, misfortunes or natural disorder are not only defined as a basis for community solidarity, but also as a metaphor for disagreement and political hostility between social categories, e.g. between the Islamic conservatism and the more liberal middle-class Muslim believers. In day-to-day social situations ideological differences have become aspects of individuals' social identities, frequently leading to conflict, and in extreme cases to public violence such as in 1989. The concept of *mosibat* or *bala* denotes misfortune as a result of too much sin. Sin is destructive to individual well-being and is believed to create social and ecological disorder, with drought as a consequence.

The idea is that God is angered by ingratitude, arrogance, immoral behaviour, and particularly by non-veiling. Heavy rain and drought are both believed to be caused by social disaster (*bala*), bringing negative consequences to the whole community. In March 1989 in daily Ramadan lessons, the preacher Zaki raised the unveiling question as usual. This time an attendant supported her view and defined it as a cause of a recent natural misfortune. Reproduction of Islamic order in ongoing political, social, and economic life has produced a new form of cultural complexity which is acted out in various social arenas such as religious meetings.

SOCIAL OBLIGATIONS

Freedom and equality are concepts which have been very much misused by the modern world. There is no doubt that human progress depends to a large extent on freedom and equality, and a society which creates artificial inequalities and places unnatural obstacles in the way of human freedom slowly degenerates and dies out. But it is equally true that real freedom does not lie in unrestricted license and presupposes as its inevitable corollary certain wholesome natural restrictions. Similarly, equality cannot mean a total obliteration of diversity arising from the natural and inborn differences between man and woman.

Real equality can be based only on an inequality of function where each individual and each sex is entrusted with the tasks to which its natural endowments and inherent qualities qualify it most. The Western civilisation has placed undue and exaggerated emphasis on self-assertion and self-expression for the historical reason that its fundamental concepts arose out of a struggle against artificial repressions.

The result is that the assertive and expressive tendencies of human beings have brought about internal conflicts which threaten to its foundation the very structure of civilisation. A balance between self-expression and self-repression, freedom and order, uniformity and diversity should be achieved to put human society on a stable basis. If this is true in the large spheres of human relations, it is equally true in the sex relations of men and women. An expert on sex psychology like Havelock Ellis says: 'We have always to remember that the whole art of living lies in a fine balance of expression and repression. For repression - understood in a wide sense and not merely in the special sense sometimes given to it by psychoanalysts - is as central a fact of life as expression. We are constantly at the same time repressing some impulses and expressing other impulses. There is no necessary penalty in the repression, for it is essential to expression.

Islam has placed certain restrictions on men as well as on women in order to regulate their sex and family life both of which it regards as the foundations of a stable and progressive civilisation. The restrictions on men and women differ in accordance with their varying functions in society. To the extent that these functions differ in the case of the two sexes, their rights and responsibilities also differ and the restrictions they are required to observe also differ. The advocates *of a bald and dead equality* who do not believe in the functional differentiation of the sexes will cite them as a proof of unequal treatment. Actually, these restrictions arise out of the different social responsibilities of either sex. If it is true that motherhood is one of the essential responsibilities of women, that sexual aberration in women leads to more complications and more serious consequences than the misconduct of men; if, again, it is true that men and women differ in the types (not degrees) of their natural gifts and that the physical powers of women are attuned to particular types of work only, then it is easy to see that, within the general framework of fundamental sex equality, their rights, duties and the channels of their self-expression and self-repression should also differ.

Saner intellectuals even among the Westerners have always recognised the functional differentiation between the two sexes. They also admit that women are better fitted for particular types of work than men, and ill-suited for other tasks. For example, the American authoress of *Male and Female*, Margaret Mead, discussing this point in connection with her researches into the life of savage tribes, writes: 'Thus if the theorist about men and women's natural work-rhythms had based his theories on *Jatmul*, he would easily have come up with a picture of man as the lineal descendant of a nomadic hunter, capable of strong output of effort, but demanding long periods of recuperation, and a picture of women as better fitted by nature for the routine tasks of everyday life, unresisting and unrebelling against a world in which their work was never done and their hands were hardly ever at rest.' Proceeding further, the same authoress says: 'If research finally demonstrates any genuine difference in the capacity to tolerate monotony, or to benefit by working in irregular spurts of energy, we still have to consider whether the most felicitous results are obtained by constructing a society in which women's work, while more monotonous and demanding, is also keyed up to the cycle of menstruation and pregnancy, and men's work, less monotonous and demanding, is the work that can be depended upon in any emergency, since men are subject to no such periodic rise and fall in capacity as women. Possibly we may find instead that if all work is keyed low enough so that women do not suffer too inappropriate demands during their periodic fluctuations in capacity, but men are not prevented from constructing crises if they find them congenial, the gain in adaptation of rhythm between the sexes may be greater than any loss that comes from not pitching the work-rhythms of each sex as perfectly as possible to their distinctive periodicities.'

Now this periodic rise and fall in the capacity of work among women is an undeniable physical fact that alters their function in society and excludes them from certain kinds of work. A civilisation which keeps this fact in view in the allocation of rights and duties will naturally suggest different social restrictions for women with a view to preventing them from transgressing their natural sphere of duties.

A more important physical factor which has a decisive bearing on the functions of women and marks out a different path of life for them is the physical periodicity of women arising from menstruation. Menstruation is by no means an ordinary phenomenon of local manifestation. It is but the most obvious symptom of the general monthly waves which periodically flow through a woman's body, affecting to a greater or lesser extent all her organs. The observations of a great many medical authorities have shown that during the process of menstruation most significant physical and mental changes are observed in women. The whole nervous system of women is affected during this period and it is the nervous system upon which depends the normal functioning of the general physiological well-being of women. Vemilow in his *Biological Tragedy of Woman* says that women's mental equilibrium is upset during the period of menstruation. He records his observation that a woman street-car conductor pulls out the wrong tickets and is muddled in counting the change. A menstruating moto-woman drives the street-car slowly and with hesitancy, becoming confused at crossings. The lady typist's fingers strike the wrong keys. The woman dentist cannot find the proper instrument. An actress is not in the right mood and makes wrong gestures. Writing in *Man and Woman*, Havelock Ellis observes that there is at this period greater impressionability, greater suggestions and more or less diminished self-control.

It is at this time that sudden caprices, fits of ill-temper, moods of depression, impulses of jealousy, outbursts of self-confession are chiefly liable to occur. At times menstruation produces abnormal and diseased conditions. There may be so high a degree of physical pain and disability that the woman is really an invalid for several days every month. On the basis of these facts Havelock Ellis had to utter a note of warning that 'it is no longer possible to regard the physiological periodicity of women and the recurring menstrual function as the purely private concern of the woman whom it affects'. Such a view necessarily leads to the conclusion that the public activities work and employment of women must be conditioned and limited by their physiological peculiarities. It cannot be that men and women are treated as equals in the field of industrial employment or in the matter of political activity. If an attempt is made to create an artificial equality which in fact does not exist, it is likely to break down with serious consequences.

Motherhood is another important factor in the life of women which conditions, limits and particularises their sphere of activity. In the modern world, a large number of well-to-do women, under the influence of a wrong conception of equality, have increasingly turned away from this noble life-vocation. Various theories and suggestions have been propounded to prove that motherhood is not essential to the life and happiness of women and that alternative institutions can be evolved which will free the mothers from the burden of rearing and training their children, thus allowing them greater liberty of movement and enabling them to share with men the larger activities of social and political life.

While no sane person will maintain that women should be kept confined to domestic life or should in no case participate in the wider spheres of collective activity, many will agree that the duties of motherhood form the primary concern of a woman's life, and a society which allows its female members to plunge into the wider spheres of life at the cost of their primary avocation is bound to suffer from maladjustment. It is only women who are already past the age of motherhood and can easily spare time and energy for other duties that should be really welcome in the political and industrial fields. But by far the largest number of women cannot escape, *if they ace to fulfil their function in society—the burden of their primary biological and social responsibility*. Of course, the more fortunate among them, by reason of their economic condition or limited family, can do, if they are so minded, part-time work in other fields but not in a way which might disturb their main functions. The saner elements among Western writers and thinkers have not overlooked this aspect of the matter and we shall give a few brief quotations from them.

Writing about the depth of maternal instinct in women, Havelock Ellis says: 'Most people, certainly most women, feel at moments, or at some period in their lives, a desire for children,' and in women the longing for a child may become so urgent and imperative that we may regard it as scarcely less imperative than the sexual impulse. Van de Veide writes: 'To be a woman means to have the desire to become a mother both physically and mentally.' He admits that 'there are women, and presumably always have been women, although their number may be relatively very small, who feel such a strong antagonism to motherhood that they refuse to marry for that reason,' but he adds: 'The absence of the maternal instinct in the modern woman is really nothing but a pose. The maternal instinct exists in spite of this, although there may be only one child .... Where it really is repressed, because some women think it fashionable, or because of decadence or love of pleasure, it will also be, seen that such repression has its revenge sooner or later. A more than temporary repression of the mother instinct is, practically speaking, impossible.'

A prominent American authoress Margaret Mead writes in, *Male and Female*: 'Women may be said to be mothers unless they are taught to deny their child-bearing qualities. Society must distort their sense of themselves, pervert their inherent growth patterns, perpetrate a series of.. outrages upon them, before they will cease to want to provide, at least for a few years, for the child they have already nourished for nine months within the safe circle of their own bodies! The same writer quotes the experience of a psychiatrist working in the United States who said: 'I have never seen a woman who was socially and physically able to have children and who refused to have children, who did not suffer psychologically from that refusal.'

Writing about the nursery and other institutions for the education of children in order to relieve mothers of their educational responsibilities, Havelock Ellis says in his book, *On Life and Sex:* 'The idea has been put forward (first of all by Plato in the famous fifth book of his Republic) that the infant should be removed from its natural parents and placed in the hands of nurses skilfully trained in all the science and art of modern hygiene in general and puericulture in particular. Certainly, it is possible to find innumerable parents who are completely and lamentably ignorant of this science and this art. This may be specially so in those lands of communistic tendency, like Soviet Russia, where the Platonic ideal is most commended.

But to be content to leave the mothers in ignorance and to train up in the knowledge of the duties of maternity a body of women who are rot intended to be mothers, except for other women's children, seems a perverted attempt to escape the difficulty. It is not calculated to benefit, and still less to render happy, the real mothers, the artificial mothers or the children. An institution on so unreal a foundation cannot possibly compete with one on a sound biological basis which is just as susceptible to any necessary cultivation and development as the other.... The legitimate method of approaching the problem-as is constantly becoming more widely recognised-lies in training the real mothers and, so far as possible, before they have begun to be mothers.... The establishment of Schools for Mothers, in some countries facilitated by law, constitutes a noble step along this path.'

In regard to the advisability and fitness of woman for work in the wider sphere of social activity, Havelock Ellis expresses an opinion which agrees with our own view which we have given above, namely, that women who have had the experience of motherhood and whose maternal duties are over have more justification as well as ability to take part in such activity than those whom motherhood calls for dedication to domestic duties. Writing in his book, *On Life and Sex,* Ellis says: 'There is nothing that is so much needed as the "maternal in politics," or in all sorts of non-political channels of social service and none can be better fitted for such service than those who have had an actual experience of motherhood and acquired the knowledge that such experience should give.

There are numberless other ways besides social service in which mothers who have passed the age of forty, provided they posses the necessary aptitudes, can more profitably apply themselves than in hampering or pampering their adult children. It is by wisely cultivating their activities in a larger sphere that women whose chief duties in the narrower domestic sphere are over may better ensure their own happiness and the welfare of others than either by fretting and obstructing or by worrying over their own children who are no longer children. It is quite true that children may go astray even when they have ceased to be children. But the time to implant seeds of virtue, the time to convey a knowledge of life, was when they were small. If it was well done, it only remains to exercise faith and trust. If it was done ill, nothing done later will compensate, for it is merely foolish for a mother who could not educate her children when they were small to imagine that she is able to educate them when they are big.

Writing about the desirability of close mother-child relations during the period of infancy which is completely non-existent in collective social institutions where women, other than mothers, take care of children, Dr. Westermarck writes: 'According to Havelock Ellis, the mortality of artificially fed infants during the first year of life is seldom less than double, and sometimes as much as three times that of the breast-fed, or even more. He also points out that the advantages for an infant being suckled by its mother are greater than can be accounted for by the mere fact of being suckled rather than hand-fed, bemuse the infant's best food is that elaborated in his mother's body. This has been shown by Vitray, who found from the statistics of Astel-Dien at Lyons that infants suckled by their mothers have a mortality of only twelve per cent, while in the case of infants suckled by strangers the mortality rises to thirty-three per cent.'

It may be said that the progress of science may so lighten the manual burden of women that even after discharging their full responsibilities at home, mothers may be enabled to spend a larger and larger portion of their time outside their homes in social, political and industrial activity. While nobody would grudge such a situation, provided: it means equal facilities for all mothers and not merely for a few born with silver spoons in their mouths, it is after all not so certain that the increasing use of mechanical devices would bring about the desired change. The following quotation from Margaret Mead is worth-reading in this connection: 'There was a time also when in the first fine flush of laundries and bakeries, milk deliveries and canned foods, it did look as if

American life was being enormously simplified. A vacuum cleaner was a great addition to a home that kept the standard of a carpet-sweeper and a broom, laundries were a godsend to a household whose routine of sheet-changing was geared to the old-fashioned wash-tub, and bakeries to homes in which the making of bread had dominated one whole day. But just as our new medical palliatives are creating new vulnerabilities and new disease states, so the new equipment has not led to more leisure, more time to play with the baby, more time to curl up and read by an open fire or to help the P.T.A., but has merely combined with other trends in making the life of the American home-maker not easier, but more exacting. Most urban living women do not realise that, as the Bryn Mawr report shows, house-keeping activities consumed 60-65 hours a week in a typical farm family, 78.35 in urban household in, cities of over 100,000. This was in pre-war days, and in a world that has been moving steadily towards a forty-hour week on the job.'

Now, if these facts are true, they show that even the mechanical improvements of an industrial civilisation cannot release mothers for whole time work outside their homes, and a pattern of social life which seeks to make men, and women equal in this respect is bound to produce unpleasant consequences. There remains one final argument to justify the full participation of women, in fields other than the sphere of domestic life. It is said that special gifted women should be given full opportunity to utilise their gifts for social and political service and to that extent they should be absolved of the responsibilities of motherhood and domestic life. This is true. But it should not be overlooked that special gifts can be multiplied and passed on to future generations on a wider scale, if the specially gifted woman undertakes the responsibilities of motherhood. So the argument in favour of exempting such women from the burden of motherhood falls down, because the social service which such women can render may be more effectively rendered if they can become proper mothers. A woman who has borne two gifted children and brought them up under her gifted training really does greater service to society than if she exercise her sifts in other ways. Of course, if she can combine motherhood with social or political service, nothing should be allowed to stand in her way, because then her utility will increase tenfold. But motherhood is the essential vocation of a woman's life which should not be sacrificed for any other consideration.

It is in view of all the facts and considerations we have stated above that Islam has laid down certain social restrictions both on men and women. Some of them are common to either sex, while some are different and arise from a particular conception of womanly duties. On the whole, the Islamic pattern of life is one in which woman has her main functions confined to home life. This does not mean that she is completely debarred from going out or taking part in wider activities, as the old-fashioned Muslims maintain. But there is no doubt that Islam disapproves of a social pattern in which women neglect their primary and essential functions or plunge into wider spheres of activity at the cost of their primary duties. Women who have the time and the ability to do useful service in the social or political field are not prevented by Islam to enter these fields, provided it does not prejudice or impede their functions at home. Let us now examine in more detail what these restrict ions are which Islam places on the liberty of men and women in, the interest of sexual purity and the stability of family life.

Another restriction which is common to both sexes is the compulsory duty of keeping certain parts of the body covered. These parts which should be kept covered in any case and not exposed to any person, except to the wife or the husband, or when medical or other pressing necessities require exposure, are called *Satr*. For men, the portion of the body beginning from the knees and extending to the navel has been fixed as *Sam*. A tradition of Daraqdtni reported by Abu Ayub Ansari says: 'What is above the knees and what is below the navel should be kept covered.' Another tradition reported by Ali states: 'Do not expose your thighs to anyone and do not look at the thighs of a living or dead person.' For women the entire body, excepting hands, feet and face, is included in the Satr. A tradition of Abu Daud says: 'When a woman reaches the age of puberty, no parts of her body should be kept exposed except the face and the hands extending to the joints of the wrist.'

Just as men have been forbidden to wear pure silk to prevent luxurious living, women have been forbidden to use thin clothing which, instead of covering and hiding the features of their body, makes them all the more prominent. Asma bint Abu Bakr, the sister of the Prophet's wife, Aishah, once came to the Prophet wearing a thin dress which did not properly cover her body. The prophet at once turned away his look and said: Asma! when a woman has reached the age of puberty, it is not proper that any part of her body should be seen except her face, hand and feet.' Another tradition states: 'God has cursed those women who remain naked era after putting on their dress.' Similarly, the corpus of traditions collected by Muslim contains one which states: 'Women who remain naked even after putting on dress and draw others into temptation or walk and move in an alluring manner shall not enter paradise, nor get even its scent.'

There are some special restrictions on men circumscribing their freedom of action with a view to guarding their chastity and sexual purity. The entry of men in the houses of other persons is forbidden except with the permission of the inmates. The Quran says: 'O men who believe! do not enter the houses of other people until you have asked their permission and when you do enter, salute them' (xxiv. 27). Further, with a view to guarding against the possibility of men finding the female members of their own house without proper covering, it is laid down that no male member should enter his house at night, in the early morning and during midday time of siesta and rest without previous notice. The Quran says: 'And when the children among you have attained to puberty, let them seek, permission as those before them sought permission' (xxiv.59). Strangers of the male sex are required to be circumspect, if they have to ask for something from the female inmates of a house.

The Quran says on this point: 'And when you ask of them any article, ask of them from behind a curtain; this is purer for your hearts and for their hearts' (xxxiii. 53). Another restriction is that no man or woman is permitted to remain alone with a member of the opposite sex except his or her partner, but women who have passed the age of child-bearing or those with whom, owing to intimate blood-relationship, marriage cannot be contracted are excepted: for example, brothers, sisters, parents, nephews, nieces, etc. A tradition reported by Aqabah b. Amir states. Do not go near women when they are alone. One of the Ansar asked: What about, the husband's elder and younger brothers? The Prophet said: 'Intimacy with them is to be avoided as death.' Another tradition says: 'Do not go near any woman in the absence of her husband because Satan is circulating as blood in your veins.' Amr b. Aas reports a saying from the Prophet: 'The Prophet of God forbade us to go near women except with the permission of the husband' (Tirmidhi).

Tirmidhi gives a further tradition saying: 'No man should from this day go near a woman unless there are one or two persons with, him.' Touching of women is also forbidden, except in cases of grave emergency endangering life or health. A tradition says: 'if a person touches a woman with whom he has no legitimate relations, his hands will be burnt on the Day of Judgement.' Whenever a woman or a party of women came to the Prophet for taking the pledge of Islam, he refused to stretch his hands. Once Umaymah bint Ruqayqah came with a few women to take the pledge and asked the Prophet to give his hand. The Prophet refused saying: 'I do not shake hands with women; verbal declaration, is enough for them.'

All these restrictions on men are intended to guard sexual purity. If chastity is of any real and lasting social value, there is no doubt that such restrictions are justified, as they prevent men and women of various disposition from failing into temptation. For those who have already been corrupted and become used to sexual indecency, these and other restrictions are of no avail.

We now come to special restrictions on women. Two of them we have already mentioned, namely, that women should not display their beauty and finery to anyone else except their husbands and a few intimate relations with whom they cannot enter into marriage: for example, brothers, fathers, nephews, etc., and that shall not strike their feet in such a way as to draw the attention of men.

The modern 'civilised' society has taken precisely to those forms of dress which expose and do not conceal a woman's beauty. The Quran which regards chastity as one of the basic moral and social values has directed its injunctions against these ultra modern forms of dress which are meant more to reveal than to conceal. The justification for these restrictions lies in the hidden springs of sex psychology. Let us quote Van de Velde again on this point. He says in *Ideal Marriage*: The male costume of modern times is not as a rule specially sexually accentuated.

The exact contrary is the case with female dress, which of late has followed primitive and tropical patterns, and aims not at concealing but at enhancing physical charms. From the earliest times, and even when it had to serve as covering from intense cold, it has tended to accentuate and follow the lines of secondary sexual characteristics. Examples are numerous: for instance, the low-cut bodice -'decollete' of the seventeenth and eighteenth centuries: take corset, which in its original form literally lifted and pressed forward the bosom, in a dangerously painful fashion; and the wasp-waist, which was constructed in order to emphasize the curves of the bust and the hips. Or, again, the 'Tournure' or 'bustle' of the eighties, which was at first only meant to discreetly indicate the roundness of the feminine posterior-in itself an important sexual attraction, but which became so exaggerated and unwieldy that it ended by giving the ladies of the most fashionable society a deplorable resemblance to Hottentots.

Fashions such as those of the Directoire and contemporary periods, which, instead of uncovering the largest possible amount of epidermis, drape the covered portion in light and clinging fabrics, which suggest rather than conceal outlines and give additional suppleness to movements, have a particularly alluring effect — much more so than that of nudity. Women have always recognized and utilized this form of charm in their veils shawls and shawl-dances, etc.

In view of these facts, it is impossible not to agree that the Quranic restrictions on female dress are not only rational but necessary.

One of the Quranic verses quoted above states that women should stay at home and not wander about displaying their beauty and finery. This verse does not mean that they should never go out and remain in perpetual confinement, since otherwise the Quranic injunctions about dress and movement of women would become meaningless. The injunction emphasises the fact that their home should form the centre of their interest and activity and there should be no unnecessary intermingling of the sexes in daily life. This interpretation is supported by a famous tradition of the Prophet in connection with Umar's objection against the appearance of the Prophet's wives outside their homes. Once Sauda, a wife of the Prophet, came out on some private business. Umar recognised her and complained to the Prophet that she was not observing the Quranic restrictions, whereupon the Prophet replied: 'They are permitted to go out for satisfying their real wants.'

Apart from restrictions on dress and speech, as indicated above, women are also forbidden to use scents or perfumes when going out. A tradition from Tirmidhi's collection states: 'The Prophet of God said that a woman who uses scent or perfume when passing through streets is a profligate woman.' A tradition of Muwatta by Imam Malik says: 'When a woman goes to mosque for offering prayers, she should not use perfume or scent.' Here again Islam has shown great insight into sex psychology. Perfumes and odours play a great role in exciting sexual emotion. The subject has been discussed in detail by Van de Velde in his *Ideal Marriage* in which he explains how women have always known the sexual effects of odours and perfumes and utilised them for different purposes. Van de Velde goes so far as to remark: 'I am of opinion that experts who use perfumes as aphrodisiacs for their own emotions - perhaps without being fully conscious of this aim - are generally women.'

Within the home also men and women are required to observe certain rules of decency. Although the sex relations of husband and wife are not subject to any kind of restrictions, the Prophet has given directions that even in their utmost privacy, husband and wife should conduct themselves with decorum and refrain from acts of mere animality. Thus, according to a tradition of Ibn Majah, the Prophet is reported to have said: 'Whenever one of you goes to his wife, he should not uncover himself completely like asses.' A wife of the Prophet, according to Tirmidhi, reports that she never saw the Prophet completely naked. The same ideal of decency and chastity finds expression in the restrictions placed on men and women in their family life. These are explained in the following Quranic verses: O you who believe! let those whom your right hands possess and those of you who have not attained to puberty ask permission of you three times: before the morning prayer, and when you put off your clothes at midday in the summer, and after the prayer of the nightfall; these are three times of privacy for you; neither is it a sin for you nor for them besides these times, because some of you must go around waiting upon others; thus does Allah make clear to you the communications, and Allah is Knowing, Wise.

Now, the question is whether this Islamic pattern of sex life is compatible with industrial efficiency and military preparedness, two factors on which in the modern world depends the collective self-preservation of a community. We shall discuss each of these factors separately.

In regard to industrial efficiency, it should be borne in mind that all efficiency, interest and dynamic energy in men and women depend, to a very great extent on a healthy and happy private and family life. We have already discussed the question whether it is possible to dispense with the institution of the family and shown that, on the testimony of Western thinkers and sex psychologists themselves, it is very difficult to envisage a time when the family will disappear as an organised unit of collective life. If the family is a permanent feature of human civilised life and cannot be satisfactorily replaced by alternative institutions, it is self-evident that its stability and betterment should have the first claim on a nation's attention. If the family becomes disorganised and is not able to throw out healthy and happy individuals, not only will industrial efficiency disappear, all other spheres of human activity will suffer a setback on account of ill-equipped, unhealthy, irresponsible and unhappy individuals who come to these fields.

A pattern of collective life which weakens and disorganises the family, in the interest of increased material and industrial productivity, is certain to suffer on the whole and, keeping all other factors in mind, more than others from social and economic maladjustments, because it undermines the very foundation on which the individual's health and efficiency depend. Unhappy, ill-adjusted and uprooted individuals lacking the drive, initiative and moral idealism, which only a healthy and happy family life can create, will hardly be productive in the full sense of the word, materially or spiritually, in any field of life they enter. Before we form any opinion as to the desirability of bringing women in the industrial field as whole time workers, let us consult the experience of industrialised countries. It would seem that the entry of the female sex in the industrial field has had positively harmful results on the 'family organisation of Western countries. Dr. Sallivan observes in his book *Akoholism*: The employment of women in the ordinary industrial occupations not only involves a disorganization of their domestic duties, if they are married,, but it also interferes with the acquisition of housewifely knowledge during girlhood. The result is that appalling ignorance of everything connected with cookery, with cleanliness, with the management of the children, which makes the average wife and mother in the lower working classes in this country one of the most helpless and thriftless of beings, and which, therefore, impels the workman whose comfort depends on her, not only to spend his free time in the public house, but also tends to make him take to alcohol as a necessary condiment with his tasteless and indigestible diet.

Both directly and indirectly, therefore, the employments that withdraw women from domestic pursuits are likely to increase alcoholism, and, it may be added, to increase its greatest potency for evil ... namely, its influence on the health of the stock.

Again, Arnold Toynbee, the renowned British historian, says in an article published in March 1949 issue of World Review: Certainly our recent efforts to solve our 'problems in strictly materialist terms have failed and made caricatures of all our brave plans. 'We have made enormous strides,' we say, 'in the development of labour-saving machinery,' and so we have. But one of the odd results of this progress is that women today are overworked as never before. Wives in America can no longer get household help or afford to devote themselves exclusively to the home. As a result the woman of today does two jobs: one as wife and mother in the home, one as employee in the office or factory.

During the war in England, this double working of women was almost universal. And such a trend is not a hopeful one. In history the ages of disintegration were unusually the ages in which women had left the home. In fifth-century Greece, the high point of classical history, women stayed in the home. But after Alexander's time when the city states were breaking up, there was a feminist movement like our own.

Commenting on the female craze to copy and imitate men and prove themselves equal to their power and capacity, Oswald Schwarz remarks in his *Psychology of Sex*: If women try to compete with men they try the impossible, impossible because it is against their intrinsic nature and against the trend of history. The best they can achieve is equality in action in such superficial strata as, for instance, the economic sphere.

Sensible Western thinkers have never approved of the existing sex and social patterns in Western countries. Their ideas and opinions are much more akin to the pattern of life advocated by Islam. For an example, we quote Anthony M. Ludovici who writes in his famous book, *Women, A Vindication*: It seems eminently desirable to emphasize more than we have emphasized in the past the ideal of matrimony for every woman up to a certain age, and bring home to parents that marriage is what they must train them for... Anything else that she may do must always be second best to this; and those who, by misrepresentation and appeals to vanity, persuade her while she is quite young that there are callings better than, or at least as good as, motherhood for, her, are enemies not only of women but also of the species.

The same book also contains the following passage: Immersed as woman obviously is up to her, shoulders in the business of life and its multiplication, let it be said openly and unequivocally that all those who teach her that any other business is her business, although who, in the face of the dilemma of modern problems, confuse her with tales about a true womanhood away from life and its multiplication; all those, in short, who beguile her with promises of happiness, contentedness or even comfort, without her primary adaptation to man and the child, are liars both unscrupulous and criminal.

It is clear from the above quotations that the promiscuous herding together of men and women in factories, besides disorganising family life, has been productive of other evils such as alcoholism, sexual laxity, etc., which, in their combination, have more than nullified the benefits arising from increased industrial productivity. All this should not be taken, however, to mean that Islam desires women, to be wholly confined to domestic life. There is no such restriction in Islam on the activities of women. They are free, to do any work that benefits themselves or their society either materially or spiritually, provided, first, they do not neglect their primary duties as wives and mothers, and, secondly, observe the rules of decency explained above. In general, this means that part-time activities, other than domestic ones, are most suitable for women, if they can spare time and if such activities do not lead to too much intermingling with men., Cooperative family concerns in which a number of women belonging to different families or to one large family take part, are ideally suited for mothers and wives. If it becomes necessary to engage male workers in such undertakings for supervision, teaching or training, men of advanced age can be selected for the purpose. Part-time work in factories can also be performed by women if there is a separate section exclusively meant for them. Women whose maternal or domestic functions are over and who can do whole time work in other fields are not debarred from outside, activities. Such is, the pattern of Islamic social life and it is one which, without breaking up or disorganising family and home life, gives full scope to the abilities and energies of the female sex.

Let us deal now with the question of military preparedness and Islam's attitude in respect of the participation of women in military service. Individual and national self-preservation in time of crisis and emergency alters the normal course of life and individuals as well as communities are forced to deviate from their principles of life when the threat to their existence becomes too serious. In consequence, they have to do things which they would never like to do in the normal course of their existence. It is the sign of a virile individuality and virile civilisation that even if it has to deviate under the pressure of extreme emergency from the standards of conduct that it holds dear, it does so most unwillingly and only in the measures required by the necessities of the situation-neither more nor less; and when the threat to its existence has passed, it hastens to revert to its original pattern of conduct. Islam, being a practical religion and claiming to be the natural way of life, recognises that situations may arise where things otherwise unlawful may have to be legalised as a temporary measure, but it takes care to ensure that its followers do not develop a liking and relish for illegality under flimsy pretexts. Therefore, while it allows temporary relaxation of normally accepted standards, it enjoins on Muslims not to regard them as more than passing concessions and to make use of them except to the extent made absolutely necessary by the requirements of the situation. Examples of this attitude are found in the Islamic commands with regard to wine and exposure of the private parts of a Muslim male or female. Wine has been absolutely prohibited by Islam, but if a person on the point of death can be saved by being made to drink wine, its use is legally justified. Similarly, Islam has given strict injunctions to its followers not to expose their private parts under any circumstances. As explained above, the Prophet even enjoined on married couples not to become completely naked during sexual intercourse.

But if a man or woman is threatened with extreme danger of ill-health or one's life is in peril and the threat to life or health cannot be averted except by exposing one's private parts before a doctor for medical treatment, such an act becomes fully legitimate. Islam has adopted that same attitude with regard to the intermingling of the sexes in times of extreme national emergency or during an actual war. During such times, it relaxes all the restrictions as and when required and to the extent made necessary by the situation. When the emergency has passed, the normal restrictions are again made operative. But even during a war or emergency, Islam requires the Muslim males and females to follow as far as possible the rules of decency and avoid unnecessary intermingling. According to the Islamic attitude of life, the Muslim individuals, male and female, and the Muslim brotherhood exist not for mere self-preservation and self-enjoyment. The primary object of human existence in general and of the Muslim community in particular is to live and act for the preservation and growth of moral values and to uphold the spiritual ideals of social fairplay, justice, decency, cleanliness in thought and action.

Sexual purity and chastity are among the fundamental social values upheld by Islam. In themselves they may appear to be of secondary importance, but they affect one's social conduct, one's ideas of justice, honesty and fairplay and in fact one's whole gamut of action in a thousand and one ways. They are, therefore, regarded by Islam as occupying a position of primary importance in its total scheme of values. How is it possible then for a community which claims to be the guardian of morality and spirituality to sacrifice them for the sake of safeguarding and ensuring a bare carnal existence. Suppose the Muslims ensure their self-preservation at the cost of these or other moral values, would it be a soul-satisfying existence? As Jesus Christ, one of the greatest Prophets of God, remarked: 'What does it avail if a man gains the whole world but loses his own soul?'

In view of these facts, Islam has enjoined, while permitting temporary relaxations, that great care should be taken during an emergency to see that these relaxations are neither misused nor used in a way which is unnecessary for individual and national self-preservation. As far as possible, intermingling of the sexes should be avoided even in times of war and resorted to only to the minimum extent compatible with the needs of collective self-preservation. Keeping in view these safeguards and precautions, let us explain the freedoms granted to women during a national emergency.

During the early period of Islam when the Muslims were engaged in a life-and-death struggle with the forces of disbelief, women used freely to take part, in helping the warriors of Islam. Short of actual fighting which was unnecessary for Muslim women, because the women on the other side too did not join battle, they did everything such as nursing, carrying food and water and looking after other needs of the army. Bukhari quotes a tradition stating that when the Prophet received wounds during the battle of Uhud, his daughter, Fatima, dressed up his wounds and carried water to him. It is clear that, under these conditions, she could not have observed any normal restrictions on the dress and movement of the female sex. Similarly in the chapter on Jihad and Siyar, Bukhari states on the authority of Anas b. Malik, that during the battle of Uhud when the nonbelievers inflicted a crushing defeat on Muslims, Aishah, the wife of the Prophet, and Umm Salim, an other Muslim lady, raised up their gowns to the knees and carried water to the wounded.

This shows that the normal restrictions on the dress of the females can be abandoned during a war to the extent made necessary by the exigencies of the situation. Again, a tradition found in the Muslim's collection states: Umm Atiyyah says: 'I took part in seven battles with the Prophet of God, and I used to cook food for the warriors, supply them with medicines and dress up their wounds. Anas also reports that the Prophet usually took with him in war Umm Salim and other women of the Ansar and these women administered medicines to the wounded and kept them supplied with drinking water. That the Prophet saw nothing objectionable and even approved of women fighting for Islam is evident from another tradition also which says that the Prophet used to visit the wife of 'Ibadat b. Samit who was related to him. One day the Prophet slept in her house and on waking up began to laugh. The wife of 'Ibadat asked him as to why he laughed. The Prophet said that he saw in a dream a number of men and women travelling in a ship and heading for a battle with the non-believers. The wife of 'Ibadat requested him to pray that she be one of those warriors. Accordingly, the Prophet prayed for her. During the reign of Muawiyyah, the wife of 'Ibadat actually voyaged to the battlefield, but when she landed on the coast she fell down from her horse and died.

All these reports establish the fact that women are permitted to take part in war with men. There is nothing to prevent women from participating in actual fighting if this becomes necessary. During the Prophet's time the Muslim women did not do actual fighting because it was not necessary, if the other side also did not employ women to fight its battles. But the Muslims may be faced nowadays with enemies who recruit women in regular fighting service. Should this happen, Muslim women can also do actual fighting as Islam does not prohibit it.

Only one question remains to be discussed. Modern war requires intensive training both for actual military service and for auxiliary services. How can Muslim women be trained in the art of war and nursing, etc., if intermingling of the sexes is to be avoided? The obvious solution is to train initially a batch of women advanced in age for military and auxiliary services with the help of male experts. When a sufficient number of women have acquired skill in the different fields of military or medical services, they can train a large number of women without the help of men. Thus, intermingling of the sexes can either be avoided or reduced to the minimum extent possible.

SOCIAL REFORMS

There are certain principles which are to be followed by the individuals in the society. No society can allow the opposition or rejection of the principles, because the non-compliance amounts to rebellion against the society. If any society gives up these principles or fails to enforce them, it will disintegrate.

The principles are meant for the women because, when the Islamic society was developing in Medina, the Islamic State had entered into a treaty with the people of Mecca, on account of certain diplomatic considerations, undertaking not to give shelter to any of the Quraish against their wish. The Muslims could afford asylum to only such women who wanted it. In this background, the Holy Quran has explained the conditions to be followed by a woman in order to become a part of the Islamic society. However, the Muslim men are no exception to these rules.

The distinct characteristics of Islam is that it creates a refined society. It becomes incumbent upon every Muslim to follow the principles of Islam strictly in order to make his own life safe and respectable. It is not possible to lead a peaceful and respectable life without adhering to the principles prescribed by the Shariah.

Force of Ideology

For the enforcement of an ideology, a society must have three powers : The force of ideology, the force of collective thinking and feeling and the force of law. The force of Islamic ideology is the only capable force to wipe out the evil from the surface of the earth and establish a pious society all over the world. The other ideologies have failed because they are man-made and devoid of

Natural laws. The world has tried all possible laws made by man and achieved nothing. On the contrary there prevails disturbance and uneasiness. Therefore, the world has no other alternative but to adopt Islamic laws for the peace and good of mankind.

The man-made laws demand the obedience to the man in authority. Therefore, the people easily ignore these laws and indulge in evil practices. Besides, these laws fail to punish and change the offenders. Whereas, the laws of Islam demand the obedience to Allah, the Creator of all. It is the fear of Allah that keeps man away from the evil practices. The man, who loves Allah, would never like to displease Almighty Allah.

Islam does not permit any kind of evil under any circumstances. Moreover, the Islamic law cannot be changed by man because he has no authority to do so. Islam disbands the jungle law and enforces the law of Islamic Shariah for the establishment of good and refined society. Islam makes the man and the woman morally high and cultured.

Moral Values

Undoubtedly, the society which is based on such lofty ideals and piety, gives prime importance to moral values. Such a society is the noblest in the world. The men and the women of such a society bear high moral character, and such is the Muslim society. The moral values help men and women to ward off evil and lead virtuous life. In this Islamic society, the individuals respect each other and never become hurdle in any way. The man, who possesses high moral character, is an asset for the society because he not only himself remains good but also helps in the prevention of evils in the society. He has great regard, specially, for the women. The moral values also make the human conscience strong.

The physical conditions of the woman are different from those of the man. Therefore, Islam also enjoins strictly the marriage of the woman. And the stress is the same as that of the man. However, Islam does not permit the plurality of husbands for the woman, but has made the provision for the continuity of her conjugal life. It never deprives her of her legitimate right of sexual satisfaction. In case she is separated from her husband owing to his death or divorce, Islam lays stress upon her second marriage after the passage of the requisite period of 'iddat'. The History of Islam shows that the second marriage of the women was performed very easily during the period of the Holy Prophet (S.A.W.) and the Khulafa-i-Rashideen (R.A.A.).

Aatika-bint-Zaid was married to Hadrat Abu Bakr's (R.A.A.) son, Abdullah. Due to some reasons, Hadrat Abu Bakr (R.A.A.) advised his son to divorce his wife. Though, Abdullah divorced his wife to please his father but he was very sad because he loved her very much. When Hadrat Abu Bakr came to know of this fact, he gave his son permission to re-marry her. After the second marriage, Abdullah was martyred in the battle of Taif. It is related that Zaid-bin-Khattab married Aatika after the martyrdom of her husband. When he was also martyred in the battle of Yamama, Hadrat Umar (R.A.A.) married her. And after Hadrat Umar (R.A.A.), Hadrat Zubayr (R.A.A.) married her. After his martyrdom, Hadrat Ali (R.A.A.) offered her to marry but she herself refused.

The aim of marriage in Islam is to enable a person to lead virtuous life and to create healthy environments in the society. The marriage can be successful only if there is harmony between husband and wife. It is also essential that they must be capable to satisfy the sexual need of each other. Islam gives the full right to the spouses to divorce each other in case the other party lacks the capability for proper discharge of sexual functions. Hadrat Umar (R.A.A.), Hadrat Ali (R.A.A.') and other Companions opine that not only the sexual incapability but also the diseases like blindness, leprosy and lunacy are the valid grounds for divorce.

On the one hand, Islam emphasises the discontinuation of the conjugal relation, which fails to fulfil the requirement of the marriage and on the other hand, it encourages the spouses to adhere to the bonds of marriage which help in leading a virtuous life. Unless there is love between the spouses and they satisfy the sexual wants of each other, the marriage cannot be successful. Besides, the strained relation leads to evil practices.

The marriage is considered a firm bond in the Islamic society. It is based on the natural wants of a man and a woman. Hence the sanctity of the Nikah cannot be violated under any circumstances. Though, Islam allows divorce but only on solid grounds. The marriage cannot be dissolved on trivial matters.

Social Responsibility

It is but natural that an individual leaves his or her impressions on the society as a whole. The person of a good moral character leaves good impressions on the society and if the person happens to be of bad character he or she leaves bad influence on the society. Thus, a good person helps in the establishment of a good society and a person of bad character spoils the good society. Therefore, it is not possible to have healthy environment and good society in the world unless every individual realises that it is his or her duty to protect the good character of the society.

Islam creates a sense of duty in an individual and reminds that he or she is the real architect of the good society. Moreover, it is not enough for an individual just to be good but it is also his or her duty to correct and improve others. An individual bearing good moral character plays an important role in the building of a good and healthy environment. Such an individual saves others from the moral degeneration.

The pressure of the society is always strong. And if it remains strong, no one would dare to disobey its set principles. If overall environment of the society is bad then all sorts of evils would creep in and the situation would go beyond control and the moral values would die.

Islam keeps the sense of morality alive in the society, hence it would not tolerate any kind of immoral act of an individual. Once a woman, who had scented her clothes, was passing through a road. Hadrat Abu Hurrayrah (R.A.A.) saw her and asked, "Are you coming from the mosque?" She replied "Yes". He further asked, "Have you applied this perfume for going to the mosque?" She replied in affirmation. According to Islam, it is the duty of man to protect moral values of the people who are socially related to him. This responsibility becomes vital if relation is closer. The chastity of the relative and the woman-neighbour must be protected. Any violation in this respect would amount to unpardonable sin.

Hadrat Abdullah bin Masood (R.A.A.) says that a man asked the Holy Prophet (S.A.W.), "Which is the greatest sin?" The Holy

Prophet (S.A.W.) replied, "The greatest sin is to associate someone with Allah, Who alone created you." He asked, "Which is the lesser sin than this?" The Holy Prophet (S.A.W.) replied, "After that, the greatest sin is to take the life of your baby thinking that it will take away the part of livelihood (and you would starve)." He again asked, "Which is the greatest sin after these two." The Holy Prophet (S.A.W.) replied." The adultery with your neighbour woman (Bukhari, Muslim and Mishkat).

Once the Holy Prophet (S.A.W.) asked one of his companions, "What is your opinion about adultery?" The companion replied, "Allah and his Messenger (S.A.W.) have forbidden adultery and it shall remain forbidden until the Day of Judgement." The Holy Prophet (S.A.W.) said, "The adultery with ten women is lesser sin than the adultery committed with his neighbour's wife."

Guiding Principles

Woman has to realize her real position in the Islamic society which aims to establish the environment free from all evils. She is the architect of the domestic life. Therefore neither the state should assign her such duties which are injurious to herself, nor she has the right to destroy the domestic life and take part in such activities which may prove harmful to herself, her house and the society. She is not supposed to solve the political problems but look after the affairs which are solely meant for her.

Obedience

Islam is the complete code of life and provides guidelines for every aspect of human behaviour. Its main object is to relieve man from slavery of man and 'establish the sovereignty of Allah over the entire mankind. It leads to peace and tranquillity. For this reason man has been assigned superiority over woman in certain respects.

The husband has this right because he himself is responsible for the maintenance of his wife and children. However, if the husband is unable to provide the necessities of life for her children, the wife is permitted to look for and earn money for the maintenance of the family. Besides, as Allama Ibn Abedin (R.A.) says, "There are certain expenses of the wife for which the husband is not bound, hence, the wife can work at home and earn money to meet such expenses." He has further said the husband can prevent her from doing such extra hard work which affects her health. It is the right of husband to keep his wife hail and hearty and beautiful."

Restrictions

A Muslim lady is allowed by Shariah to leave her ' home with the permission of her husband to perform her religious, educational and social services, but she should keep in mind the fact that she has been restricted from mingling with the male strangers. Islam confines her to home because her presence amongst the men who are strangers gives rise to moral degeneration. If a woman breaks the law of Shariah and enters any field, with however good intentions, her step will be considered against the principles of Islam because it leads to troubles and destruction.

As it has been said before, Islam aims to establish a society free from all evils and provides peaceful living for the whole mankind. Therefore, it is absolutely essential to keep the men and women separate in all matters whether educational, cultural, martial, social or political. Thus, according to Islamic Shariah, women are not allowed to mingle with other men. As a matter of fact it is not possible to have healthy environment in any society if the intermingling of men and women are allowed. Hence prevention is better than cure. In Islamic society neither co-education nor co-cultural programmes are allowed. A Muslim woman is not permitted to take military training along with other men. Nor she can participate in games or recreation with men. Whether it is a market place or an assembly hall, Islam considers intermingling of the two sexes at any place, as undesirable. Women attended the sermons of the Holy Prophet (S.A.W.) but separate seating arrangements were made for them. They never sat alongwith the men. Islam is the Deen for all times. Hence even in the modern times women can participate freely in all activities and functions, within the limits of the Shariah provided separate arrangements are made for them.

In War

War is a big obstacle in the way of human life. It stops progress and brings devastation. In such situation the entire nation is involved and the circumstances take such turn that it becomes impossible to apply the normal laws and principles. The rules that are framed for normal conditions, do not remain effective in an emergency.

The war creates such dangerous and dreadful situation that the set rules become ineffective and every individual has to become active and helpful for the cause of Islam and Muslims. So the participation of women in war also becomes inevitable. This does not mean that the law 'women should not mingle with men' is broken but automatically suspended to some extent for the time being during the emergency.

The Holy Prophet (S.A.W.) and his companions had to face very critical situation during wars. In the first place they had not yet attained the political stability in the country and in the second place they were numerically less and had not enough equipment to fight.

On the other hand, the enemies were in large number and well equipped. They also brought a large number of women with them who encouraged the men to, fight and also, provided medical aid to the sick and the injured. But the Muslim women remained attached to the domestic duties only, therefore they knew nothing about war. Ultimately the participation of Muslim women in war became inevitable.

The fact cannot be denied that Islamic states may have to face such situation in every age. So the women, within the limits of the Shariah and above mentioned conditions, can serve the cause of Islam and their country directly or indirectly. Islam is the practical Deen and will remain ever dynamic. Its laws are for the entire mankind and for all times. It controls the activities of men and women for the welfare of the entire mankind. Its target is always to uproot the evil.

Women in History

Woman has achieved an important and significant place in the history of Islam. But the West has done a great disservice to the history by distorting and mis-interpreting the facts of the Islamic history. The freedom that West has given to woman is not the freedom in real sense of the term. In fact, it is a licence and an attempt at exploitation of woman for the satisfaction of man's sensual desires only. This kind of freedom has made the Western society corrupt and evil.

The Western culture teaches woman to rebel against her own home and encourages her to become a plaything for the men in the so-called modern society. Whereas, Islam has given her the freedom of equal rights, honour and dignity. The main place of her activities is her home. Besides, she is allowed to leave her home when the necessity arises. The freedom of women by West brings disgrace to her, whereas the freedom granted by Islam elevates her status and she becomes an honourable member of the society.

The West has painted a very wrong picture of a historical event. After the martyrdom of Hadrat Uthman Ghani (R.A.A.), the administration of the state was greatly disturbed. When it became difficult to bring to book the assassins of Hadrat Uthman Ghani (R.A.A.), Hadrat Aishah (R.A.A.) entered the arena of politics and endeavoured to enforce the laws of Shariah on the culprits. Her struggle for the cause of Islam brought her to the stage of leadership which is the right of man alone. It was an emergency and there was no man to lead the Muslim nation and fight the forces opposing Islam. The situation was so grave that she declared war even against Hadrat Ali (R.A.A.) who tried to confront her.

The West has interpreted this event wrongly and derived very mischievous conclusions from it. The Western historians base their arguments on this particular event of the Islamic history and maintain that Islam has granted equal rights in the field of politics, that is, a woman can become the leader of the nation. Hence, her participation in politics and social activities cannot be prohibited according to Shariah. They say that men and women can intermingle freely in every sphere of human life. But this notion is absolutely false and baseless. It is a fabrication to defame Islam.

It is a fact that Hadrat Aishah played a leading role on account of unavoidable circumstances. That was an exception and does not make a rule. The rule remains the same that woman cannot be assigned the leadership of the Muslim Ummah. Women was never allowed to play this role during the time of the Holy Prophet (S.A.W.) and Khulfa-i-Rashideen (R.A.A.).

The teachings of Islam restrict the activities of woman to her home and allow her to leave it only in inevitable circumstances. The leadership of the nation was never assigned to woman nor she ever claimed it. Though the Holy Prophet (S.A.W.) and Khulfa-i-Rashideen (R.A.A.) faced great difficulties and hurdles, yet woman was never entrusted with any responsibility for their solution.

During the long period of Islamic rule, a number of battles were fought but woman was never made the commander-in-Chief of the Muslim army. Woman was never appointed as a Governor by the Holy Prophet (S.A.W.) or by any of his four Caliphs. She was not assigned any responsible post in the department of finance or the judiciary. After the demise of the Holy Prophet (S.A.W.) the Muslims never elected any woman as their Caliph.

America is the most advanced and prosperous country of the world. If one or two persons are found there poor, it would not make America a poor country. Similarly if Hadrat Aishah (R.A.A.) played a leading role in the politics of her time, it would not mean that Islam allows the leadership of woman. The act of an individual cannot become the rule of the Shariah.

4

Islamic System of Family

The importance of the large-scale ideological and economic factors in the everyday life situation of the individual, and the way in which this ideology has opened up the possibility of divergent adaptations and a new household economy. Moreover, the burden that economic changes place on adult males (who still are the main providers in most families), as well as career married women, has increased.

This has complicated and intensified the tradition of child-rearing, cooking, washing, cleaning the house, taking care of the family and social networks, as well as the time spent on purchasing goods and supervising children after school. The large-scale economic reforms, and the new household economy, have affected the life of family members in different ways. The form and the rituals of household activities in everyday life are central themes in the following section.

The economic crises of the Islamic state and the new ideological demands have incurred cumulative and overlapping perspectives. This has left a narrow range of options for young and ambitious couples, forcing them to seek opportunities outside the home country, as exemplified by Mahry's extended family.

Marriage and higher education has traditionally served as a passage for social and economic independence, although it has often been the case that newly-weds stay in the house of the wife's or husband's father for a while, before establishing an independent household. For ten years Halima, a 44-year-old female school teacher, shared a residence with her sister-in-law before she and her husband could save enough money to buy one of the two-room flats offered to school employees.

Marriage has always been an economic security for the wife, and the husband is traditionally responsible for the economic security of the family. The reality of the current socio-economic situation for the average lower and middle-class category, is such that extra economic support is necessary, either from the wife-particularly in the case of young married couples-or from parents.

A young family's economic independence and higher social status, such as in the case of Mahry and her siblings, depends upon occupation and further education. Mahry and her family had less chance of obtaining higher education because of the increased number of applicants, and also because of new Islamic ideological criteria for the selection of religiously active candidates. A new mode of adaptation, and a new economic niche, has emerged for family members who are able to take on additional roles.

As a result of constant price increases on household goods, the consequences of these economic niches have affected males and females differently. Managing the household economy is difficult in lower and middle-class families, even when the breadwinner (often the man), has previous work experience, or higher education. Families are dependent on a single income from employment in the public sector, such as teacher or office work jobs.

Grown-up children, despite their higher education, are economically dependent on their parents, who returned home from abroad during the Iranian revolution in 1978. This dependency may be permanent for some, thus placing a burden on the parents. In post-revolutionary Iran, large numbers of urban middle and higher-class Iranians left home.

Two distinctive, significant and completely new household structures emerged in post-revolutionary Iran. These were: (a) the extended household composed of parents and married children who shared a residence, and (b) the households consisting of elderly couples who remained in Iran, while their children left home and took permanent residence abroad. The former household composition is common among families where a majority of the members stayed in Iran, and only a few moved abroad. The latter household composition consisted of elderly couples who voluntarily lived alone at home, visiting their children only once in a while abroad. These are often better-off couples, contrasting dramatically with the lower and middle-class extended household, where parents accommodate a married daughter or son and their families.

To maintain the economy of daily life many young educated men started a business of their own, or with other male relatives. The inevitable solution for lower and middle-class families was to have two members of the family in employment. Alternatively the breadwinner of the family would take two jobs, one in the official sector and another in the private sector. In the case of Mahry, close and distant male relatives were employed as civil servants, teachers, low-ranking army officers, social health personnel, etc. Due to the high cost of living they worked in their spare time as independent taxi drivers, as salesmen buying and selling land, as dealers in foreign currencies or rationed goods, or as shop assistants. In comparison, women were either housewives or, as is the case among a few middle-aged women, they were employed as nursery teachers, computer assistants, students, social health workers or, like Mahry, they worked with sewing and embroidery.

Most of the young families in the community, either rented rooms that cost them half of their salary as state employees, or they shared a residence with their parents or a close relative in order to save money. Many were also dependent on others for economic support, directly or indirectly, in the form of cash, household subsistence, and goods. Such socio-economic insecurity, along with the poor educational opportunities for themselves and the problems facing their children, as well as the general political harassment, has led many of these middle-class families to join the flow of migrants of the 1980s.

Household work is not only a distinctive personalised domain, but is also a part of the larger economic and post- revolutionary ideological development, as well as being a focus of change. Domestic work in post-revolutionary Iran involved a series of new tasks and more intensive work schedules for women.

Adaptability of household members to changing conditions depended on the availability of facilities and resources. A married woman explained that due to the intensive work schedule and, for example, the lack of communal facilities, she had to do the laundry at night when water was more easily available, and the shopping before sunrise so as to be able to prepare the mid-day meal for the family. This example illustrates how the mode of work among women mainly concerned with 'domestic' tasks has intensified due to broader political and economic conditions. One could hardly escape the daily observation of lower and middle-class women (often mothers), accompanied by small children, waiting impatiently for several hours in queues, in order to purchase hygienic supplies of milk, foods, and other 'domestic' items, at a more reasonable price than in the open market. Commonly they were worried about the daily household routines; for example, one waiting in such a queue told how worried she was at being delayed in preparing the noon meal for her husband and children coming home from work and school.

Foreign goods, such as electrical appliances, were very expensive and considered as luxury items by lower middle-class families. Moreover, these items provided a new form of enterprise for well-off families. Being able to sell foreign goods in the home market greatly boosted the income of such well-off families. The extended household has to some extent solved the problem of married children who are not able to establish an independent household without economic support from their parents.

High prices of household equipment and house rent made it impossible for young families with average economic means to establish an economically independent household. However, such an intensive relation and extended household dependency has increased family conflicts dramatically, particularly in already controversial relationships such as between daughter-in-law and mother-in-law.

Career options are limited for young members of lower-class families. Petty trading seems to be an acceptable strategy for boys. Wheeler-dealers, and street vendors, are two forms of economic activity adopted by recent school-leavers. Bazar-e azad activity has opened a series of channels through which household items rationed by the state flow into the black market. Such enterprises, and the extra income earned, are often considered insecure, illegal, not quite respectable and even immoral.

Middlemen, such as wheeler-dealers, after spending long hours in queues, buying goods such as cigarettes and eggs from the cooperatives shops, and then selling them at black-market prices. This type of occupation may serve as a source of income for young and middle-aged male members of low-income families. For families with low incomes, daily petty trading is not a permanent enterprise.

Self-employment yields more income than a low-paid permanent job. Establishing a business requires both economic and social capital, without which it is difficult to obtain goods to sell, or to rent a shop. When renting a shop a deposit is paid. The price has increased with inflation from around 50 thousand tomans in 1979 to an average of one million tomans in 1990. This means that it is virtually impossible to establish a permanent business. It also means that large profits can be made from letting shops, houses, flats and rooms. Those who have parents with a large capital may set up a small business.

While the father is still alive, they will be allowed to enter the family business as part of their eventual inheritance. The street-corner traders sell items such as dollars, cigarettes, rationed foods, and stockings. Dast-farosh is an enterprise open to even those with little capital, and is often a second source of income for individuals such as a grown-up son, or a head of a household. Any form of self-employment to supplement the limited household income, is justified on the grounds that multiple sources of income are necessary. Since a single-income job in the public sector cannot meet all of the household's real expenditures, the idea of a second job has become widely accepted.

Resourceful entrepreneurs will be able to provide for family consumption, as well as accumulate considerable wealth. In contrast, permanent business activities are generally open only to better-off middle-class merchants and craftsmen, and other traditionally independent producers and distributors. These are often cooperative family businesses jointly owned by close male relatives, such as a father and his sons, brothers, cousins and in-laws. This contrasts with the petty trader who sets up his business independently. Recently, because of restrictions, male shopkeepers are forbidden to sell female lingerie, or to open female hair-dressing salons.

As a consequence, female shopkeepers and co-partnership with a female relative has increased. The open market makes non-rationed items available to the public, such as electrical appliances, clothing, and domestic goods, as well as scarce medicines. The scarcity and long queues have forced many people to purchase items in the black market.

The rise in prices of local commodities may be explained by: (a) the government extra export policy for earning foreign currencies; (b) the rise in the exchange rate for dollars; and (c) the two devaluations of the rial. Devaluation of Iranian currency has been of particular importance for the family household economy, since family incomes are in the form of riyals. Subsequently they are the hardest hit by inflation, exchange rates, and the black market policy of the state.

Broad structural and economical changes, such as the rationing system for the distribution of goods, has encouraged the development of a new transactional pseudo-occupation niche. Some of these new enterprises are considered immoral, in terms of their transactional and insecure nature. Self-employment and free-enterprise activities are considered to offer greater opportunities for meeting the daily increases of expenditures. Government employees, who are particularly well educated, and with fixed low wages, have become very disappointed with the monthly income of their permanent jobs. It is not adequate to cover their household expenses, such as rent. The difference in the earnings of these well-qualified government employees, and those whose main source of income is selling dollars in the black market, has marginalised the former category both socially and economically.

Wages for average civil servants and employees in official sectors, such as education, have remained relatively the same as they were before the revolution. According to a study by Behdad, in 1980 there had been an increase in the official minimum wage and a change in the rate of income tax to 12 per cent.

Most workers were affected by the new law stipulating minimum wages, the exception being urban workers in large firms. It must be keep in mind that family economic viability in post-revolutionary Iran is a problem for most government employees, hence the interest in free business and double waged jobs.

The most profitable enterprises involve trading in foreign currencies and goods, such as dollars, pounds, gold, household items and land, and money lending. Thus, the families that had invested capital in such commodities as land, houses, cars, gold, shops, etc., prior to the outbreak of the war between Iran and Iraq in 1980 are now in position. Expansion of the black market has an advantage as it further benefited those who have access to foreign currencies, imported goods, and are able to travel abroad frequently.

Land ownership has always been an important source of local identity and power in Iran. After the revolution, long-term investment in land has more than ever become an important form of capital, as well as a strategy for rapidly accumulating wealth. The dramatic rise in land prices since 1980 has applied even to the purchase of the isolated land outside the city limit, which is not even supplied with electricity and water.

An example of rapid social mobility through land ownership is the case of an educated civil engineer. He qualified in England in the 1970s. He and his family returned to Iran shortly after the Iranian revolution in 1980. He started to work for his former employer, where he had previously been employed in a junior position. Due to his high foreign qualification he was soon offered jobs in different cities, including one in a province where he received high wages due to the difficult geographical conditions. Shortly after he returned home from England he bought a piece of land at a low price. The land was on the nonresidential periphery of a town without electricity and water supplies. It cost him 60 tomans per square metre in 1980. However, inflation increased its value to 5,000/6,000 tomans per square metre in 1989.

In the long term ownership of land is highly beneficial, the rapid increase in value making it a secure investment. The demand for land has particularly increased as a result of demographic changes. These can be explained as follows: (a) rapid population growth; (b) the continuous migration from small towns and nearby villages to large towns. The rapid expansion of towns toward the city limits increased the value of cheap and isolated land from 20-60 tomans per square metre in 1979, to 6,000 tomans per square metre in 1989-90. Such land could not, however, be used for building a house until it had been included within the town's official boundaries.

The profit from land ownership was greater than from the ownership of fruit gardens, the latter providing only a small annual income for urban middle-class and business families. This was the common enterprise that led to the serious destruction of the famous orchard land in Shiraz. The grape and apple farms changed into building sites, thereby bringing a high profit to their owners. It would be interesting to evaluate the impact on agricultural production.

Land confiscated during the revolution has been sold cheap to religio-politically privileged community members, such as war veterans, employees of the Islamic institution for rehabilitation, and to families of martyrs or hostages. In recent years government supporters have been favoured for the redistribution of economic and social opportunities, such as obtaining employment, education, rationed goods and land. Special allocations have been given as the rewards for their support. Thus, economic advancement has been possible not only for those who have accumulated capital under the former regime, but also for those who have gained high status as first-class citizens in the Islamic regime, whatever their class background may have been.

Gifts of gold signify sets of kinship relations and are part of large chains of acts distinguishing close relatives, high-ranking guests and close friends. The value of gold is both an objective and a subjective cultural phenomenon, and concerns the relations between people on various levels. Gold has always been associated with prestige and high status and is often exchanged as valuable gifts among Iranians. There is a strong tendency for women to own some gold, receiving and giving in accordance with expectations.

The saving and management roles women play within the family in this context is considered to be related to their orientation toward the future. Gold functions for women both as prestigious ornaments, and as a status symbol. Gifts of gold signify a 'proper' bride and provide capital for the family and her husband. While purchasing land has remained the principal investment and economic transaction for men, gold has played a similar role for women. The constant rise in the value of gold, along with inflation, has meant that its importance not only as solid capital, but also as a status symbol, has grown.

The common strategy is to buy as many articles of gold as possible when the prices are low, and then sell or exchange these items when the prices have gone up. Accumulation of gold is considered a wise policy, both from the point of view of the individual and the family.

Gold is a significant gift requested by the bride. The amount to be received is often agreed upon at the time of engagement. Gold jewelry, or a number of gold coins, may be agreed upon as being a part of, or the entire *mahryeh*. The increasing tendency among middle-class brides to have mahryeh in gold coins than riyals is because gold is more stable in price and more likely to rise in value than fall.

The quantity of gold received as wedding presents depends on how wealthy the relatives are, and the number of guests. Such gifts may also be given on other significant occasions, such as at the birth of a child, during the first pregnancy, upon obtaining a higher degree, or on the Iranian New Year in March.

The young married women were considered inexperienced, and were constantly advised by their mothers and sisters about future relations with their husbands and their families. Planning a secure future, the mothers advise their daughters to buy gold instead of toys and decorative items, and to be concerned about the future. Such issues have become important lessons given by mothers to their married daughters.

The importance of the gift of gold as capital is revealed at times of family crises. It is increasingly common for married women to give their savings to their desperate husbands to start a business or purchase property. Such a form of economic support brings extra recognition and respectability for the wife. The husband is often willing in return to register part, or whole, of the purchased property in her name.

On one occasion Farid, a 30-year-old married housewife, proudly exclaimed how she sold all of her wedding jewelry and the children's gold to give tomans to her husband, so he could purchase a piece of land that was especially offered to him at his place of work. Her husband in return registered the land in her name. Another situation in which a woman's gold reserves may be vitally important to the whole family is exemplified by Mahtab, an elderly mother with a family of ten, who was forced to seek shelter in Shiraz during the Iraqi bombardment of Abadan in 1981. The only property they could bring with them was her gold (one kilogram). Soon she decided to sell it, despite the market rate being low, because she considered it important to provide the necessary clothing and accommodation for her daughters, and to protect the family. The only thing she had been reluctant to sell was a ring that had once belonged to her mother.

A third example is that of a 55-year-old woman, who sold all of her gold jewelry and borrowed money from her oldest daughter, in order to visit two of her children living in Norway. To her the value of the visit was worth more than her gold. She thought, what would be the use of saving when she might never again have the chance to see her children and grandchildren?

The distance, and the high cost of the journey, signified the importance of the visit and, and as she put it, 'it may be the only chance in my lifetime'. She had to insist on the importance of such a visit since her old husband thought that it was more important to take care of the house, and was thus reluctant to give her any financial support. Finally she alone provided the money for her journey to visit her children. She frequently talked about this as an event to gain respect.

A fourth example is that of a couple educated abroad, who had recently returned home and needed to pay for the transport of their household goods from Germany to Iran. The wife, Shahla, decided to sell her own gold, as well as her daughter's, to pay the required sum. She considered the household items to be of equal value to the gold since these were enormously expensive and scarce in Iran. Her mother, Mahtab, proudly returned to this case, telling others how her daughter managed her family life, thus presenting her daughter as a good wife to a good husband.

Contributions to the family economy in times of crises would allow the wife to emphasise her honourable identity and enable her to negotiate with her husband. The latter may, as noted, often agree to reward his supportive wife by registering some property in her name.

Some women insist on keeping some of the gifts of gold received through their own lineage by transferring it to their daughters or daughters-in-law, or to their mother's lineage (sister's daughter). Such a form of gold exchange signifies sets of kinship relations in which the wife competes with the husband's for support. Thus, women often adopt far-sighted perspectives on the value of gold, a view that their husbands may not necessarily share, but from which they often benefit.

Dowry consists of household goods that the bride will bring to her husband's house. Mehr is a sum of money or valuable items such as gold and land that the husband pledges to pay the bride upon marriage. This amount will be written as a legal document for the bride's security, and may become a legal debt upon the bride's request. These two forms of payment play important roles in the dynamics of the marital relation, giving a woman a high degree of security and also a deterrent for a divorce.

It is generally assumed that the larger the dowry (i.e. consisting of kitchen utensils, carpets, bedroom furniture, etc.), the greater is the respect shown to the daughter and, thus, the greater is the prestige gained in the eyes of the husband's female relatives. Due to the open market prices of dowry items people purchase presents through the newly established Islamic state marriage institution, which offers a few items for those newly wed. These might include items such as a stove, a machine-made carpet, and an oil heater. Two or three items were sold to each newly married couple in 1989.

The better the daughter's education, job and appearance, the less pressure is placed on the parents to provide an expensive dowry. This point of view was expressed by at least ten of the working women, aged between 30-45, including 4 teachers (1 nursery, 2 school, 1 university), 3 hairdressers, 1 social worker, 1 accountant, 1 office worker. Of these two had resigned, one of whom was Narges, a 40-year-old woman and former accountant, the other being a teacher who had several times taken leave to avoid the political stress associated with her working conditions.

Working women have often purchased household goods either through the cooperative institution where they worked, or when such goods were available at a special price. Six of them had been working before marriage. As part of their dowry they brought these goods to their husband's house without putting economic pressure on their parents. The average parent, with several marriageable children, may find themselves in serious economic difficulties, unable to provide a dowry for their daughters. However, some parents, in order to reduce these expectations, will give a little dowry to the daughter and in return agree for a simple wedding party and a smaller gift of gold.

In order to reduce the expenses of the groom, a one-day celebration for the two phases of the wedding is the most usual form of marriage. The first phase of the wedding party starts with the *aqad* ceremony, in which the Muslim marriage contract will be written. At that time the close relatives of the bride and the groom are invited, and a warm meal will be served at the expense of the bride's family. In the afternoon the second phase of the celebration, known as the wedding party, will be held. Then dinner will be served to a large number of guests, including distant relatives, friends and close neighbours. This part will be held at the expense of the groom. The wedding marks a recognition of the Muslim marriage contract. It is seldom the case that a bride moves to live with her husband before the second phase of the marriage celebration.

Devaluation of the rial brought a series of dramatic changes to families and the household economy. The reduced value of riyals provided grounds for parents of brides to request higher *mehr*, to guarantee more security for women at the time of divorce. The average mehr requested by the bride's family increased from a few hundred thousands before the revolution, to 3 million for the average middle-class family in 1989, and to 10 million in 1994. Knowing the existence of such a threat causes the girl's family to request a higher amount of mehr.

In the past, the mehr was so low that initiating a divorce today has been easy for some husbands, being only a matter of paying an insignificant amount of cash to the wife. The predicament of a woman facing divorce due to low mehr, can be illustrated in the case of Narges. In 1970, when she married, her mehr was 100,000 tomans; (a high sum at that time). When she divorced in 1989 the average mehr was 3-5 million tomans; among the better educated and well-off families. Her husband thought it was an easy matter simply to give her the total amount of 100,000 tomans in cash, thus fulfilling the sole legal condition for a restricted third-degree divorce. For the husband this equalled the price of a pair of car tyres.

The high amount of mehr today makes it impossible for husbands to pay it to their wives in case of divorce. However, to women the sum is more a matter of status, providing them with more power and ability to negotiate with the husband in case of divorce. Family insecurity and the increasing number of divorces on one hand, and the continuous devaluation of riyals on the other, induces parents to increase their demands of mehr, thus hoping to guarantee greater security for their daughters in marriage.

STATUS IN FAMILY

The legal, moral and social status of woman is not affected in any way if she engages herself in the maintenance and upliftment of the home. Islam, on the one hand, safeguards all her rights by law and on the other, instructs society to render her a kind and fair treatment. Islam creates such an environment that whatever position woman assumes, she holds it with all her dignity and honour. As long as such an encouragement prevails, no change can ever occur in her honour and dignity. There are three prominent positions of woman at home — a daughter, a wife and a mother. Islam bestows great rank and position on her in all her three roles. No one can pull her back from this high position while she remains in the fold of Islam.

Mother

Islam assigns the highest rank, after Almighty Allah and His Prophet, to mother. Islam instructs man to give just and fair treatment to both father and mother and commands him for their obedience because both of them confer benevolence on him. But, in the Quran and Hadith, reference to the great benevolence of mother occurs more evidently and prominently.

In all the works of child upbringing like feeding, nursing, education and training, the father participates with mother. But it is only the mother who bears all the pains and troubles of pregnancy and delivery individually. To bear the burden of pregnancy for nine long months, to give birth to a child after a great struggle of life and death and to feed her child out of her own blood and to lead a life of full care and strict precaution in all these stages is not at all an easy task. Father does not undertake all these hardships and does not bear all this pain. Therefore the benevolence and favours of mother on man are more than those of the father.

There are several Hadith which draw our attention towards rendering great service and obedience to mother and to behave politely with her. Some of its precepts are being discussed here.

Prophet Muhammad (peace be upon him) instructed man to give fair and just treatment to both father and mother. But the Prophet stressed the fair treatment more to mother.

Some of the people are of the opinion that since mother is weaker than father, hence the Prophet (peace be upon him) instructed man to serve and obey the mother much more than the father. Probably it is also true. However, the fact is, mother confers more benevolence on man than father and therefore she deserves more attention and obedience.

In traditions, disobedience to parents is included in Kabair, i.e., great sins.

The just and fair treatment to mother is regarded as a means of atonement for one's sins and the attainment of Paradise.

Service to mother is superior to the service to father. It is next only to the mother that the position of any other person can be determined. Hadrat Abu Hurrayrah relates that a person questioned Prophet Muhammad (upon whom be peace): Who deserves my polite behaviour most? The Prophet replied: 'Your mother'. The man asked: Who (deserves) the next? The Prophet replied: 'Your mother'. The man enquired for the third time that who deserves the next? The Prophet made the same answer:

'Your mother'. When the man repeated the same question for the fourth time, Prophet Muhammad (peace be upon him) said, 'Your father.'

There is one more Hadith according to which a companion of the Prophet asked him who deserved the greatest right for his decent and just treatment. The Prophet replied: 'Your mother'. The man asked who stands next to her? The Prophet replied: 'Your mother'.

The man asked the same question for the third time. The Prophet gave him the same answer again. When he put the same question for the fourth time, the Prophet replied: 'Your father', then whoever stands as much nearer to you in relations deserves as much decent treatment.

Qadi Ayaz states that some people say that both mother and father deserve just and fair treatment. But mother deserves more rights for service. Imam Nawawi says that this opinion is the correct one since most authentic Hadith support it. Harith Muhasbi says that consensus seems to be that in matters of service from children mother has more rights than father.

There are different Traditions on the question whether the polite behaviour with mother should be double or triple? Imam Tahawi says that in this connection those Traditions are more authentic in which it is said that a man should offer kind and mild treatment to mother three times more than what he should offer to his father.

Imam Ahmad says that father should be obeyed, but as far as the fair treatment is concerned, out of the four parts, three belong to mother.

Islam does not stress the legal rights of mother and father alone but also prescribes a kind and decent treatment to them. Islam holds that the legal rights of parents should be observed heartily and with love and devotion and should not be regarded as burden. It also unfolds the fact that apart from the legal rights, one should give as noble and humble treatment to parents as possible and in this treatment again, mother deserves more affectionate treatment. Mother should be offered better behaviour than what is offered to father.

Wife

In Islam woman possesses an independent entity of her own. Because of Nikah, neither her personality gets dissolved in the personality of her husband nor does she become his subject or servant. When she holds some new responsibilities after marriage, she becomes the owner of some new rights at the same time. As she cannot refuse these responsibilities, in the same manner her rights cannot be taken away from her.

Now let us see how Islam views the relationship between wife and husband and what legal and moral basis Islam provides for this relationship.

What is suggested is that there should be a relation of love, sympathy and affection between husband and wife. It is all their natural urge indeed. If hostility and animosity take the place of love and affection, it is against nature on which Allah Almighty has created them.

There is always a head of any minor or major institution. The structure of the family and the relationship among its members and its problems are more complicated and varied than all the other institutions and their problems. Order and discipline cannot be there in a family in the absence of its head. If there is no head of a family or no one is responsible for a family, it would definitely get disorganised. In Islam, man obtains the position of a head of the family for several reasons. This does not mean that man has acquired unlimited and whole and sole authority on his wife and that she is merely his subject. It actually means that while it is the responsibility of woman to accept her husband as a leader and obey and follow all his 'lawful demands', she also enjoys her rights. It is compulsory and obligatory for a man to perform these rights rather to pay all her dues.

Woman, while accepting the superiority of man in domestic life, gains and enjoys all rights of maintenance allowance, residence, alimony, and education and training and several other rights. If man falls short of performing all these rights of woman, she can secure them through law.

Islam exhorts man not only to discharge the legal rights of his wife but to behave with her decently and justly. Nice treatment with wife is required in every condition. Sometimes man dislikes the face, temperament and habits of his wife, which affects their relationship. In such cases man is instructed to consider the better aspects of his wife because if he dislikes one aspect of hers, there can be then praiseworthy qualities in her. Therefore it is the demand not only of morality and nobility but also of wisdom and sagacity that man should keep far-reaching interests before him and should not spoil the cordial relationship with his wife. Sometimes a certain thing appears unpleasant to man, but in it are hidden unaccountable aspects of goodness. In this connection, Islam lays down such a noble and ideal rule that cannot be found anywhere else.

A lucid elucidation of such a polite behaviour with wife can be found in the sayings of Prophet Muhammad (peace be upon him).

Hadrat Muawiyyah Qushairi once enquired about the rights of wife of the Prophet (peace be upon him). In reply the Prophet said: That you should give her food when you eat, clothe her when you clothe yourself, not strike her on the face, and not revile her or turn her out of the house (if separation becomes necessary) but live separately within the house itself (temporarily).

The same Tradition is expressed again in some other words: Feed her what you feed yourself with, her clothing should be of the same standard as yours, do not beat or abuse and rebuke her.

First, husband should follow the same standard of eating and drinking, clothing and dressing for his wife which he keeps for himself. It is unjustified if he keeps a high standard of life and compels his wife to subsist on a lower standard. Secondly, in association and relationship with her, his performance should be honourable. He should not treat her harshly or cruelly.

If any action of woman looks unpleasant or disagreeable, Prophet Muhammad (peace be upon him) advised man to endure and to have patience because this unpleasantness may prove temporary. Where some act of hers is unpleasant, some other acts may be pleasing to heart. To express lament and to show hatred and to be enraged at the slightest provocation will spoil mutual affectionate relationships for ever. Hadrat Abu Hurrayrah relates that Prophet Muhammad (peace be upon him) said: A believer must not hate a believing woman; if he dislikes one of her traits, he will be pleased with another.

Sometimes man demonstrates high morals and displays good conduct with others but his behaviour with his wife is reproachable even though his wife who is his life-partner is most deserving of polite and decent behaviour. Hence the man whose behaviour with his wife is just and fair is regarded as the best man. In a Tradition Hadrat Abu Hurrayrah relates that the Prophet said: The believers with perfect faith are those who have the best disposition and the best of you are those who are best to their wives.

In a Tradition, showing courtesy and love to wife and children is regarded as an attribute which completed faith (Iman). Hadrat Aishah related that Prophet Muhammad (peace be upon him) said: Among the believers, the man whose moral is best, has the perfect faith and who behave with his wife and children with more love and affection.

In another Tradition Hadrat Aishah relates that Prophet Muhammad, upon whom be peace, said: The best of you is he who is the best to his family, and I am the best among you to my family.

Islam regards the standard of relationship between husband and wife free from contention and strife as commendable. Wife should try to keep her husband delighted and contended, to obey him in rightful works and to safeguard his honour and dignity and wealth and property. On the other hand, husband should consider such a chaste and virtuous wife to be an excellent asset of life and should offer more decent and polite behaviour to her.

Hadrat Abu Hurrayrah says that Prophet Muhammad (peace be upon him) was asked about the attributes of a virtuous and righteous woman. The Prophet said: 'The one who pleases (her husband) when he looks at her, obeys him when he gives a command, and does not go against his wishes regarding her person, or property by doing anything of which he disapproves.'

Hadrat Abu Amama relates that Prophet Muhammad (peace be upon him) said: 'After fear of God, a believer gains nothing better for him than a good wife who obeys him if he gives her a command, pleases him if he looks at her, is true to him if he adjures her to do something, and is sincere towards him regarding her person and his property if he is absent.'

Hadrat Abdullah b. Umar b. Aas says that the Prophet said: 'The whole world is to be enjoyed, but the best thing in the world is a good wife.'

Hadrat Umar asked Prophet Muhammad (peace be upon him) that Allah Almighty forbids to store gold and silver, what type of wealth, then, we should keep with us? Prophet Muhammad (peace be upon him) said: 'Each one of you must possess with you, a thankful heart, a God-remembering tongue, a (Muslim) believing wife who assists him in the works for Akhirah (eternal life).'

It is quite evident from the above Traditions what type of relationship Islam wants to promote between husband and wife. If such a type of relationship exists between them, both of them will be assistant and well-wisher of each other, their life will be pleasant and ideal and all the unpleasant problems of rights and demands which cause disturbance and destroy the domestic life would never occur in their life.

Daughter

Before the proclamation of the Prophethood of Prophet Muhammad (peace be upon him), parents were much proud of their sons and they were supposed to be their great asset, because they gave more strength to their tribe and they were assistant in their great exertion in the field of finance. But daughters were considered to be burden on them and they were supposed to be the cause of ignominy or disgrace and on their very mention their heads dropped in shame. The Quran portrays a very graphic picture of the feelings of a parent on the birth of his daughter at that time.

One of the results of these obnoxious feelings for daughter was that some tribes used to bury their daughters alive. The Quran vehemently criticised the murdering of children and regarded it a capital offence and put an end to this abhorrent practice once and for all. The Quran says that on the Last Day, one would have to answer for the hard-heartedness to God. Islam inculcated totally different feelings for girls in place of their barbarous and brutal feelings.

The first and foremost that Islam says is that it is the will and wish of God that favoured some with children and to some He debarred and to some He gave only sons and to some He favoured with daughters alone and to some He blessed with both sons and daughters. None of this case is a cause of honour or disgrace or cause of dishonour or ignominy. All this is a natural phenomenon representing as it does the boundless knowledge and wisdom of God. Those who consider it a standard of dignity or ignominy are cavilling at His wisdom.

There is exhortation in Islam for the proper nourishment and sustenance of daughters. It is regarded as a good deed and a means for the attainment of Heaven.

In Traditions, the upbringing and nourishment of two or three daughters or sisters or even one daughter or sister is referred to as a means for entering Heaven. From this the reward or requital to the person who brings up more than three daughters or sisters can be well realised. Hadrat Utba bin Aamir relates that Prophet Muhammad (peace be upon him) said: 'Whoever has three daughters, and bears with the miseries in their connection, feeds and clothes them with the earnings of his labour, they will become a curtain on the fire of hell, for him.'

Hadrat Abu Hurrayrah relates that Prophet Muhammad (peace be upon him) said: Whoever has three daughters and he bears with the difficulties and financial problems, in connection with them, Allah will make him enter Heaven, for courtesy towards them.' Abu Hurrayrah reports that a man enquired if he has two daughters (and bears with the difficulties in connection with them). The Prophet replied, 'Even if he has two daughters (Allah will bless him with Heaven)'. A man asked, if he has one? The Prophet said (He will) even if he has one.'

Hadrat Abdullah bin Abbas relates a similar Hadith that Prophet Muhammad (peace be upon him) said: 'If anyone takes care of three girls or the like number of sisters, training them and showing kindness to them till God enriches them, God will guarantee him paradise.'

Hearing such a great reward, a man humbly enquired Prophet Muhammad (peace be upon him) that if anyone renders the same service to two daughters or sisters in the same way does he get the same reward? The Prophet replied, 'Yes, he would get the same reward'. The one who relates the above Hadith says that if the man would have enquired for one daughter or sister, the Prophet would have given the same reply.

It shows that for providing nourishment and giving proper training to one daughter or sister a man deserves a seat in paradise. If he nourishes and brings up more than one daughter or sister, his rank may be raised accordingly.

It is stated in the Hadith that with the good nourishment of daughters, they should also be given good education and training and should also select a good match for the marriage and should continue fair and just treatment with them. Hadrat Abu Sayeed Khudri relates that Prophet Muhammad (peace be upon him) said: 'Whoever nourishes three daughters, educates and trains them, gets them married (and afterwards) offers a gentle behaviour to them, for him there is heaven.'

Generally more love and affection is showered on sons in feeding, clothing, education, training and in every respect more preference is accorded to them. This is total injustice and oppression. In Hadith such a treatment is forbidden and condemned.

Hadrat Abdullah bin Abbas relates that Prophet Muhammad (peace be upon him) said: 'Whoever has a girl, who has neither buried her alive nor gives a mean treatment to her and not even gives preference to his son over his daughter, God will make him enter Heaven.'

In all these Hadith on the proper nourishment, education training, arrangement of marriage and equal treatment to daughters or sisters, glad tidings is given for liberation from Hell and the attainment of Heaven. One who does not have faith in God and the eternal day and one who gives all importance to the present world alone does not realise the significance of these Traditions. But the very goal of the believer (Momin) is success on the Judgement Day. There is all what he wishes in this goodness for a believer.

With the inducement of the proper care for girls, this conception is also laid down that she is not worthless or valueless as the world considers her, but she is the most valuable boon of nature. The love and affection which she possesses in herself, a boy does not have it.

Hadrat Uqba bin Amir relates that Prophet Muhammad (peace be upon him) said: Do not hate girls. They are comforter and much precious.

Such a teaching for a fair and just treatment of girls is an example which is found nowhere. According to Islamic law, if the child does not own any position and does not have any proper means for living, his maintenance is obligatory on his father. In accordance with this rule, the maintenance or allowances for daughters is obligatory on his father till her marriage and in the absence of his father, it is necessary for her nearest relative to ensure her maintenance. After marriage, the responsibility of her maintenance shifts to her husband and on the death of her husband or in case of divorce and if the woman is not self-sufficient in financial matters, the responsibility goes to her children or in case she has no children, the responsibility for her maintenance falls on her nearest relative. This is a legal right and in the Tradition its importance is well emphasised.

Hadrat Suraqua bin Malik relates that Prophet Muhammad (peace be upon him) asked him: 'Shall I not show you what is the greatest charity. He said: Messenger of God, certainly show (it). The Prophet said, 'To be grateful to your daughters who (after becoming widow or being divorced) is sent back to you and there is no one save you, her earning man.'

The Companions of the Prophet were so thoughtful about their widows and daughters that it can be well understood from this example that Hadrat Zubayr endowed some of his houses. In the details of this endowment the following statement was also included.

Whosoever of his daughters (being divorced or by becoming a widow) would come back to her house, she would stay in it.

Neither she would put it in loss nor would she be put in loss. If she is self-sufficient in respect of finance without depending on her husband, she would not have any right in it. In this way, in the family system of Islam, the legal right of woman are secured; and on the moral ground also she enjoys a place of honour and dignity.

SANCTITY OF THE HOUSE

Whereas Islam has promulgated rules and regulations for all actions and deeds, it has also set some principles for entering the houses in order to maintain the sanctity of home-life. It is not permissible to enter a house without seeking permission of the head of the family.

In the places not used as residences such as schools, guesthouses, monasteries where there is no restriction to go or in the houses where no one resides, one may enter without seeking permission. If, however, restrictions are imposed on the entry of some persons, they should not go therein.

Supposing there is none in the house, even then you have no right to enter a house which is not meant for general public use. Moreover, if the permission to enter is not granted, it is futile to insist and to enter forcibly in the house. It is a great sin and offence. It is also against moral and ethical principles. So the Ulama are of the view: If the entry is refused one should neither insist for permission to enter nor ask that purdah should be observed. He should also not wait as all these acts are against good etiquettes. He should not knock at the door. The author of *Kashaf* has explained his view while commenting upon the above verse.

There are many advantages of seeking permission to enter a house. In the terminology of Hadith it is called Istidhan. It is an obligatory duty in Islam and one must act upon it. No one knows how much harmful it is to himself or to the family if anyone enters the house suddenly. It is just possible that someone may be naked, his glance may suddenly fall on him/her. It is, therefore, proper that no one should enter the house without seeking permission. If a number of married sons and daughters of the same father are residing in a house, it is necessary to seek permission before entering so that the inmates of the house may become alert and recompose themselves. The principle should be observed in entering the female apartment. The Holy Prophet (peace and blessings of Allah be upon him) instructed his Companions to seek permission before entering a house. Many such events have been mentioned in the Ahadith where the Holy Prophet instructed his Companions to act upon this principle.

A person who belonged to Bani Amir once went to the Holy Prophet (peace and blessings of Allah be upon him) who was in the house. When he arrived at the door of the house, he said, May I come in? When the Holy Prophet (peace and blessings of Allah be upon him) heard his voice, he said to his servant: Go to the person who is outside and teach him the way to ask permission in accordance with the Shariah. Ask him to say: Assalamo Alaikum! May I come in? That person heard the instructions which the Holy Prophet (peace and blessings of Allah be upon him) was giving to his servant and said: Assalamo Alaikum! May I come in? Thereupon the Holy Prophet (peace and blessings of Allah be upon him) gave him permission and he came in.

Hadrat Kuldah bin Al Hanbal (Allah be pleased with him) said: I went to the Holy Prophet (peace and blessings of Allah be upon him) and entered without saying Assalamo Alaikum. Thereupon he said: Go back and say: Assalamo Alaikum! May I come in?

It is clear from the above Ahadith that the correct way to ask permission is that one should first say Assalamo Alaikum and then ask permission to enter. To seek permission without saying Assalamo Alaikum is not correct. It is also evident from the above Ahadith that one should ask permission thrice and if there is no response even at the third call one should not insist and return.

There is another incident relating to the Holy Prophet (peace and blessings of Allah be upon him). He went to Said bin Ubada and asked permission thrice after saying Assalamo Alaikum. When he had no response he returned. Meanwhile, Hadrat Said came to him running and took him to the house.

It is necessary for the visitor to ask permission first so that he could not see any one of the inmates of the house all of a sudden. It has been narrated that once the Holy Prophet (peace and blessings of Allah be upon him) was sitting in the house and scratching his head. Someone came and began to peep in. When the Holy Prophet (peace and blessings of Allah be upon him) knew it, he became very angry and said: Had I known it, I would have had his eyes torn out. Is he not aware: The visitor, must therefore not stand in front of the door; he should remain at one side.

Hadrat Abdullah has reported that whenever the Holy Prophet (peace and blessings of Allah be upon him) went to anyone he stood at one side of the door and said: Assalamo Alaikum! In those days curtains were not hung at the doors of the houses. If it is hung, there is no harm in standing in front of the door; but etiquettes demand that one should not ask permission to enter standing just in front as thus there is every possibility of seeing the inmates of the house.

It has been mentioned in a Hadith that a person came at the door of the Holy Prophet (peace and blessings of Allah be upon him) and asked permission standing in front of the door. The Holy Prophet (peace and blessings of Allah be upon him) beckoned him to stand at one side of the door as the law of seeking permission has been made due to gazing in.

It is forbidden to peep in from fissures of the doors or that of the windows as the very purpose of seeking permission is thus violated.

If he seeks permission to enter after saying Assalamo Alaikum and the inmate of the house asks who is he, he should tell his familiar name. It should not be said: 'It is I', as the person cannot be recognized in this way. The Holy Prophet (peace and blessings of Allah be upon him) does not like that an ambiguous reply should be given.

Once Hadrat Jabir went to the Holy Prophet (peace and blessings of Allah be upon him). He (the Holy Prophet) asked: Who are you? He said: It is I. The Holy Prophet (peace and blessings of Allah be upon him) disliked the reply and said: What do you mean by this I, I. The Companions of the Holy Prophet (peace and blessings of Allah be upon him) also taught their followers the way tc seek permission and exhorted them to act upon it.

The permission to enter the house should also be asked from the *mahram* such as mother and sister, etc. It has been stated in the verse regarding 'Istidhan' that a woman from Ansar came to the Holy Prophet (peace and blessings of Allah be upon him) and said: I am in such a condition that I do not like any one, even my father to see me; but these persons come and go in this state.

Thereupon the verse a particular was revealed. Various instances have been narrated in Ahadith from which it is evident that *mahrams* are also required to ask permission as no body knows about the condition in which the women would be sitting. In my opinion one should not enter without permission even if there is only wife in the house as she might be naked and no body likes to be seen in a state of nudeness.

A person asked the Holy Prophet (peace and blessings of Allah be upon him): Is it necessary to seek permission from mother? He said: Yes, permission needs to be sought from mother. He said: I live with her. In other words, she is not required to observe purdah from me then why is it necessary to ask permission? The Holy Prophet (peace and blessings of Allah be upon him) said: Ask permission from her also. He said: Even if you go to your mother you ask permission. Would you like to see your mother naked? He said: No. He (the Holy Prophet) said: That is why I say that you should seek permission before seeing her.

Hadrat Zainab (Allah be pleased with her) says: Whenever Hadrat Abdullah bin Masud (Allah be pleased with him) came in for some need, he first stopped at the door and coughed and then came in. He did not like to come in suddenly. Zainab was the wife of Hadrat Abdullah bin Masud.

Hadrat Abu Ubaidah says: When Hadrat Abdullah arrived he asked permission loudly at the door. Hadrat Imam Ahmad bin Hanbal says: When a person enters the house he should cough loudly or strike his shoe with force so that the inmate of the house may know that some one is coming.

The purpose of Assalamo Alaikum for three times is that the inmates of the house may know about the arrival of the visitor. They may become alert at the second and may grant or refuse permission at the third.

Ibn Al-Arabi is of the view that it is an incumbent act to ask permission before entering the house of others. As regards one's own house, it is not an incumbent duty. If, however, mother and sisters are living there, he should cough and then enter. At the door he should strike his feet so that the women may become aware of his arrival. Sometimes even mother and sister are in a condition that it is not proper to see them.

According to Imam Malik, it is necessary to ask permission before seeing the mother or sister. It was again and again enquired from Hadrat Ibn Masud and Ibn Abbas whether it is necessary for the persons to ask permission from the mother and sister residing with him. He said: No one likes to see his mother naked, then why do you insist on this question.

If you ponder over the Islamic rules and regulations you would come to the conclusion that they are not only rules of wisdom and freedom but excellently safeguard modesty.

We are constrained to say that these rules and regulations of entering the houses which have been explained by the Holy Quran and the Ahadith ~ and practically followed by the noble Companions of the Holy Prophet throughout their lives are being overlooked by the Muslims of today. These rules and regulations need to be revived and enforced in our home-life.

It is an admitted fact that the Divine Law is the most effective safeguard against immorality and debauchery. After the commandments relating to grown up and adolescent boys in the Holy Quran the Ahadith have also explained that the children too have the capability to think. So far as *ghair-mahrams* are concerned, it has already been explained that it is necessary to observe strict purdah from them.

It is, however, allowed to expose the face and palms of hands in need; but if there is any fear of evil or mischief, these parts should also not be exposed. From mahrams purdah is for the whole body except face, palms of hands, arms, head and shanks, etc., which remain ordinarily exposed but it is not allowed to expose these parts unnecessarily. The servant is also a ghair-mahram and it is necessary to observe purdah from him. An infidel maid-servant also comes under the definition of a mahram.

What we want to tell you is that the young boys and maid servants who fall under the category of mahrams should also ask permission to enter at special times as during these times men and women do not generally exercise proper care and vigilance in observing purdah.

Some commentators have written that the instructions of Istidhan in the first verses are applicable to the other people and strangers and those contained in this verse pertain to the relatives, that is to say, to the mahrams. According to some scholars the instructions contained in the verse are for the common men and for all times and those contained in the above verse are for specific persons and for specific times and this view is correct.

The word *malik* used in the above verse means a maid-servant as Abd which stands for servant is according to the Shariah a *ghair-mahram*. A servant is permitted to come among men; but he is not allowed to go among women. The mahram on whom there is ordinarily no restriction to come are also not permitted to come during the special times, the detail of which has been given above. These preventive measures are based on prudence and wisdom.

The immature children are also required to ask permission to come on reaching puberty. Previously they were required to seek permission if they wanted to come in at specific times. The practice which is in vogue in India and Pakistan that those children who come in without restriction during childhood and before puberty come without asking permission even after attaining puberty and the women do not observe purdah from them is absolutely wrong and against the Shariah and should be put to an end. There is no ambiguity about this rule that the children when they come to puberty must also ask permission as the concession enjoyed by them in childhood now no longer exists.

Uptil now the children were required to ask permission at three specific hours; but on attaining the age of puberty they are also required to ask permission at all times like the other people as in childhood and in the adolescence period they were neither aware of the implications of purdah nor women had any attraction for them and vice versa; but now there has occurred a change in them; their feelings and sentiments have awakened raging a tumult in them. Women might also feel attracted towards them. Now the rule which is applicable to the grown-up persons is to be applied to them. Maulana Ashraf Ali Thanvi has added the following comments: And when the children among you reach the age of competency or be nearing this age, they should also ask permission like the grown-up persons. Allah, the Exalted has revealed clear verses. He is all-knowing, All-Aware. The above commandment has been repeated to emphasize the advantages of the rules of seeking permission. It has been explained above that for women it is necessary to observe purdah of the whole body except her face and the palms of her hands as is evident from the above verse so that no one should have any misconception about the implication of these words. It may be pointed out that although there is no *satr* of face and hands, yet they should not be exposed to a stranger if there is fear of evil and mischief. The aged women may, however, not cover their faces and hands although it is better for them to do so.

It has been ordained even for the aged women not to display their decoration. It is evident that Islam does not allow the parts of the body which come under the given definition be remained uncovered without any reason. Maulana Ashraf Ali Thanvi has written: One thing we must understand. Although there is no satr of face and hands in the strict sense of the word, but it is not permissible that women should freely display their faces and hands to strangers as there is fear of evil and mischief. The satr of these parts of the body also becomes incumbent except upon the aged women who have lost attraction for men and have no hope for marriage, only such women are permitted to expose their face and hands and according to some their feet but they are not permitted to display their decoration. So far as a young lady is concerned, it is necessary for her to observe satr of these parts if there is fear of evil and mischief, but it is permitted to expose these parts in case of necessity or genuine excuse. It is, however, better that purdah should be observed.

BIRTH CONTROL

Birth Control in its modern form was not practised in the early days of Islam. No doubt, infanticide, abortion and other methods of getting rid of unwanted children were prevalent in

Arabia, as in other parts of the world, and Islam forbade them completely. The Quran said: 'Do not kill your children for fear of poverty; We will provide for them and for you.' The question is whether this injunction can be applied to modern methods of birth control which do not amount to killing but aim at the prevention of conception. But this is not the only vital issue. There is the further question whether Islam would have approved of artificial methods for limiting population, if such methods had been used in its day.

No clear-cut instructions are available either in the Quran or in the traditions of the Prophet. We will have to decide them on the basis of the general tenor and spirit of Islamic teachings, and the moral considerations involved therein. The Quran's own accepted method in deciding such doubtful issues is to weigh the good and the evil of a habit, institution or way of life, and condemn it if its evil is likely to exceed the good and vice versa. For example, in prohibiting the use of alcoholic liquor, the Quran says: 'Its sin and evil far outweigh its benefits.' Thus the Quran recognises that there are some benefits also in the use of wine but condemns it because the evils of it are more numerous and more dangerous. Proceeding on this basis, let us analyse the argument, for and against birth control.

Among the foremost advocates of birth control in modem times Havelock Ellis stands most prominent, apart from Margaret Sanger. In his book on *Life and Sex* he has devoted a whole chapter entitled 'The Individual and the Race' to prove the thesis that birth control is a social necessity and serves the interest of the race. Let us give a few quotations from this book.

Stressing the eugenic aspect of birth control, Ellis says: It is often said— I have said it myself—that birth-control when practised merely as a limitation of the family scarcely suffices to further the eugenic progress of the race. If it is not deliberately directed towards the elimination of the worst stocks or the worst possibilities in the blending of stocks, it may even tend to diminish the better stocks since it is the better stocks that are least likely to propagate at random. This is true if other conditions remain equal. It is evident, however, that the other conditions will not remain equal, for no evidence has yet been brought forward to show that birth-control, even when practised without regard to eugenic considerations-doubtless the usual rule up to the present has produced any degeneration of the race. On the contrary, the evidence seems to show that it has improved the race.

Examining the effect of birth control on the health of mothers, Havelock Ellis writes in the same chapter.

There will probably be a longer interval between the birth of the children, which has been demonstrated by Ewart and others to be an important factor not only in preserving the health of the mother but in increasing the health and size of the child. The diminution in the number of children renders it possible to bestow a greater amount of care on each child. Moreover, the better economic position of the father, due to the smaller number of individuals he has to support, makes it possible for the family to live under improved conditions as regards nourishment, hygiene and comfort. The observance of birth-control is thus a far more effective lever for raising the state of the social environment and improving the conditions of breeding, than is direct action on the part of the community in its collective capacity to attain the same end.

Socialists also come in for scathing criticism by Havelock Ellis, because they are opposed to birth control.

Put social conditions on a sound basis, the people on this side often say, let all receive an adequate economic return for their work and be recognized as having a claim for an adequate share in the products of society and there is no need to worry about the race or about the need for birth-control; all will go well of itself. There is not the slightest ground for any such comfortable belief.

And further the same writer says:

This prejudice against birth control is based on the ground that bad economic conditions, and an unwholesome environment are the source of all social evils and that a better distribution of wealth or a vast scheme of social welfare is the one thing necessary. . .. It is certainly impossible to overrate the importance of the economic factor in society or of a good environment.

And it is true that eugenics also, like birth-control alone, can effect little if the economic basis of society is unsound. But it is equally certain that the economic factor can never in itself suffice for fine living or even as a cure-all of social and racial diseases. Its value is not that it can effect any of these things but that it furnishes the favourable conditions for effecting them. He would be foolish indeed who went to the rich to find the example of good breeding and, as is well known, it is not with the rich that the future of the race lies. The fact that under any economic system the responsible personal direction of the individual and the family remains equally necessary, and no progress is possible so long as the individual casts all responsibility away from himself on the social group he forms part of.

In another book, *Psychology of Sex*, Havelock Ellis says:

The necessity of birth-control is now generally recognized, not only by those who do not desire to have children, but by those who do. The reason is that, both for the sake of the mother and for the health and well-being of the off-spring, it is desirable that births should be properly spaced, allowing at least an interval of two years between births, while there are various legitimate reasons, economic or other, why those who marry early do not see their way to become parents immediately. The child, therefore, however much desired, should come at a time when the parents are best able to receive it and to care for it. Moreover the days of large families are over. For the sake of the family and in the interest of the nation and the race, an average of between two or three for each married couple suffices. The hygienic conditions of civilization should be ample to keep up the population. When for any good reason, such as the health of the mother or the existence, in either parent, of a bad heredity which should not be carried on, conception cannot be allowed, then strict birth-control is compulsory.

So far we have quoted arguments in favour of birth control. Now let us see the other side of the picture. It must be recognized that over-population is not the only evil which has to be fought against and controlled. A falling birth-rate and a diminution of population is at least an equally serious evil. In the decline of civilisations, under-population and not over-population, is a common symptom. This is true of the Roman civilisation which was faced with serious depopulation in its period of decline. Similarly, one factor in the defeat of modern France against Hitlerite Germany was lack of manpower. This was emphasised by Marshal Petain in his speech on the morrow of French defeat. The reason is that love of luxury and comfort among the richer classes and fear of poverty and insecurity among the poor make them unwilling to bring more children in the world, This tendency has been greatly facilitated by the use of birth-control methods. As Margaret Mead has pointed out in her book, *Male and Female:* 'Every human society is faced not with one population problem but with two: How to beget and rear enough children and not to beget and rear too many?

The definition of "enough" and "too many" varies enormously.' The same writer, pointing to the growing sterility among men and women, adds: 'There seems to be a deep-seated belief that conception is an almost automatic process, and that unless drastic measures are taken every sexual act will result in a child. The story of the king and the queen who had no children is replaced by jokes based on contraceptive failures. Even in the face of rising sterility rates and the occasional sterility clinic, the popular mind is still focussed on how not to have children rather than how to have them.' On this evidence, in some countries the widespread use of contraceptives is creating a serious danger of depopulation, apart from facilitating and widening the range of extra-matrimonial illicit sexual relations which is undermining the stability of the home and the family. 'Let us quote Dr. Westermarck who says in *Future of Marriage in Western Civilization*: 'While the knowledge of contraceptives may increase the marriage rate, it also facilitates extra-matrimonial intercourse, the great frequency of which is, in our days, regarded as another indication of the doom of marriage.'

The cult of birth control was one of the by-products of the Malthusian theory that the rate of increase of population is far in excess of any increase in the means of subsistence and if it is allowed to go on unchecked, a point will come when most of the human race will have starved out. This false theory has been exploded, since then, but its influence on the minds of people everywhere is still so great that, they overlook the danger of depopulation. As Stefansson said in 1925: 'According to the false Malthusianism of Malthus himself, we should all have starved to death sometime ago .... But here we all are, alive; prosperous and sceptical of the prophets, of doom.' What Malthus and his supporters overlooked was that humanity is infinitely creative, if it does not lose its spiritual moorings or sink into gross and sordid materialism.

The productive powers of man have increased at much faster rate than his numbers. If they have failed to make him happier and contented, it is because, in the mad race for power and wealth, they are being put to destructive uses. As science and knowledge increase, the earth will support more and more of human beings, provided man's spirituality and vision also expand in the right direction. There was never really any danger of population increasing faster than human productivity. Even the available space on earth for human habitation is not so limited as many people imagine. Geographical explorations are opening, up new areas with immensely rich resources which can be made fit for human habitation with the help of scientific power at the disposal of man. This theme has been very brilliantly treated by Parker Hanson in his book, *New Worlds Emerging*.

We give here a few quotations from this great book which will show how much habitable space and available resources are still to be tapped by mankind. Discussing the methods which have been and can be used for meeting the threat of over-population, Hanson says: 'Throughout history and prehistory, man has met his ever recurring problem of over-population, not in any one way but by a complex, interrelated application of three distinct lines of effort, namely, migration, change of social and economic organization, and technical invention.' Strikingly enough, Hanson does not mention birth control as one of the methods for meeting the danger of over-population, because no really great and creative civilisation has ever resorted to birth control except in its period of decadence. The three methods referred to by Hanson are still open to humanity. With regard to the first of these, migration, let us study his conclusions.

Turning to the economic aspect of the question, we must emphasise one factor which the advocates of birth control seem to have lost sight of. It is that every child who comes into the world remains as an economic burden on his parents and society only so long as his creative faculties are undeveloped. As soon as he becomes creative—and all individuals properly educated are creative — he pays back to his family and society more than what they contribute towards his growth and development. If lack of economic resources or a defective and unscientific education does not release his latent creativity, it is not the fault of his maker but of the social system in which he is born. As far as Nature is concerned, it never really brings a fresh individual in society without implanting in him the seeds of creativity and endowing him with capabilities of enriching his society materially, and spiritually.

Properly brought up and scientifically educated, every human being is capable of creating more wealth than he can possibly use for his individual needs and of giving back more than what his parents have invested on him. From this point of view the birth of every child is an addition to social wealth for which humanity ought to be thankful to God. It is not a cursor to be eliminated and fought against. When people begin to prevent the birth of children and are afraid of every new addition to human population, it is a sure sign that the society in which they live has ceased to be creative and the acquisitive spirit has so far acquired ascendancy over the mind of the people as to destroy the economic equilibrium of society.

In a nation which enjoys economic health and provides equal opportunities for all its members, nobody should be afraid of having an extra child. It is social and economic injustice and the accumulation of wealth in the hands of an uncreative oligarchy of politicians, officials, traders, industrialists and landlords which reduces the common man to poverty and makes him unwilling to add to his burdens by bringing into the world more mouths to feed. The advocacy of birth control really springs from a subconscious desire to keep intact the socio-economic organisation of an unjust society. It is always a convenient device of the privileged classes when they feel that they cannot prevent the growth of disaffection among the poor without radical changes in the economic structure of society. In the circumstances they feel that a further deterioration in the economic situation of the poor cannot be arrested without the widespread use of birth control. So, instead of cutting down their own privileges and lowering their own luxurious standards of living, they offer the palliative of birth control to the people low down in the scale of life.

Havelock Ellis has attacked the socialists for opposing the use of birth-control methods. But, apart from eugenic considerations, he produces no convincing arguments as to why, instead of exterminating the human race partially or wholly, society should not be so reorganised economically as to remove the fear of poverty on account of procreation. As regards eugenics what Havelock , Ellis seems to forget is that the application of eugenic principles will lead to much interference in private and family matters. It is the State, after all, which will decide who shall procreate and to what extent particular stocks shall be encouraged to propagate themselves and what shall be withheld from so doing. Is there any guarantee that the State will not misuse its authority for political ends or that the sordid interests of a small group, holding power in the State, shall not determine the application of eugenic principles to the prejudice of its opponents. And again, how will the State or any other corporate body enforce its decisions on unwilling persons?—A secret police force to watch the operations of birth control and report to the authorities. — Surely this is an absurd idea!

The most serious evil which is likely to attend the spread of birth-control methods is that once people get used to artificial family limitation; there will be nothing to prevent them from carrying that limitation to its furthermost extent and reducing the population to a dangerously low extent. There is no limit to which love of ease and luxuries may not carry a people when they once become addicted to these things. Is there any real need for providing more incentives towards life of irresponsibility? Human nature is already ballasted with this tendency, and for this very reason procreation in man creates its own natural checks. As soon as a couple feel that more children will mean extra burden, they take necessary precautions, as far as they can, to prevent more births. To provide artificial checks and push human beings on the road to pleasure-loving and irresponsibility is tantamount to committing national suicide.

When race extermination has become the rage and unwillingness to suffer and sacrifice for the sake of the family and the nation has become deep-rooted, you can do nothing effective to reverse the process or change the habits of a people within a reasonable distance of time. To introduce such dangerous methods in a nation without an eye on future consequences and psychological reactions on the mental and spiritual attitudes of men and women is the height of unwisdom. A few fleeting advantages should not blind us against far more effective and permanent national and moral injuries. A people using birth-control methods on a large-scale may have more comforts, better standards of economic prosperity and wider educational opportunities, but they are also likely to be incapable of making big sacrifices or undergoing great hardships for any ideal-social, religious or national. Can such a people survive in a world where these very qualities ultimately determine the chances of survival? The fear that bigger families will mean more hardships and a tougher economic struggle should be balanced by the consideration that it is through struggle, sacrifice and hardship that great individuals as well as nations have achieved success and glory and left their imprint on the sands of time.

Very few among the great men of the world and not one among the great nations of the earth initially had those comforts, luxuries and facilities which the advocates of birth control consider to be necessary for the health, happiness and progress of human beings. A small measure of poverty, provided it is not extreme and such as to freeze and corrode the human soul, provides an ideal incentive to progressive effort for creative individuals and nations than all the wealth and comforts sought after by the friends of race extermination. No great creative spiritual or cultural accomplishment has ever come from the rich who wallow in luxury, waste, extravagance, greed, acquisitiveness and ungodly arrogance.

It is the poor individuals and nations that have throughout history lit the lamp of spirituality, culture and high scientific achievements. No great soul was ever afraid of moderate poverty. Let us not be carried away by the slogans of a decrepit civilisation. A society which does not allow the majority of human beings to be reduced to abject poverty in order to provide wealth and luxury and comfort to a privileged group has little need of birth control. Let all people live a life of simple habits, let them have freedom from the ever-recurring threat of starvation, let them be provided with the necessaries of life, even without its superfluities, and, finally, let them be creative in thought and deed, not acquisitive in spirit and attitude, and every fresh addition to the human population will but increase the wealth, happiness and virtue of mankind.

5

System of Marriage

'There are three essential elements in every normal marriage,' says Dr. Westermarck in his book, *The Future of Marriage in Western Civilization*, 'the gratification of the sexual impulse, the relation between husband and wife apart from it and procreation of children.' Let us see what is the angle of vision from which Islam looks at marriage and what is the central value in it which it stresses more than any other. Let it not also be forgotten that, unlike Christianity, which looked upon marriage as if it were a necessary evil, Islam regards it as a most sacred institution and makes it incumbent on every Muslim man and woman, unless prevented by valid physical or economic incapacity, to lead a married life.

The Quran has constantly used the word Mohsin for chaste men and Muhsinat for chaste women both of which come from the Arabic root Him meaning 'fort'. The underlying idea is that marriage safeguards and protects chastity in the same manner as a fort protects the garrison within from a besieging army.

From the above quotations it appears that Islam recommends marriage because, first, it helps men and women to lead a life of chastity, that is, it secures them against promiscuous sexual indulgence; secondly, because it prevents the formation of secret sex relations. These two values are the cornerstone on which the institution of marriage rests and Islam's conception, of woman's rights in marriage flows logically from them.

Let us see what the social importance of chastity and open sex relation is as opposed to secret love. In modern times, the ideal of chastity has lost hold on man and it has been claimed by some, even among men of science and learning, that chastity is by no means a very important social value and that happiness in marriage as well as the proper upbringing of children need not suffer from sexual promiscuity on the part of either partner. Some would go to the length of abolishing the family system in order to secure the release of men and women from the bonds of conjugal fidelity. It is presumed by these people that alternative methods of bringing up children can be organised more efficiently. It is difficult to bringout the importance of chastity as a social value unless we discuss all such proposals and ideas.

Let us first deal with the importance of conjugal fidelity and its healthy effects on the happiness of the family and the health of society. Islam has made no distinction in this respect between man and woman; both are equally punishable under the law of Islam if they are guilty of sexual laxity. But, in practice, public opinion has always, even in Western countries, taken more alarm at unchastity in women than in men, the reason being that the disturbing social and family effects of a woman's misconduct are deeper and more widespread. Discussing this inequality of treatment as regards men and women, Dr. Westermarck says in the *Future of Marriage in Western Civilization.*

But there are also more special reasons for that inequality between the sexes. It was a doctrine of the Roman jurists that adultery is a crime in the wife, and in the wife only, on account of the danger of introducing strange children to the husband. . . . It has been argued that the danger of confusion of pregnancy has disappeared with the development of methods for preventing conception, but it is anything but certain that the lovers trouble themselves about contraceptives. Von Krafft-Ebing writes [in his book *The Modern Family*): 'The unfaithfulness of a wife, in comparison with that of a husband, is morally much more weighty, and should be more severely punished legally. The unfaithful wife dishonours not only herself, but also her husband and her family....' 'The man,' says Kisch in [Die Sexuelle Untreue der Frau], 'can make a lapse in this marriage without the consequences of it being necessarily of vital importance; he can at any moment do remorseful penance without the mischief he has caused being irreparable.

The infidelity of the wife poisons the soul for ever, shakes the foundations of the harmony between mother and children, makes the legitimacy of the latter uncertain, and leads to an irreparable rupture of the 'domestic life.' Hedwig Wega observes that while the adultery of the husband is in many cases a purely social act, which need not spoil marriage, that of the wife is in no case merely bodily attachment. Stendhal remarks [in his book on Love] that where love is absent, the fidelity of a married woman is something contrary to nature, but that, 'with love there, one has no taste for any mate but that of the beloved fount.' He also writes: 'The difference between infidelity in the two sexes is so real, that a woman of passion may pardon it, while for a man that is impossible!'

These are some of the consequences of female unchastity, but so less grave are the consequences which follow from the sexual irregularities of men. We shall again quote Dr. Westermarck who says:

> *However useful sexual intercourse may be to the unmarried, it has also its disadvantages. It may give venereal diseases to him who practises it; and it may be fraught with serious consequences for the female partner.... The illegitimacy of birth affects the offspring even more than the mother. The death rate for illegitimate infants is very much higher than for legitimate ones.... Another result of them is the comparatively large number of criminals among the children of unmarried parents, who grow up in so unfavourable circumstances. The way in which they have been treated in the Western world is a disgrace to its civilization... It certainly seems both absurd and unjust that the legal rights of any citizens should be influenced by the judgments which society passes upon their mothers; but however much legislation may improve the condition of illegitimate children, it cannot make them equal to those under which most other children develop. Family allowances may be granted, to their mothers where the father is unknown or indigent, founding institutions may provide them with an education that is the best possible in the*

> *circumstances, but nothing can compensate them for the lack of an adequate home.*

It may of course be argued that all such evils can be avoided through the use of contraceptives. Dr. Ellis maintains that the much smaller rate of illegitimate children in England, compared with the rate of such children in Germany, is due to the wider adoption of methods for preventing conception, but when we hear that their number is rapidly increasing in Germany, in spite of the fact that contraceptives are used on a large scale in all classes we can by no means feel reassured that extra-matrimonial procreation will some day become an anachronism. Strictly speaking, however, the censure to which the unmarried mother is subject refers to something else than the birth of the child; this event is an impressive and conclusive testimony of an act which itself is considered degrading.

The above quotations should suffice to establish the fact that immodesty and unchastity have a serious disturbing effect on married happiness, family ties and the proper development of children. Apart from these effects, conjugal infidelity breeds jealousy, one of the most destructive human passions, both individually and socially. There are people who try to minimise the effects of jealousy, and regarding it as a relic of primitive barbarity foresee its disappearance with the spread of education and enlightenment. Dr Westermarck himself is one of those who believe that with proper education this primitive feeling would disappear, but even he has been forced to admit that there is one kind of sexual and conjugal jealousy which is not traceable to primitive barbarity.

This kind of jealousy, he says, arises from the uniqueness of the relationship between two persons and the endeavour to stamp this uniqueness on the whole relationship, sexual and moral. If this is true, civilisation and culture may be expected to increase this kind of jealousy rather than refuse its proportion. Let us see what Dr. Westermarck himself has to say on this subject. He writes:

> *The jealousy of a man, particularly a civilized man, differs from that of a male animal, apart from any feeling of injured rights ownership or any other right.*

> *It is coloured by the nature of his love, It is accompanied with humiliation, because the loss of possession to which jealousy refers or the failure to obtain it, is of such a nature as carries with it a lowering of a man's self valuation. There may also be envy of what the other has obtained by depriving him of it. There may be fear of another man's offspring being born into the family. But there is one characteristic common to sexual jealousy in all its forms, namely, that it is an angry feeling aroused by loss, or fear of the loss, of the exclusive possession of an individual who is the object of one's sexual desire. It is impossible to suppose that the feeling of anger will ever disappear, however ugly and useless it may be. How violent ... it sometimes is among ourselves is illustrated by the fact that in analysing 188 murders committed by some persons in England, a prison commissioner recently found that the highest number, 46, were due to jealousy.*

But even when the infidelity of a husband or wife does not give rise to the angry feeling of jealousy it causes deep sorrow; and I think it can be demanded of a: spouse to consider whether he or she has a right to inflict such suffering upon the other party. Helene Stocker observes that the refined feeling of love implies instinctively an obligation to avoid, as far as possible, making the beloved person feel pain. It is true, as Bertrand Russell said, that love, is a generous emotion. But it is not generous to the person who has to suffer for his generosity towards another.

Communist-minded persons in our country who really desire to maintain their capitalistic way of living under the garb of communism have spread the false idea that Soviet communism does not attach any importance to the ideal of feminine chastity, because all such ideas and values are really the product of outmoded religious teaching. But a writer of the eminence of Havelock Ellis writes: 'There has been an erroneous idea abroad in the world that the Bolsheviks believe in sexual intemperance and promiscuity in sex relations, an idea no doubt based on the chaos which inevitably resulted at first when the new regime was so suddenly inaugurated. That disorder much distressed Lenin himself, who was entirely opposed to promiscuity and all mere physical indulgence, and held that the highest human elements entered the love relationship. It is Lenin's doctrine which now permeates Soviet society.'

The same writer tells us that unchaste women command little respect in Soviet society. It would almost seem that the polyandric woman whom, in the opinion of some Western persons, Soviet conditions favour, is there unduly depreciated.... Blonsky points out that the depreciation of polyandric women is shared by men, even the men who form temporary relationships with them, for men are inclined to look on such women as a convenient means of satisfying sexual needs, simply as substitutes for prostitution, and feel for them no high regard.

That, Blonsky considers, is an influence making for the degradation of polyandric woman whose life courses are not usually, happy. It is unnecessary to add that the monoyandric woman, who is peculiarly adapted for motherhood and family life, will not be easily deprived of that career.

It is sometimes argued by those who wish to lead a life of unlimited sexual indulgence that there is no reason why a man's sexual desires should be tied down to one woman, why he should be put under an unnecessary obligation to bring up a family with all its cares and responsibilities. To such persons Havelock Ellis replies: 'It used sometimes to be asked: What has posterity done for me that I should do anything for posterity? The question was wrongly put.

"Posterity" is only another name for mankind, and when we pose the question rightly, there can be no dispute about the answer. If we put aside the part that belongs to nature or God we owe everything to mankind. All that we are, all that we possess in civilization, we owe to the everlasting aspiration and struggle of mankind before us, and to the slow accumulation of knowledge and art on the topmost level on which we now stand. Our immense debt to mankind in the past can only be repaid to mankind in future. It is our privilege, if we do not regard it as our duty, to pass on in even finer shapes the great traditions which have been handed to us.'

Such passages enable us to understand why Islam insists on marriage both for men and women. Without married life involving the care and education of children, human personality can never find its full development and the great traditions of religion, culture and civilisation cannot be passed on to the future generation. It should also be remembered that children contribute as much to our education and personal self-development as we contribute to their proper growth and upbringing, so that it can be safely asserted that a childless man is necessarily a half-developed man. Then there is an additional consideration. If human individuality is a value of some importance, then it is not only necessary for every person to develop his individuality to the fullest extent possible but also to transmit it for the future use of mankind by bringing into the world fresh individuals who will retain at least a part of his individual characteristics.

It is possible, however, to admit the necessity of procreation and the importance of chastity as a cementing and healing bond in family life and yet maintain that by abolishing the family and evolving alternative institutions for the training and upbringing of children, we may allow a large amount of sexual latitude to men and women without any serious social disturbance. Such methods were tried in Soviet Russia for some time and, though the Soviet Republic has widely abandoned them, their echoes are still heard even in our backward country. It is true that if once we can get rid of the family and evolve other means for the preservation of human race and the education of children, modesty, chastity and all other such values lose their necessity. But what is the possibility of success in this attempt? Is it possible to abolish the family or is it rooted in our social nature? Let us deal with the question, as it has a very important bearing on the rights of women versus men.

There are three biological tendencies common to men and animals which form the foundation of family life and which cannot be overthrown now or in any conceivable future. They are the impulse of sexual attraction which leads to mating, the tendency to a close and enduring comradeship with the opposite sex and the instinctive impulse of mates to care for their offspring. Even an authority like Havelock Ellis admits that 'it is vain for even the most conservative of human beings to lament the failure of marriage, it is futile for even the most light-hearted of radicals to hope to get beyond it. The family is at the root of our bisexual constitution, and needs no formal institution.

Again the same writer says, 'it has too often been forgotten that the family possesses this manysided flexibility and has in different ages and lands shown endless variation of shape in adjustment to varying social conditions. Those who overlooked this essential fact have frequently cried out in rebellion against the whole conception of the family. Because they themselves have chanced to come out of an unhappy family life. Though the excellent qualities they have, notwithstanding often displaced, so far show that even an unhappy family life may have happy results they impetuously demand the complete abolition of the family. Havelock Ellis also replies to those who believe that the economic independence of woman achieved by her in modern society, her increasing participation in civil and industrial life and the growing use of contraceptives will in the end lead to the disintegration of the family. He does not believe in any such consummation and says in his essay on the 'Renovation of Family' that these factors, instead of abolishing family, may even strengthen and purify it, if they are well handled.

Institutions like the maternity home, the nursery school and the kindergarten which are increasingly taking over the functions of the home have encouraged a large number of people to believe that as this process goes on to its perfection, the family will soon become unnecessary as a social institution. Those who harbour such notions should not turn a blind eye to evils which are likely to arise from the disappearance of personal and intimately affectionate relations between the parents and children. Mechanical instruments involving depersonalisation of human relations are a source of danger to the growth of human personality. This aspect of the matter is well brought out by Margaret Mead in her book *Male and Female*. Writing about American mothers, she says: 'Birth in America is ideally, more and more frequently and actually in a hospital.

This means that but for a few exceptional cases, the father is absent and the mother has been given over to the care of professionals, doctors and nurses. For months before the birth she has been preparing to leave her home and her husband, not for the home of her parents or her brothers, as in many primitive societies, but for a strange, segregated spot, where she and many other women unknown to her will live together, giving birth among strangers. When the baby is born, it is against the force of gravity, on a delivery table designed not to let the child's own weight assist the birth but rather to facilitate the ministrations of the obstetrician. Its first cry is often induced by a vigorous slap.

The mother, deep under an anaesthetic dose, does not hear this cry, although recent research has suggested that the cry has a function in making her uterus contract. The infant is taken away to a row of cribs; its lips, ready for sucking, are left to press helplessly against each other. The primary bodily capabilities with which the child enters the world are initially unrewarded. It can suck, but no breast is given it; it can cry for help, but no one holds close and feeds it. Its body is wrapped completely in soft cloth, the first lesson in expecting cloth to intervene between one body and the next. The second lesson will come when it is taken to its mother, at the proper hour for its birth weight, neatly laid out on a moving table, and placed against her fully clothed body, with the carefully sterilised breast exposed just a few inches, and persuaded to suck.

This persuasion is often a grim business, the nurse knows how to take the baby, who very often is so exhausted with hunger that it no longer wants to eat, and, holding it by the scruff of the neck, puts it on the mother's breast. Whether it eats or not, it is supposed to be taken away again after the appointed number of minutes.

The mother is left sometimes worried and enraged because the baby would not eat, having very doubtfully enjoyed in routinised cloth-developed experience. During the nine or ten days that follow, the mother handles her baby clothed, and only at regular hours. The father does not handle it at all. Breast-feeding is frequently abandoned altogether, and by the time the child goes home, the mother, if not the baby, has learned that contacts between mother and child have a certain form.

The failure of milk, the failure of the baby to nurse, the obstetrical and paediatric pressure towards at least supplementary feeding are all natural enough in a setting where the new child is treated as if its health and well-being depended on the machine - like precision with which it is fed and on what it is fed. The mother learns impatience with her milk, which is too rich or too weak, too much or too little, pouring through nipples that are inverted or sore or otherwise unobliging. She can turn with some relief to the bottle and the formula, the reliable rubber nipple with a hole that can be enlarged with a pin, the graduated bottle into which just the right formula at just the right temperature can be measured.

No recalcitrant individual unregulated body here, to endanger her baby's gain in weight, the chief criterion of its healthful existence. At once or in a few weeks, most American mothers reject their own bodies as a source of food for their children, and, in accepting the mechanical perfection of a bottle, reaffirm to themselves, and in the way they handle their babies, that the baby too will be much better the more it learns to use that beautifully mechanical bottle accurately on time, in the right amounts, the more it accepts an external rhythm, and abandons its peculiar rhythms that it brought into the world.

'For primary learning experience, that is, the physical prototype of sex relationship, a complementary relation between the body of the mother and the body of the child is substituted by a relation between the child and an object, an object, that imitates the breast but which is not handled as either part of the mother or part of the body. If the mother holds the baby as she gives it the bottle in most instances it becomes an implement, an extension of her hand so that it holds food, rather than an extension of her breast. At what age the child distinguishes the exact difference between a glass bottle and a rubber nipple, loose in space, and a human breast, we do not know, but the mother experiences the difference from the state, and her experience is available to the child, in her voice, in her hands, in the very tempo of her being. She is not giving the child herself; she is faithfully, efficiently providing the child with a bottle, external to both of them substituting for a direct relationship mediated by an object.'

This ironic description of an ideal delivery in an ideal hospital shows how the substitution of mechanical inventions for direct human contacts retards the growth and mars the personality of the child. Evidence is not lacking to prove that institutional care of children is a poor substitute for home life. A White House Conference on Child Health and Protection held in America in 1930 declared that 'institutional care for the most part has produced uninspired individuals poorly adjusted to the outside world.' Dr. Nimkoff writes: 'We can show that normal family life is indispensable to the proper development of the child's personality.'

Floyd Dell writes: 'Institutional life at its best has been notoriously drab and barren in comparison with ordinary family life. Institutional life has been found to fail in developing individual powers and in furnishing incentives for growing up. It has characteristically turned out spiritless creatures who do not know how to get along in the outside world. The best modern institutions for children now model themselves upon the parental home and try to give what it should give. Even at their best, however, these institutions, when they replace the private, home entirely, are regarded as makeshifts, as poor substitutes for a real home with real parents. And real home and real parents are known to be so important to the child's development that it is more and more the practice that only as a last resort are homes broken up and children taken from parents.'

We thus find that the family, as the basic unit of social organisation, is likely to outlast the forces tending to destroy it. A stable family life is necessary not only in the interests of society, not only for the happiness and moral development of the husband and the wife, but also for the proper growth and development of future generations. Conditions and forces which tend to shake the stability of the family should be countered and removed in the interests of the society and the individual. If these basic facts are admitted, chastity becomes a value of the highest social importance to be safeguarded at all costs. And from this conception and pattern of family life, the mutual rights and obligations of men and women can be determined with more scientific precision and greater justice than from an abstract conception of equality which does not keep in view the practical requirements of family organisation.

Islam has built its system of rights and obligations for men and women not on a vague and abstract conception of sex equality but on a doctrine of basic sex equality qualified by actual biological sex differences and the practical needs of a stable family organisation. With this background in view, we proceed to discuss the rights and obligations of the female sex as defined by Islam.

In order to ensure a happy home and a really stable family life, Islam has assigned to marriage the status of a contract dissoluble if ,either party develops grievances against the other leading to a final and irrevocable break in their mutual relations. It is not as in Christianity, a sacrament indissoluble except by a difficult process and under very extraordinary circumstances. This may appear, at first sight, to be a factor operating against family stability, but in fact it is designed to safeguard it. There is really no virtue in keeping two persons tied together to save appearances, when their relations have deteriorated beyond all hope of reconciliation. An unhappy marriage resulting in interminable quarrels fails to realise the primary object of the union which brought the partners together, besides increasing the probability of illegal sexual relations outside marriage. It also tells upon the health and education of children. It is, therefore better both socially and morally that the husband and the wife should be allowed to part with each other if the breaking point has been reached in their mutual relations.

Therefore, marriage in Islam is not indissoluble but a kind of contract in which specific rights and obligations may be undertaken besides those already implied in marriage. These rights are justifiable in a court of law. It is open both to the husband and the wife to enter into agreement prior to marriage on matters which they consider important for the regulation of their future relations. Such agreements shall be parts of the marriage contract and adjudicable in law-courts, provided they are not repugnant to the basic rights and obligations of husband and wife as stated by Islam. Thus, Umar, the Second Caliph, says: 'When a person marries a woman and the woman stipulates that she would not be taken out of the town or city of her residence, it is necessary for the husband to abide by the stipulation' (Tirmidhi, p. 385). Imam Ahmad and Imam Shafii also hold the same opinion. But Ali, the Fourth Caliph, says:,'

The conditions laid down by God take precedence over the, conditions set by man,' which means that, in his opinion, such a condition is repugnant to the basic terms of marriage. Sufyan Thabri and other scholars of Kufah also hold the same opinion. Whatever the differences among the scholars on this point, they relate to the point whether this particular stipulation is or is not repugnant to the basic terms of marriage contract as defined by Islam. There is no disagreement on the point whether a woman can insist on inserting terms of her own in the marriage contract. All are unanimous that she holds this right. Thus, the author of *Nail al-Autar* (Pt. VII, p. 64) says: 'The wife can lay down conditions prior to marriage relating to her way of living, her food, house and dress, according to the social status of the husband and that her just rights shall not be whittled. Similarly, the husband can lay down these conditions: that the wife shall not go out from home without his permission, that she shall not refuse sexual intercourse with him and shall not use his property and possessions except by his permission.'

Just as a man can stipulate that his wife shall not go out except by his permission, it is open to the woman to insist that she shall not be prevented from going out of her home on suitable occasions or for her economic or social needs, so long as this action does not disturb the work of her husband or the proper upbringing of the children. All these matters come within the scope of the marriage agreement, but since some of them are not easily justifiable, much depends on the actual relations of the husband and the wife after marriage and their mutual understanding. All these things show that the wife does not lose, under Islam, her separate legal personality, but retains full possession of it. She can sue her husband in a law-court if the implied or express terms of the marriage contract are violated by the husband.

This is in direct contrast to the position of woman under Christianity. Professor Mansfield, writing in his book, *The Legal Rights, Liabilities and Duties of Women*, states: 'The first great principle of Scripture, the unity of husband and wife, is repeated by the law. They are, in law, one person. Upon it, as observed by Blackstone, depend nearly all the legal rights, duties and disabilities acquired by marriage.' The English Common Law, as interpreted by Blackstone, whose commentaries governed actual legal decisions both in England and America for a very long period, assigned the same position to a wife in relation to her husband. It was only with the greatest difficulty and by resorting to parliament any legislation or equity courts that the wife was able to secure a few rights over against her husband. From a strictly legal viewpoint, the position of women among the Muslims has been really enviable when compared to that of their counterparts in the Western countries.

In order to safeguard the economic position of women after the marriage, Islam has made it legally obligatory on the husband to pay her a reasonable amount as dower. The amount to be fixed, as dower depends on the agreement between the two parties, but, in any case, the object is to strengthen the financial position of the wife, so that she is not prevented, for lack of money, from defending her rights.

No marriage can be regarded as legally valid, according to Islam, for which dowry has not been stipulated. If the amount of dowry is not fixed, the wife is entitled to proper dowry (*mehr-i-mithl*), even if the marriage was contracted on the express condition that she should not claim any dowry. In determining what is 'proper' dowry, regard is to be had to the amount of dower settled upon other female members of her father's family such as her father's sisters.

Regarding the amount of dowry to be fixed, Islam has given a wide, latitude to men and women. It can be as low as possible or as high as the parties may desire. Ibn Majah and Tirmidhi report from Amir ibn Rabia that a woman belonging to the tribe of Banu Fazarah married a man for a pair of shoes. The Prophet asked her whether she was really happy over that much dowry.

The amount of dower may be fixed either before or at the time of marriage or after marriage, and can be increased after marriage. A contract of dower can be made by a father on behalf of his son, if the latter is a minor. The wife may remit the whole or part of dower. Such remission is valid though made without consideration. If the dower is not paid, the wife and, after her death, her heirs may sue for it. The wife may refuse to live with her husband and admit him to sexual intercourse so long as the dower remains unpaid. If the husband sues her for the restitution of conjugal rights, before sexual intercourse has taken place, non-payment of dower is a complete defence to the suit, and the suit will be dismissed. If the suit is brought after sexual intercourse has taken place with her free consent, the court can issue a decree for restitution conditional on payment of the dower, to the extent only of a share of the dower debt proportionate to his share of the estate. When a widow is in actual possession of the property of her deceased husband, she is entitled as against the other heirs of her husband and as against the creditors of her husband, to retain possession of the property until her dower is satisfied. The fact that a widow is in possession of her husband's property under a claim for her dower is no bar to a suit against the other heirs of her husband to recover the dower debt, but she must in such a suit offer, to give up possession of the property.

Further, to secure a strong economic position for women, Islam has given them full property rights. A daughter gets half the share of property allotted to the son, half of the entire property of her father if there is no other son or daughter; and if there is more than one daughter but no sons, the daughters share among them equally two-thirds of the entire property. A widow is entitled to one eighth of the property left by her husband, but if there are no children by the marriage, she receives one-sixth. No distinction is made by Islam between movable and immovable property. The whole, including both kinds, is distributed to the heirs in their fixed proportions. It may be said that by giving the daughter half the share of a son, Islam has let down the position of women, but it should not be forgotten that a woman may also receive dower and property from her husband in which case her inequality is more than compensated for. Moreover, there is no obligation on a wife to sustain her husband economically, while the husband is under a legal obligation to provide for his wife. Thus, the inequality of women in the share of inheritance is matched by a corresponding increase in the economic burden of men, which makes the two sexes equal in respect of their economic rights.

One of the most essential factors of a happy marriage is the right of free choice by either party. Islam has given this right both to men and women. The Prophet insisted on a number of occasions that a person wishing to marry a woman should have a look at her before finally consenting to marriage. Thus, Abu Hurairah reports: 'A man came to the Prophet and said, "I intend to marry a woman of the Ansar." He said, "Have a look at her, because sometimes there is something defective in the eyes of the Ansar." Jabir reports that the Prophet said: 'When one of you seeks a woman in marriage and then if he is able to have a look at one he wishes to marry, let him do so' (Abu Daud). Mughira b. Shubah reports: 'I sought a woman in marriage. The Holy Prophet asked if I had seen her. "No," said I. He said: "Then look at her, because it is more proper that love should be cemented between you." The jurists agree that this right to have a look at the prospective partner is equally eligible for the members of the female sex. According to Imam Abu Hanifah, it is lawful to have a sight of the bride and the bridegroom. Imam Malik holds that it is lawful with the permission of the bride. Imam Shafii and Imam Ahmad are of the opinion that a look at the prospective husband or wife is lawful with or without the permission of the other.

Freedom of choosing one's partner for life has been extended both to men and women. No marriage in Islam can be valid without the consent of either partner. According to a report from Abu Hurairah, the Prophet said: 'A previously married woman shall not be married till she gives her consent, nor a virgin be married till her consent is sought.' They asked: 'How shall her permission be known. He said: 'If she remains silent.' A report from Ibn Abbas, collected by Muslim, states that the Prophet said: 'A previously married woman is more a guardian for herself than her guardian and a virgin should be asked permission about herself, and her permission is her silence.' Abu Hurairah further reports that the Prophet said: 'A grown-up girl shall be asked permission about herself. If she is silent, it is her permission; and if she declines, there shall be no compulsion on her.'

The presence of two witnesses is necessary to make a marriage valid, because open declaration of marriage constitutes its soul and essence. According to a tradition of Tirmidhi reported by Ibn Abbas, the Prophet declared: 'Those women are adulteresses who marry themselves without the presence of witnesses! Umar was once told that a certain marriage had been performed with one witness only. He said that such a marriage amounted to clandestine relationship which was illegal. If he had knowledge of it beforehand, he would have dealt stern punishment to either party.

Guardianship is regarded by some as necessary for the marriage of a woman. There are some traditions in which the presence of a guardian has been made an essential condition precedent to the marriage of a girl. Thus, Bukhari gives a tradition stating: 'There is no marriage without a guardian.' This is probably meant only for minor girls. Imam Abu Hanirah, the greatest and the most popular jurist of Islam, holds that a marriage, whether of a widow or a grown-up virgin, is permissible even without a guardian. Imam Shafii's and Imam Malik, however, hold that guardianship is necessary for the marriage of a woman. As marriage depends essentially upon the choice of a woman, the presence of a guardian, even if not required by law, can be regarded necessary only in the sense that he undertakes to watch the interests of the minor or the grownup girl who is to be married and to see that she is not disadvantaged by reason of sex in the settlement of the terms on which marriage is contracted.

This interpretation is supported by a tradition contained in Kitab at Nikah of the collection made by Tirmidhi. The tradition states: Aishah said, the Prophet of God declared: 'Marriage of a woman is invalid without there being a guardian.' He repeated this three times and said that if the husband of such a woman had sexual intercourse with her, she should receive her dower and if, after the performance of the marriage, the two quarrel, then the ruler of the Muslims is the guardian of the woman who has no other guardian. The reference here to the recovery of dowry and the possibility of quarrel as well as recognition of the right of the State to take up the functions of a guardian all point to the fact that the Prophet had in mind the necessity of safeguarding the interests of women by making the presence of a guardian essential. In a society which, until the advent of Islam, had been ridden by sex inequality and where women had been treated as mere chattel, it was always possible, despite the teachings of Islam, that a single woman without a guardian or a patron should find herself at a disadvantage in the settlement of marriage terms. So the Prophet deemed it essential that, if there be no guardian for a woman, the State should become her guardian with a view to ensuring equality and justice at the time of marriage contract and thereafter. No other interpretation is possible in view of the fact that the final say in all matters has been accorded to women themselves and not to their guardians, a fact which is attested by the authentic traditions of the Prophet himself.

A very significant' report which throws a flood of light on the complete liberty of choice and repudiation extended to women by Islam in the matter of their marriage is found in the traditions collected by Nasai. The reporter is no less a person than Aishah, the wife of the Prophet. She says, 'A girl came and stated that her father had given her in marriage to his nephew and she disliked him. I told her to wait till the Prophet arrived. When the Prophet came, I told him the full story of the girl. He at once sent for the father of the girl and inquired of him whether the facts stated were true, after which he told the girl that she was at liberty to choose or repudiate her husband. The girl replied saying that she chose to retain her marriage, And that she wanted only to know whether women had any rights in the matter.' Another tradition from the collection made by Ibn Majah states: 'Ibn' Umar says: Uthman b. Mazun left behind a young daughter. My uncle, Qudamah, married her to me, and did not even consult her. When the girl came to know of this, she disliked this marriage and wished to marry Mughira b. Shubah. So she was married to Mughira.'

All these traditions furnish conclusive proof that a girl is as free in Islam as a boy to choose or repudiate her partner and that the Prophet's insistence on there being a guardian before a woman can be married was intended to safeguard her position and rights in a society which was not yet completely free from the dominance of the male sex and in which a lonely woman ran a chance of being outwitted by clever men and left without the necessary protection.

The legal equality of men and women in Islam is a fact which has never been in dispute among the Muslims. There is no legal right belonging to man for which a corresponding female right cannot be cited. But the ideal of sex equality or any other kind of equality cannot be wholly given effect to by the law. Specially is this true of the relations between husband and wife which in their very nature refuse to be covered and guided wholly by legal injunctions and principles. Real equality between the sexes depends much more on social opinion and national traditions than on legal commands. Even in Western countries where the claim for complete equality between the two sexes has been pressed to extremes, formidable difficulties have been experienced by legislators to translate the ideal into the actual. Mary Beard, after giving a detailed account of the attempts made in America to give equal property rights to men and women, mentions a long list of legislative failures to give effect to the principle of equality. The following extract from her book, *Woman as Force in History*, will give the reader an idea of the intricate and evasive nature of the ideal of sex equality. Writing about the legislative changes made in America with respect to women's property rights, she says:

> *A Married Women's Property Act was, therefore, simple in principle. But in application the terms of such an Act were difficult to draw. Despite the theory of independence and equality which was supposed to furnish guidance in drafting the Act, law reformers and lawmakers actually confronted a paradox: The wife is to be treated as if she is a single woman in respect of her property, but in marital relations she has obligations not assumed by single women and is no more of a single person than her husband is; for both are entangled in a network of duties not imposed on single persons. Is the wife free to use her property as she pleased while the husband is in straits to support her and their children? In what, if any, circumstances is the wife to be under obligation to support the family in part or whole? Is the owner of the home, whether husband or wife, to be allowed to sell it at will, without the consent of the other party to the marriage contract, and turn the family out of it? These*

> *and a hundred other questions taxed the adroitness of law-makers and were answered by men and women in many different ways. No mere declaration of equality could dispose of them in a few words. At no time or place did it prove possible to write one Married Women's Property Bill which could settle all these questions.*

The same writer goes on to say:

> *In their efforts to clear away anachronisms and to bring the law abreast the advance in civilization, legislators did not, indeed could not, treat a man and a woman who had chosen to marry and bring children into the world as if they were perfectly free and entitled to be wholly whimsical with their respective properties and earnings, without regard for obligations due to each other. Nor could legislators overlook the rights of their children, their creditors and their more or less distant relatives. All lawmakers recognized the fact that husband and wife had to surrender some freedom by virtue of their very marriage contract. How much and what kinds of freedom? ... On the point of how to realize the ideal of equality, men differed and women differed and provisions of law running into hundreds of pages reflected their doubts, uncertainties and aspirations.*

Furthermore, after statutes were enacted, the application of the principles in them to human controversies which arose in law and equity, led to a positive risk of variations. The more general the principles, the more difficult it was for men and women as litigants and for courts as tribunals of adjudication to agree on the meaning of principles as governing concrete cases. Especially is this true of novel cases not specifically contemplated or provided for in the written laws. And novel cases were and are perennial and striking features of life and law.

How far Married Women's Property Acts and kindred legislation fell short of covering in concrete anticipation the numerous problems that arose under them is indicated by the following types of questions raised and adjudicated in various jurisdictions of the United States after the process of abolishing common-law doctrines had been started. In order that the readers may decide for themselves, if they can, how these questions should have been answered under the theory of separate property rights and equality, the answers given to these questions by the judges in affirmative opinions, negative opinions, and diversities of opinions, are left to the readers' imagination.

Does the Married Women's Property Act relieve a husband of obligation to support his wife, even if he has become bankrupt and she is earning money?

If the wife leaves the husband without good reasons and returns home voluntarily at a later date, is the husband to pay the bills which she had incurred for her support during her absence?

Can the wife lawfully waive the husband's liability to support her with a view to helping him pay his debts to creditors?

If the husband employs his wife at wages otherwise payable to someone else, may she be deprived of the money or the property in which it is invested on the ground that it is actually her husband's?

May the wife take her separate property, enter business, and, without his consent, compete with her husband's who is legally liable for her support?

Where under a new statute the husband is forbidden to use even gentle force to restrain his wife, may he lawfully restrain her from committing a crime?

If the husband carries on a gambling business in his wife's house, may she be liable for his crimes committed therein?

There are a thousand other questions likely to arise in the married state to show the limitations of law in governing husband and wife relations. Even if perfection in legislative acts were possible and the marital relations of men and women could be placed on a footing of full equality, that would not automatically ensure actual equality in day-to-day relations. Human relations in general and marital relations in particular are governed and regulated far more by customs, traditions and the spiritual and moral outlook of human beings than by legal enactments and commands of the sovereign. Law alone is an insufficient guide and measures in gauging the extent to which a civilisation gives effect to the ideal of sex equality. To understand in full the attitude of a community towards the relations between the two sexes, we must look to its general moral teachings, as distinguished from legal provisions. Let us judge Islam from this angle and see how far it adds to the social dignity of women and ensures their equality in its social precepts, moral principles and spiritual directions.

The same generosity towards women is enjoined by the Prophet in his traditions. A report from Abu Hurairah says: 'No believer should be angry towards his wife. If some of her qualities are displeasing, there will be many other qualities worth appreciation' (Nail al-Autar, p. 125). Aishah, the wife of the Prophet, reports: The Prophet of God said: 'The best of you is he who is good to his wife' (Tirmidhi). On the occasion of his last pilgrimage, the Prophet advised the Muslims to treat their women kindly and added: 'You have no more rights against them except that if they are guilty of manifest lewdness, you can ask them to leave your beds and strike them softly; if they improve their conduct, do not leave them helpless, because there are some rights for you over against them and some rights for them over against you. The duty of a woman is that she should not allow anyone to enter your house whom you dislike, nor spoil the bed which is your preserve and the duty of a man is that he should feed, clothe and treat his wife generously' (ibid.).

According to a report from Abdullah b. Umar, the Prophet declared: 'The whole world is a thing to be made use of and the best thing in the world is a virtuous wife' (Muslim). On his deathbed, the Prophet's last words related to the duty of offering prayers and safeguarding the rights of women and, slaves. About women he said: 'Women are like prisoners in your hands and you have taken them on trust from God and the word of God has made their private parts lawful for you; so be careful towards the treatment of women.' On another occasion the Prophet is reported to have declared: 'The Angel of God advised me so many times about women that I became convinced that it is not lawful for a man to divorce his wife, except when she commits adultery' (Irshad al-Muhtaj, Huquq al-Azwaj). A report from Bahz b. Hakim states: 'I inquired of the Prophet about his teaching in respect of women. He replied: "Feed them as you feed yourselves, clothe them as you clothe yourselves and do not beat or scold them' (Kanz al-Unimal). According to Aishah, the Prophet's wife, he said about women: 'They are like pleasing roses,' meaning thereby that their grace and tenderness deserve special regard from men (ibid.). In regard to domestic duties, Islam has relieved women of all manual drudgery.

According to strict Islamic injunctions, it is not obligatory for a woman to cook the food for her husband or children, or to wash their clothes or even to suckle the infants. A woman may refuse to do any or all of these things without this being made a ground of legal complaint against her. If she undertakes these duties out of her regard for the husband, it is an act of sheer grace. It is reported that a man once came to Umar, the Second Caliph, with the intention of bringing to his notice certain complaints which he had against his wife. When he reached the door of Umar's, house, he heard the Caliph's wife railing against him. Hearing this he went back as he thought that the Caliph was himself in the same predicament and could, therefore, be hardly expected to set matters right for him.

Umar, coming out of his house, saw the person going back. So he called him out and inquired as to the purpose which had brought him to his house. He said that he had come to him with some complaints against his wife, but turned back on finding that the Caliph himself was subject to the same treatment from his wife. Umar said to him that he patiently bore the excesses of his wife, because she had certain rights against him. 'Is it not true that she cooks my food, washes my clothes and suckles my children, thus relieving me of the necessity of employing a cook, a washerman and a nurse, although she is not in the slightest degree responsible for any of these duties? Not only that, I enjoy peace of mind on amount of her and I am protected from committing the sin of adultery. In view of all these advantages, I put up with her excesses. You should also do the same.'

This tradition makes the wife co-equal of her husband in home affairs. She is as much responsible for the conduct of domestic affairs; as the husband. Only in larger matters affecting, the total welfare of the family, the husband is given a degree of superiority, since two coordinate authorities with equal powers are likely to lead to clashes and conflicts such as may destroy the balance and poise of family life.

Social Bond

Marriage in Islam is regarded as a strong bond and a total commitment to life, to society and to being a respectable human. It is a promise that the married couple make to one another and to God. This undertaking on the part of the married partners would allow them to find mutual fulfilment and self-realisation, love and peace, comfort and hope. This is because marriage in Islam is essentially a righteous act and an act of complete devotion. As such, celibacy is discouraged not only for men, but for women as well. This is in consideration of the fact that their needs are equally legitimate and valid.

Islam views marriage as a natural course for women in the same way as it is for men, and probably even more so, in view of the fact that marriage guarantees women some form of economic security. It must be stressed here that this benefit for women is in no way an indication that marriage in Islam is sheer economic transaction. Indeed, the economic factor is the least aspect of the whole enterprise; the emphasis has been always on the religious qualities of the spouses.

From the collective point of view the most significant benefit is of course procreation, but not just the physical perpetuation of the human race; rather, the institution of marriage ensures that this procreative function will be both sanctified and orderly, not vulgar and chaotic. From the specifically religious point of view, having children entails the following: the realisation of God's desire, the fulfilment of the Prophet's call to marry and increase his followers' number; gaining the fruit of a child's prayer.

Muslims believe that when parents die and leave a child, his prayer would benefit the dead parents. However, if the child dies before his parents, he would make intercession on his parents' behalf. Fulfilling one's sexual desire is another important aspect of marriage. Marriage, from the Islamic viewpoint, helps control sexual passion and channel it in the right direction. Also, it functions as a shield against committing adultery and fornication, both of which are forbidden in Islam. Marriage, moreover, brings peace and tranquillity of spirit and implants love and compassion between the married partners. These are great supports for one's worship of God. Intimacy between spouses is viewed as catalyst for the development of their souls.

In other words, the intimate relationship that develops between a husband and wife is crucial for relieving the heart from its burdens and thus enables the mind to better focus on accomplishing the Divine requirements. Al-Ghazzali beautifully explains this point in the following account: 'The third benefit of marriage is that the heart finds ease through intimacy with women, because of sitting and joking with them. This ease then becomes the cause of an increase in desire for worship. For diligence in worship brings weariness, and the heart contracts. But ease acquired in this way brings back the heart's strength. Ali said, 'Do not remove rest and ease completely from the hearts, lest they become blind'. It sometimes happened that the Prophet was overcome by such tremendous unveilings that his bodily frame was not able to tolerate it.

The marital link helps the partners to work together and cooperate amicably in the management of the domestic affairs of their house; hence sufficient time could be spared to meet the Divine commandments. Therefore, the Prophet is reported to have advised his followers to choose the right spouses who would help them attain Divine blessings.

Marriage, in addition, is seen as an opportunity to develop for oneself a good and sound character as a result of the added family responsibility which both spouses have to endure during their married life. Hence, success in carrying out family commitments (which are equally regarded as divine duties) would ensure Divine reward. The Prophet said 'A man will be rewarded for what he spends on his wife, even for putting a morsel of food into her mouth'.

Also, 'Whoever performs his prayers correctly, and spends on his children in spite of his modest means, and does not speak ill against others, will be in paradise as close to me as these [two fingers of mine]'. Finally, marriage ensures social stability and a dignified form of living for both partners (the husband and the wife), probably even more for women since it guarantees their rights both as wives as well as mothers (of course alongside their fights as individuals).

Since Islam takes marriage seriously, its concern has been always to ensure that the marriage bond stays relatively stable and durable. To achieve these goals, it has laid down certain rules and regulations to meet these objectives. First, the couple have to be of proper marriageable age; also, there should be no discrepancy between their ages. It must be stressed that the claim by some scholars that the groom has to be always senior in age so as to ensure a healthy marriage relationship has no religious grounds and in practical terms does not make any sense. In fact, it contradicts the practice of the Prophet, two of whose wives (Khadijah and Sauda) happened to be older than him; despite this, the record shows that they lived in peace and harmony.

Second, there should be a degree of compatibility between the two partners in terms of social status, educational standards and physical attraction (again the claim by some scholars that the bride has to be more beautiful and more attractive than her groom is a fallacy). Third, the dowry of the bride should be of a reasonable level: neither too high, which could cause hardship for both of them, nor too low which might give the impression that the bride is of no worth. The dowry which is in its essence a gift from the groom to the bride-should be affordable and manageable so as to ensure satisfaction and happiness on both sides. Fourth, the consent of the couple is crucial for the stability and durability of the marriage. Both have to enter into the wedlock with free will and without coercion.

Compelling the couple (or even just one of them) to contract an unsatisfactory union would be detrimental to the interest of both sides and could lead to a disastrous end. Fifth, the prospective partners have to be pious and of good moral conduct. Both have to be kind, sympathetic, considerate, patient and loving, caring to one another; this encourages peace and harmony in domestic life. Sixth, the two parties have to declare, from the beginning, their intentions to keep the marital bond as permanent as humanly possible. This commitment requires that the marriage contract should be free of any hidden agenda such as casual or temporary unions.

Islam is against all marriages that have been described as experimental, casual and temporary. In a clear statement, the Prophet outrightly denounced those men and women who enjoy the frequent change of marital partners and warned against their unacceptable behaviour. Having stated the importance Islam lays on the permanency of marriage, it is essential to stress that in Islam there is no concept of 'indissoluble' marriage.

Although Islam endeavours to keep the marital link stable and intact, this does not mean that the wedlock cannot be brought to an end if there are compelling circumstances. Indeed, Islam recognises that if the marriage is not working, it is in the interest of both sides to terminate it on good terms. Hence, divorce in Islam is a legitimate act, although it is discouraged by the Prophet. Islam, as we know, encourages both men and women to marry. Just like a man, a Muslim woman (virgin or non-virgin) has the freedom to propose to a man of her liking, either orally or in writing (I wonder how many Muslim women these days would dare to initiate an oral proposal, let alone put it in writing!).

The Muslim woman has the freedom of marital choice: she is at liberty to choose her prospective husband, look at him and get to know him without coercion on the part of the father or other relatives. If force or pressure takes place, she has the right to appeal to the court to redress the wrong. Her consent is essential for the validity of the marriage contract.

The Prophet is reported to have made the following statements: 'A previously married woman shall not be married till she gives her consent, nor should a virgin be married till her consent is sought'. 'A previously married woman is more a guardian for herself than her guardian, and a virgin should be asked permission about herself, and her permission is her silence'. 'A grown-up girl shall be asked permission about herself. If she is silent, it is her permission; and if she declines, there shall be no compulsion on her'. According to Islam, a divorced or widowed woman has the right to remarry without any shame or denunciation. In fact, the

Quran allows the betrothal of a divorced or widowed woman even during her period of transition (idda). 'It shall be no offence for you openly to propose marriage indirectly to such women or to cherish them in your hearts. Allah knows that you will remember them. Do not arrange to meet them in secret and, if you do, speak to them honourably. But you shall not consummate the marriage before the end of their waiting period. Know that Allah has knowledge of all your thoughts. Therefore take heed and bear in mind that Allah is forgiving and merciful'.

Neither age nor previous marriage would impede a woman from contracting perfect matches. Many are the examples which can be cited from the early Muslim community during which women were, very often, re-married after they were divorced or widowed, and this was done without stigma or discredit. Take, for instance, Umm-Kulthum bint Uqba, an early convert from Mecca. She emigrated to Medina in defiance of her family, who tried to force her to return to Mecca, but to no avail. She stayed in Medina and married her first husband, Zaid bin Harith. When Zaid was killed in one of the battles she contracted a second marriage with Zubayr bin al-Awwam. Zubayr was rough with her, so she decided to part with him. After the separation, she married Abdul Rahman bin Auf, her third husband, and bore him two sons.

Upon Abdul Rahman's death, Umme Kulthum once more contracted herself into marriage, to her fourth and final husband, this time with the conqueror of Egypt, Amr ibn al-As. She stayed with him until she passed away. Atika bint Zaid is another good example. She was a woman of exceptional abilities who had managed to contract four marriages during her lifetime. Her first husband was Abdullah ibn Abu Bakr, son of the first Caliph Abu Bakr. He died, leaving her a fortune on condition that she would not re-marry. For a while she was content with the idea of living a celibate life, but later she decided to go against his wish and not to spend the rest of her life alone; hence her decision to accept Umar ibn al-Khattab, the second Caliph, as her second husband. When Umar was assassinated in 642 she married her third husband, Zubayr ibn al-Awwam. After his death in 656, she took her fourth husband, Hussain ibn Ali, son of the fourth Caliph Ali; by this time she was around forty-five years old. Marriage in Islam requires a contract between two equal partners. Hence in Islamic terms, the woman is to be a subject rather than an object in the marriage contract. The contract, in sum, is a legal written document between two adults, which entails an offer by one partner and an acceptance by the other in the presence of two witnesses. The Qadi, or official, usually solemnises the marriage in a mosque or court or any other location.

The consent of the prospective wife is crucial for the effectiveness of the marriage contract. Any force or blackmail on the part of the relatives would automatically render the contract invalid. The bride, moreover, has the exclusive right to stipulate her own conditions in the contract. These conditions include mainly (though not exclusively) such issues as marriage terms (the right, for example, to have a monogamous relationship whilst she is still living with her husband) and divorce terms (the right, for instance, to dissolve the marital bond at her own initiative if she deems it necessary). In addition, dowries-one initial and another deferred in case of divorce-must be specified and written down and they should be of substance. The dowry (or Mehr, in Islamic terms) belongs to the wife; it is her exclusive right and it should not be given away, neither to her family nor to her relatives. The Quran says 'Give women their dowry as a free gift; but if they choose to make over to you a part of it, you may regard it as lawfully yours'.

When the marriage is consummated, the couple assume a new relationship: that is, a husband-wife relationship. It is a kind of reciprocal and interdependent relationship. The Quran says 'And of His signs is that He gave you wives from among yourselves, that you might live in tranquillity with them, and put love and kindness in your hearts. Surely there are signs in this for thinking people'. The verse implies that in a marriage bond the two partners are a comfort to each other. They should find and enjoy peace and tranquillity in each other's company and be bound together not only by a sexual relationship but also by love, compassion and mercy. As such, both have to demonstrate mutual care, affection, respect and be prepared to make sacrifices.

There should be no servility on the part of either side, for they are two equal partners in a healthy, loving and caring relationship. The Quran eloquently illustrates this equal partnership in the following statement: 'They are an apparel to you, as you are an apparel to them'. The verse explains that just as a garment covers a person completely and provides him/her with warmth, protection and decency, in the same way a husband and wife provide each other with the necessary warmth, comfort, intimacy and protection. The realisation of these principles in actual life depends, mainly, on the way both partners react to each other.' In this context, the Quran expects them to behave in the best manner toward each other.

The husband, on the one hand, is commanded to treat his wife gently and with kindness, affection and consideration. The Prophet said 'The best of you is the best of you to his wife, and I am better than any of you toward my wife'. He is to deal with her with dignity and in an equitable manner, not to hurt or injure her feelings. He is to show her that he loves her, appreciates her good qualities and he is to give her the impression that he needs her and depends on her to attain happiness in life. Also, he is asked to ensure that his tasks as husband and father are fulfilled to the utmost. Besides, the husband has to meet his legal responsibility to provide full maintenance of the wife: a task which he has to accomplish with good cheer and gladness.

The wife, on the other hand, is similarly required to reciprocate in kindness towards her husband, treat him with respect, admire his good qualities and express her love and affection to him. Also, she is called upon to ensure that her duties as wife and mother are performed to the best of her abilities. To maintain a happy conjugal relationship, both partners must be loyal, honest, direct, and trustworthy. They should be thoughtful, sympathetic and sensitive towards each other's feelings; in particular, they must avoid raising each other's suspicions and jealousy and try to maintain their integrity as husband and wife, united together in a matrimonial link. Concerning their sexual intimacy, both must be pleasing and receptive. They should endeavour to attain and give maximum gratification.

Moreover, in order to keep the marital link intact, stable and healthy, both partners have to demonstrate their willingness to share the burden of looking after the welfare of the family. They must share the ups and downs of married life, be prepared to make sacrifices, pay attention to each other's point of view, consult each other and adopt joint decisions on important matters that affect the entire family. These joint decisions have to be delivered or enforced by the husband since, in Islam, he is the head of the family. This is based on the following Quranic verses which give the husband the right to be in charge of the family: 'Women shall with justice have rights similar to those exercised against them, although men have a degree above women. Allah is Mighty and Wise'. 'Men have authority over women because Allah has made the one superior to the other, and because they spend their wealth to maintain them'. These verses were and still are a source of much discussion and debate throughout the Muslim world, generating a host of different interpretations. These interpretations range from liberal to moderate to conservative.

Our view in this context is that the headship of the husband should on no account be a license for dictatorship; it should entail no absolute freedom on the part of the person in charge; if the husband misuses or abuses his status, the wife has ' the right to interfere to rectify the situation. After all, the whole issue of being a chairperson is to ensure the smooth running of the family. Any neglect on the part of the husband to fulfil the task which is designated to him justifies his replacement by the more able person (the wife).

However, God-conscious pairs would always act responsibly because they are aware of their commitments to God as well as to each other. Also, because they are conscious of the fact that if they live up to their promises and act rationally in their married life they would invoke God's pleasure, hence making their lives a perpetual joy and paradise. But, sadly, this kind of paradise, envisaged by the Quran and practised briefly during the Prophet's time, has hardly ever been realised.

In fact, the case has nearly always been the reverse. Slowly but surely, attitudes towards women and marriage changed. The Quranic principles which bestowed honour, dignity, kindness and respect on women were gradually eroded and went into limbo. Customs, rather than Divine laws, shaped and continue to shape the social fabric of society and govern people's attitudes towards women and marriage. The outcome has been a steady deterioration in the status of women as far as their marital rights are concerned. Take, for example, the right to initiate a marriage proposal. This has been completely abandoned: not even in her wildest dreams would a woman dare to propose orally or in writing. The disappearance of this early practice has been so total that most women, even educated ones, are not aware of its existence, let alone practise it. The right to exercise her choice in selecting a marriage partner has, in most cases, been forgotten.

Most marriages that currently take place in Muslim societies are arranged unions, during which force and intimidation are quite often employed to obtain the girl's consent. Moreover, her freedom to sign the marriage contract has been considerably curtailed. The majority of Muslim marriages nowadays are contracted through agents (guardians, especially on the part of the woman), very often a male member of the family (father, brother, or uncle), who formalises and signs the contract on her behalf. In doing so, her opportunity and right to negotiate marriage and divorce terms are deliberately denied.

In most cases, a woman is subjected to considerable pressure to avoid stipulating in her marriage contract a divorce right or any other rights which might be viewed as a constraint on the freedom of the husband. If she did so, the social pressure on her would be so tremendous that in the end she would be obliged to give up, otherwise she would be accused of endangering the whole enterprise. Divorce has become a stigma and women are always regarded as being culpable.

The prospects for a non-virgin (divorcee or widow) getting remarried is dim. Indeed, in many cases they are forced to spend the rest of their lives cherishing the memories of their dead husbands and serving the male members of their own families. Within the context of a husband-wife relationship, authoritarianism and dictatorship have replaced the ideal and equal partnership advocated by the Quran.

The husband assumes the role of ruler, superior, controller, oppressor and master, while the wife, on the other hand, is reduced to a slave, a captive, a low, inferior and submissive creature. Listen to what the so called Council of Ulama (that is, people with knowledge about Islam) of South Africa has to say about the relationship between the two spouses: 'She (the wife) should mould herself to wholeheartedly submit to his whims and fancies. His likes must become her likes and his dislikes, her dislikes. She should step out of her way to comfort him and to console him in his worries and distress. Her wishes and desires are subservient to his wishes and orders.... After all (God) has created her for her husband's comfort and peace'. The Council goes on to say 'The Shariah has accorded the husband the highest degree of authority over his wife. Likewise it will transpire that the wife has to offer the higher degree of submission to her husband... with humility and patience she should tolerate his shortcomings and even his injustice... men are the rulers of women and they have a superior rank... (as such) it is the husband's right and role to dominate and dictate (and) it is the duty of the wife to submit and serve. The wife should understand that she can never conquer her husband by confrontation and seeking to set herself up as his equal or superior'.

Concerning the financial arrangements between them, the Council stresses: 'It is significant that in spite of the wife remaining the sole owner of her wealth... (she is encouraged) to put her wealth at his disposal and pleasure'. What about his money? 'She should not attempt to appoint herself as the controller of his finances. It is none of her business on whom her husband spends his wealth'. What if the husband fails to perform his duties properly?

The Council emphasises: 'She must not adopt a legal stand and a technical attitude, demanding from her husband perfect and total fulfilment of her legal rights.... The wife has to remember that despite her husband's failure to fulfil his duties to her, she is under... obligation to obey her husband.... obedience to the husband will ensure the everlasting happiness... for her'.

The mutual responsibilities on both sides to demonstrate to each other their loyalty, honesty and respect have become exclusively the wife's domain and obligations. The husband has been deliberately left out of the equation. So whether he is honest and loyal or a cheat it does not matter. What matters most (and this is important to him and to the male-dominated society) is the faithfulness and loyalty of the wife. There is no question of reciprocity between them in this matter. The emphasis has always been on the wife, as if she is a creature with no control over her sexuality.

The word 'divorce' 'traces its origin back to the Latin derivative and conjures up the splitting of a unit, the permanent physical separation of the spouses', while the Arabic word '*talaq*' is derived from the verb *itlaq* which means to set loose, set free or to leave. Talaq, therefore, within the context of the marital link means to terminate the bond created by a marriage contract.

In every society there are ways and means which allow the marital link to be dissolved if it fails to fulfil its objective. The reasons for the dissolution of marriage are, generally speaking, common and almost universal. They apply to human society irrespective of time, place or level of civilisation from the unavoidable death of a spouse or involuntary barrenness to the trivial cooking mistake of burning the husband's food or putting too much salt in it, not to mention the man's arbitrary dislike of his spouse or capricious preference for another woman who seems more pleasing to him. So the termination of marriage is sometimes inevitable and no system can afford to ignore this reality, otherwise it is doomed to failure.

Any system which insists on the indissolubility of marriage and overlooks the fact that under exceptional circumstances the dissolution of the family becomes a necessity is static, impractical and does not respond adequately to human needs. A system under which marriage is indissoluble would inevitably lead to the abuse of marriage, because people will always find ways around it, hence defeating the whole purpose which the system stands for in the first place.

In principle, Islam regards marriage as a lifelong commitment. However, sometimes there do arise situations wherein marriage ceases to fulfil its purpose. Hence, divorce can be invoked by either side or both of them in order to accommodate the realities of an unsuccessful marriage. It, must be stressed that divorce can only be exercised as the last resort after all efforts for reconciliation between the spouses are exhausted. Therefore, in

Islam divorce is considered a necessity if the married partners are not happy. However, divorce is heavily disapproved of and discouraged.

The Quran discourages divorce in the following verses: 'And (remember) when you (Muhammad) said to the man (Zaid, Muhammad's adopted son) whom Allah and yourself have favoured: keep your wife and have fear of Allah'. In this verse there is an implicit disapproval of divorce.

In other verses the Quran clearly discourages Muslims from having recourse to a hasty divorce, even though they might be dissatisfied with their marriage partners. 'Treat them with kindness; for even if you do dislike them, it may well be that you may dislike a thing which Allah has meant for your own good'.

The Quran not only discourages divorce, but it prohibits the slandering of one's wife in order to take back her dowry 'If you wish to have a wife in the place of a (divorced) one, do not take from her the dowry you have given her even it if be a talent of gold. That would be improper and grossly unjust; for how can you take it back when you have lain with each other and entered into a firm contract?'

Divorce was also discouraged by the Prophet, who is reported to have said: 'Of all things licit, the most hateful to God is divorce,' Also: 'Let not the faithful man hate the faithful woman; if he dislikes some of her habits, he may like others.' Ali, the son-in-law of the Prophet, said, 'Marry and do not divorce your wives, for divorce causes God's throne to tremble.' These disapprovals notwithstanding, Islam concedes the possibility of divorce as the lesser of two evils when the alternative is a disastrously unhappy marriage and it devotes much attention to dealing with it both in the Quran as well as in the Sunnah.

There are many causes for divorce. If the spouses discover that they are incompatible because of their ideas and opinions, their modes of behaviour and their temperaments, then they should resort to divorce. The conflict and tension that would inevitably arise as a result of their incompatibility would certainly give rise to ill feeling and contempt between the spouses. This would adversely affect not only the couple but their children as well as their relatives and closest friends. As a way out of this difficult situation, Islam therefore prescribes divorce.

Furthermore, spouses locked forcibly in an unhappy union would surely be forced themselves—in an attempt to satisfy their sexual urge—to seek sexual intimacy outside the marriage tie, hence falling into the trap of committing adultery, which is forbidden in Islam. To prevent partners from indulging in such indecency, Islam allows the couple to be divorced so that they can go their own separate ways.

Divorce is also granted if the husband is impotent. Divorce, moreover, can take place if both spouses or one of them suffers a serious disease that renders the continuation of the marital relation either impossible or unsafe, or if the husband is put in prison for a long time or fails to support his wife.

In order for the divorce to be effective and valid, the person who is performing it has to be adult (*baligh*), sane (*aqil*), free from any confusion or coercion and full of clear and good intentions (*qasid*). In addition, the witnesses have to be reliable, trustworthy and of good conduct.

Divorce in Islam is one of those issues which has generated considerable controversy and debate among Muslims and non-Muslims alike; this is probably because it has been grossly abused by Muslims and certainly misunderstood by both Muslims and non-Muslims.

Islam is against divorce and is strongly in support of the family unit: hence, both spouses have to do their utmost to build up a strong and harmonious marital relationship. If, however, tension arises between them, they should not rush into a hasty divorce. First, they should try and make some serious efforts to save their marriage. For example, they should attempt to stand the causes of their differences and try to solve them in a private and amicable way. If this proves to be unsuccessful, then they are advised to ask representatives, one from each side, to mediate and try to restore peace between them.

The Quran says, 'If you fear a breach between a man and his wife, appoint an, arbiter from his people and another from hers. If they wish to be reconciled, Allah will bring them together again-Allah is Knowing, Wise'. The arbiters have to be close to the parties involved and command their trust and respect. They should conduct their task impartially and discreetly. Also, they should try and settle the differences between the spouses without publicity; they should especially attempt to avoid the embarrassment of revealing such issues that might be regarded (by the married partners) as very private and intimate. The decisions reached by the arbiters are binding on both spouses. However, if one or both of them refuse to abide by them, then the rulings have to be enforced by the court.

The Quran clearly protects the right of the woman in this matter. By insisting here that two arbiters one from the side of each party (the husband as well as the wife) have to be called to investigate the matter between them peacefully and objectively, it has in fact put the interests of the wife on an equal footing with those of her husband, by giving her the opportunity to present her case and viewpoint before the arbiters. This is surely a fair and just way to deal with divorce matters because it takes into consideration the interests of both sides. More importantly, it protects the weak (the wife) from being abused by the strong (the husband), an outcome which all too frequently occurs in our society these days. For example, it prevents the husband from arbitrarily divorcing his wife without any due consideration for her mental or physical well-being, a practice very often used by the husband to punish his wife in contemporary Muslim societies.

In light of the above it would seem sensible to favour and recommend the adoption of this orderly divorce process by the judicial systems of all Muslim countries for it is simple, civilised and, most importantly, authentically Islamic: it has been described and recommended by the Quran. So, it is not something foreign or alien to Islam; on the contrary, it is an integral part of the Islamic tradition. Indeed there are many examples in which divorce cases were judged according to this procedure in early Islamic history.

For instance, it has been reported that during the reign of the fourth Caliph Ali (son-in-law of the Prophet), a man and his wife approached him complaining about each other's behaviour and stating that there were gross differences between them that had made their lives miserable. Ali immediately acted as Judge and asked for representatives from both sides to be despatched to him. Upon their arrival, he commissioned them to look into the matter carefully and decide whether there would be any possibility of making peace between them.

Also, he reminded them of their responsibility and sacred duty to handle the case with tact, due consideration and impartiality. He told them that if they sensed that there was a chance that they could be reconciled then they should spare no effort in doing so, otherwise they had to be separated with honour and in dignity. When the arbiters reached a decision, Ali made it legally effective by forcing the spouses to abide by it.

If the arbiters realise that there is a good chance for patching up things between the spouses, they are encouraged to do so, but if they think otherwise, the partners have to be allowed to go their own separate ways. It is most unfortunate that such a humane understanding of the verse and such a civilised practice of it failed to materialise throughout most of our Islamic history. For one reason or another, both the jurists as well as the rulers decided to ignore and shelve it. Nevertheless, there were a few scholars who continued to stress the importance of utilising the directions contained in this verse and use them as guidance to promote legal or judicial divorce systems in the Muslim world.

As far as the representatives are concerned, Abduh explains that there are two different views: one sees that the arbiters as mere mediators with no legal authority, while the other insists on regarding them as judges with legal power to enforce their decisions. Concerning the part which states, 'If they wish to be reconciled, Allah will bring them together again. Allah is, Knowing, Wise', Abduh interprets it thus: this part means that, God favours peace and harmony between spouses and wishes that they would be reconciled, because of the emphasis Islam lays on the family unit in society. As such the arbiters are exhorted to ensure that peace can prevail between them. However, if the arbiters fail to bridge the gap between the couple, they are not to blame.

Abduh then introduces his own version. He says: 'when conflict erupts between husband and wife and proves difficult to solve amicably, the spouses are advised to take the matter to the judge of the county. The judge here has to appoint two mediators-one represents the wife while the other acts for the husband. Both representatives have to be of good character and highly respected people. The judge, after briefing them, has to send them to the spouses in an attempt to solve the dispute. If the arbiters' efforts culminate in success, then it is good news. But if they fail to bring the two spouses together again, then they have the legal power to divorce them.

The representatives, after completing their mission, have to report to the judge and the judge has to enforce their decision. It must be stressed here that the mediators—when they decide on separation have to give only one revocable divorce, so that time may be given to the spouses to reflect on their situation before final separation can take place.' Abduh's view on the judicial process of divorce found acceptance among the reformers in some Muslim countries who thought that improvement in this area was badly needed because the unlimited power of the husband to repudiate his wife was grossly abused, hence making the lives of many Muslim women unbearable. His view was, therefore, incorporated into their legal systems and helped them to introduce such reform. Tunisia, for example, was one of a few Muslim countries which decided to introduce legal, reform based on Abduh's view on judicial divorce.

The Tunisian reformers argued that; 'In the case of discord between spouses, the Quran orders the appointment of arbitrators-yet what more obvious case of discord between spouses is there than a pronouncement of repudiation by the husband? And who is then better qualified to undertake the necessary function of arbitration than the official tribunals? On this ground, therefore, the right of a husband to repuditate his wife extra judiciously, was abolished.'

Thus, all divorce actions were prohibited, henceforth taking place outside, the domain of the court. The introduction of such reform has heralded two things. Firstly, it has empowered the court with an unrestricted power to compensate the wife for any injury endured as a result of the divorce; secondly, it ensures that both spouses are treated on an equal basis in this regard.

The Quran deals with divorce issues in another verse which states:

> *Divorce may be pronounced twice, and then a woman must be retained in honour or allowed to go with kindness. It is unlawful for husbands to take from them anything they have given them, unless both fear that they may not be able to keep within the bounds set by Allah; in which case it shall be no offence for either of them if the wife ransoms herself.*

In this verse, God explains that divorce may be pronounced twice, during which period reconciliation can take place; hence it is a revocable type of divorce, since the couple can still resume their marital life if they wish to do so.

However, a third pronouncement would lead to irrevocable divorce, after which the spouses cannot remarry, unless the woman marries another person first and that person also divorces her. In this case, she is allowed to remarry her former husband if she desires to do so: 'If a man divorces his wife, he cannot remarry her until she has wedded another man and been divorced by him; in which case it shall be no offence for either of them to return to the other, if they think that they can keep within the limits set by Allah. Such are the bounds of Allah. He makes them plain to men of understanding.'

Divorce must be pronounced when the wife is in a state of purity (*tuhr*), otherwise it is regarded as invalid. The reason for not allowing the husband to divorce his wife during the state of impurity is that the husband is physically separated from her and this might induce him to press ahead with the separation. While if she is in a state of purity, he is physically close to her and in this case he might be persuaded to reconsider his decision.

Anyway, if divorce takes place, the wife has to observe *idda* or the waiting period. This lasts for three months, during which time sexual intercourse is not allowed between the spouses. By the end of this waiting period, the separation becomes final and legally effective. The reason for making the waiting period obligatory is to ensure the achievement of the following: first, to give the spouses more time to reconsider their attitudes and resolve their differences; second, to determine whether or not the wife is pregnant, for if she is expecting a child there is always a good chance that the spouses might be willing to effect a reconciliation.

Both spouses are encouraged to recognise and respect each other's rights, after the separation. In particular, the Quran exhorts the man to be considerate and kind to his former wife. Also, he is enjoined to act with due care and not allow her to be thrown out of her house. He must ensure that she may stay, if she wishes, with respect and dignity. Moreover, he should properly maintain her and give her sufficient support. Here, it must be noted that there are differences of opinion among scholars regarding the maintenance of divorced women. Some recommend that a divorcee is entitled to sustenance, which includes both the dowry as well as a financial allowance, whilst others insist that the payment of her maintenance should only continue for the period of idda, which is not more than three menstrual cycles.

Under Islamic Law, the marriage contract may be dissolved in three ways: first, the death of one of the spouses; second, by act of the husband or the wife or both of them; third, through Judicial process or a decree of court. The dissolution of the marriage contract by the husband is called Talaq (divorce), which is usually translated as repudiation. It can be done unilaterally by the husband without his having to produce any reason. This form of divorce or *talaq* has been classified (by the jurists) into three main types:

Talaq al-Ahsan: This is the most approved form of repudiation. In this kind of Talaq the husband has to pronounce one single divorce during *tuhr* or the period of purity of the wife. Then he must abstain from having physical contact with her during the waiting period. This form of repudiation is revocable. For the husband can, before the end of the idda, revoke the divorce and resume the conjugal relationship. It must be noted here that the approval of the wife is essential in this context. The husband cannot force her back, even if he regrets divorcing her. She must first give her consent before the couple can resume their matrimonial relations. In order for him to signal his intention to retain her, he may express this desire either explicitly or implicitly. The former is the preferred one, and is usually done by pronouncing the revocation of the repudiation. If, during the waiting period, one of the spouses dies, the other can still inherit the estate. If the husband allows the waiting period to elapse without reclaiming his wife, the repudiation becomes irrevocable or absolute (*bayan*).

Talaq al-Hasan: This is a less approved form of divorce. Here the husband repudiates his wife three successive times over a period of three months, once each month during the period of tuhr. As with Ahsan talaq, the husband can revoke his divorce after the first or second repudiation, but after the third repudiation the divorce becomes absolute (bayan). The only difference is that the wife cannot remarry her former husband until she has first married someone else and then dissolved that marriage. The reason for adding this condition is to prevent a hasty repudiation on the part of the husband.

Talaq al-Bidah: This is the least approved method of divorce in the Muslim world but, unfortunately, it is the most widely used. It is highly condemned by women and civilised men and regarded as sinful. Nonetheless, it is considered legally effective once it is pronounced. This form of divorce is effected by three repudiations, which may be pronounced at any time (not merely in clean periods) and without definite intervals'. It is an irrevocable form of talaq and the husband can only remarry his ex-wife after she has contracted a new marriage with a second man and dissolved that marriage (after proper consummation).

Bidah divorce lacks any Quranic support. Also, it was strongly denounced by the Prophet, who is reported to have reacted angrily when he heard that somebody had divorced his wife by the triple pronouncement of talaq in a single sitting and said 'How would you play with the book of Allah while I am alive and amidst you?' He then ordered the man to take back his wife. Nonetheless, this innovative divorce acquired legitimacy under the reign of the second Caliph Umar, who decided to make it legal in an attempt to prevent any careless use of the formula.

However, his efforts in this context proved to no avail as his decree eventually produced counterproductive results. Since then it has remained lawful and legally effective among Sunnis (the Shia do not recognise this type of divorce), and men have continued to make use of it to their own advantage. We are therefore strongly in favour of banning it outright. It is a bizarre and odd practice; most importantly, it is very degrading to the dignity of Muslim women.

The great jurist, Ibn Taymiyyah, was against it. He stated that the erratic use of such a practice (triple pronouncement on a single occasion) was invalid and had no impact on the statutory position of a marriage. His aim was to protect women, as he thought that they were victimised by such a ruling (Umar's validation of Bidah divorce). It is a shame that his position has been forgotten and disregarded in contemporary Muslim societies.

The dissolution of marriage by the wife takes two forms:

Talaq al-Tawfid, (or delegated divorce.) In this form of divorce the husband, at the time of marriage, agrees to delegate to his wife the power of pronouncing the talaq, thus allowing her to dissolve the marriage contract. It must be stressed here that once the husband consents to give his wife the right to divorce him, he is no longer in a position to reclaim it. Tawfid divorce is indeed a powerful weapon in the hands of the wife, since she can easily use it if the conditions in the marriage contract are violated by the husband.

Khula, also called ransom by some jurists Here, the wife initiates the divorce, but the husband has to agree to free her in return for repayment of part or all of the dowry or mehr. A woman, seeking khula, however, may lose her right to maintenance during the waiting period. Women's right to khula was acknowledged and respected during the early Islamic era; they were very often allowed to exercise it without fear or intimidation. For a woman to request khula she does not have to quote any specific reason; the fact that she is unhappy with her husband would be enough to grant her separation under khula.

Divorce through mutual consent is usually called *Mubaraah*. This form of divorce centres around an agreement between spouses to release each other from the marital link with no exchange or payment on either side.

The final method of dissolving the marriage contract is through a judicial process, at the instigation of either the wife or husband.

This can be obtained in the case of (a) Lian and (b) annulment.

Lian: It is the divorce by oath and it occurs when the husband accuses his wife of committing adultery without evidence. The court, after studying the case and hearing particular oaths from both spouses, would issue a decree allowing the marriage to be dissolved. This form of separation is irrevocable and the partners cannot remarry each other again.

Annulment: The annulment of the marriage takes place when the wife lodges a complaint against her husband on the basis of the following: impotence, failure to fulfil the marital obligations, maltreatment, insanity and any other causes which might justify the annulment of the marriage.

RIGHT OF SELECTION

Men have been exhorted to marry women of their choice and liking, provided they do not transgress the prescribed limits. There are some women with whom it is unlawful to marry. Some are near relatives and some belong to other religions. Except these women, man has the freedom to select from among other women. The women also enjoy the same right of choice. There is no pressure or compulsion to marry a particular man or woman. Everyone who has a grain of common sense knows that at the time of purchasing a thing costing even only a few pennies, we make sure of our full satisfaction as having made a good bargain. Who can then advise anyone to marry in haste without proper investigation? It is obvious that the thing upon which depend the lives of two people, who are strangers, cannot be taken lightly.

Islam which is a harbinger of justice and peace for the oppressed and downtrodden humanity and their greatest supporter, does not at all tolerate that the rights of the rightful people should not be restored to them. It aims at curbing tyranny and oppression with an iron hand. So the Holy Prophet (peace and blessings of Allah be upon him) declared that all sorts of persecution should be ended. He did not leave any aspect of life untouched and issued reforms in conjugal life as well. He safeguarded the rights of the downtrodden and trampled humanity by holding back the hand of the tyrant so that the husband and wife could lead a happy and fulfilled life, the real purpose of marriage.

It would be better if the rights and obligations of the husband and wife are determined in the light of the teachings of Holy Quran and the Sunnah. Both the husband and wife enjoy full rights. The only restriction on them is that none of them should transgress the limits imposed by Allah.

Islam has, within prescribed limits, given priority to the opinion of the men and women who are going to be married in the matter of the selection of a spouse. Their opinion must be sought. Before the advent of Islam, the parents or guardians wedded their daughters to men whom they did not like, by exerting undue pressure upon them, thus committing tyranny and oppression on them. Especially, the orphan girls were subjected to the worst oppression.

History bears ample proof of the fact that in the Days of Ignorance, the condition of women was most miserable. The poor creature was condemned to be a moveable property which had been bought by a man on payment of dower. After the death of her husband, the heirs considered her as their personal property and perpetrated all sorts of tyrannies on her. Islam eradicated this evil.

Just as every wise man and woman are free to decide their worldly matters after attaining puberty, similarly in the matter of marriage, Islam has given them freedom to give their proposals. Parents and other relatives can give them suitable advice, as they should, but they should not pressurise the boy or girl. The men and women going to be married should act upon the advice of their experienced and loving parents and relatives, but according to Islam, their advice is not binding on them.

> *It is far from the truth to say that in Islam women are helpless, dumb creatures. Islam has given them freedom of choice like men. In contracting marriage, the consent of a woman, attaining the age of puberty must always be sought. The Holy Prophet (peace and blessings of Allah be upon him) has said: 'A divorcee or a widow*

must not be married until she is consulted and a virgin must also not be married until her permission is sought.'
(Bukhari)

In another Tradition the Holy Prophet (peace and blessings of Allah be upon him) said: 'A woman who has been previously married (Thayyiba), has more right to her person than her guardian. And a virgin should also be consulted and her silence implies her consent.'
(Muslim)

A further probe into the above Ahadith would affirm the fact that women are not helpless but they have been given the freedom of choice by Islam and without the consultation of a woman, the marriage of a woman with any man is not permissible. Thus, consent of a woman is an essential condition of marriage and it must be obtained in all circumstances.

It is the duty of a guardian that he should first consult the woman, attaining the age of competency, regarding her proposed marriage and then begin the negotiations. Islam ordains that both the parents and guardians of a girl should seek permission from her before marriage.

But where Islam considers the permission and consent of the woman as an essential condition of her marriage, it does not do so at the cost of her sentiments of modesty and chastity. So if she is a virgin her silence implies her consent, but in the case of a woman previously married (divorced or widowed) explicit consent from her is necessary. Some scholars are of the view that it is more appropriate that it should be made clear to a virgin.

A Hadith narrates the incident of a Sahabia, Hadrat Khansa bint Huzam (Allah be pleased with her) that her father married her to a person whom she did not like. She came to the Holy Prophet (peace and blessings of Allah be upon him) and submitted a petition which was accepted by him, and he revoked the marriage.

Hadrat Abdullah bin Abbas (Allah be pleased with him) reported that a woman came to the Holy Prophet (peace and blessings of Allah be upon him) and said: 'My father has married me to a person whom I do not like.' The Holy Prophet (peace and blessings of Allah be upon him) authorised that woman to accept or revoke the marriage.

According to an incident narrated by Buraida (Allah be pleased with him) a young woman came to the Holy Prophet (peace and blessings of Allah be upon him) and said: 'My father has married me to my cousin whom I do not like.' Thereupon the Holy Prophet (peace and blessings of Allah be upon him) gave her permission to adhere to or revoke the marriage contract. Hearing this the woman heaved a sigh of relief saying: 'I have already given my consent to what my father has done, but what I want to impress upon women is that a father has no right to give the hand of his grown up daughter without her consent.'

Abdur Rahman bin Yazid and Majma' bin Yazid (Allah be pleased with them) narrated an incident. A person, namely Khuddam, married his daughter to a person whom she did not like. She came to the Holy Prophet (peace and blessings of Allah be upon him) and expressed her disgust. He (the Holy Prophet) (peace and blessings of Allah be upon him) revoked the marriage contracted by her father and then she married Abdul Baya bin Abdul Mundhir (Allah be pleased with him).

The above Ahadith bear ample testimony to the fact that it is not permissible to put pressure on a grown-up lady in the matter of marriage, but that she reserves the full right to select her husband. The sum and substance of what we have said above is that the real aims and objects of marriage i.e., morality and chastity, love and affection and multiplication of the human race should always be kept in view. The guardian and the father possess the right to get a girl, who has not yet attained the age of puberty, married to someone; but the right of the father is more essential as she cannot, in that case, exercise her option or choice on attaining the age of puberty.

However, marriage is an important matter. It should be arranged after thorough investigation. The parents and guardians should satisfy themselves to the possible extent and those who are going to be tied in wedlock should also feel contented.

Another point worth thinking about is that nowadays people do not consider it necessary to consult their parents and guardians. No doubt, the like and dislike of a person proposed for marriage is the primary factor, but the heart and passions should not be allowed to overrule the mind and one should be vigilant and not lose one's sense. Besides, in the gratification of the sexual instinct, marriage entails responsibilities which one owes to one's family, society, country and nation. One should not be concerned with one's present state only, but should also keep the future in view. It is, therefore, quite necessary to consult elderly people as they possess more experience of life. If there arises a dispute, the choice of the woman should be given priority.

Now the question remains of the case of dispute between a guardian or father and a woman going to be married; how should the matter be decided? Certainly, the verdict will be in the favour of the woman, and according to the Shariah, priority will be given to her opinion as it is she who is going to be married and the matter pertains to her modesty and chastity. The guardian is not being married nor is he to shoulder the responsibility of marriage. Then how is it that the opinion of the woman should be overlooked? There are incidents and clear decisions of the time of the Holy Prophet (peace and blessings of Allah be upon him) that he gave preference to the opinion of the woman. He revoked the marriage contracted by the father, but did not decide against the woman. It has been said in the Holy Quran:

> *"When they reach their term, place not difficulties in the way of their marrying the husbands of their choice if it is agreed between them in kindness."* *(2:232)*

In the matter of marriage, the woman has the right to decide according to her sweet will. The woman is also human, she possesses intellect and wisdom. She is not a helpless creature unable to decide any matter of her own accord.

From the above we are bound to arrive at the conclusion that coordination between the guardian and the woman is essential for arranging the marriage smoothly. The views of Hadrat Maulana Kashmiri on this subject are worth reading. Here we shall give only the gist thereof: In the case of the matters concerning the people, the Shariah has given the right to both the parties. One should decide keeping in view all the Ahadith. One-sided decisions can be wrong. For instance, in the case of Zakat, the matter pertains to both the payer and the payee. So far as the payer is concerned, there is a clear Hadith that if any collector of Zakat comes to him for Zakat, he should please him by giving to him what he demands. If he does justice, the reward will be for him and if he commits injustice, he will be liable to punishment. The excellence of Zakat is that the collector should go back cheerfully.

It has been narrated in a Hadith that the people complained to the Holy Prophet (peace and blessings of Allah be upon him) against the collector of Zakat. He said: 'Please him and give him what he asks for.' Thereupon they asked: 'O' Allah's Messenger, even if he commits injustice?' He answered: 'Yes, in that case too!'

On the other hand, the payee has been admonished: 'Beware against taking the best of the wealth of the people. Be afraid of the outpourings of the heart of the oppressed as there is no barrier between him and Allah.'

Now, ponder over both the Ahadith. According to the instructions of the Holy Prophet (peace and blessings of Allah be upon him) the collector of Zakat should be given what he demands even if he commits injustice. On the other hand, the payee has been warned to receive what the payer gives him justly and should not be arrogant. Similar is the case of husband and wife. On the one hand, the wife has been ordained to please her husband and a stern warning of being thrown into the Fire of Hell has been given for misbehaviour on her part. And on the other hand, it has been said that the perfect in Faith among you is the one who is of good manners and who is the best in behaviour towards his wife.

The same is the case of the woman and her guardian. It is impressed on the woman that the guardian possesses the right in respect of her marriage and without his consultation the marriage contract is not complete. On the other hand, it is said to the guardian that the woman has more right to her person than him and he has no right to intervene.

What can be concluded from the above Ahadith is that both are responsible and that the marriage should not be contracted without each other's consultation. The woman should, as far as possible, give due regard to the opinion of the guardian and the latter must seek the former's consent. Neither is the guardian allowed to deprive the woman of her legal right nor should the woman bring disgrace to the fair name of her family and guardian. In any case, the guardian has no right to put pressure. It is, however, preferable that he should give advice. If the girl is a minor, the guardian can exercise his will. As is evident from the Quran and the Sunnah, in the event of a dispute between the woman and the guardian, priority will be given to the opinion of the woman.

The views of Maulana Kashmiri are most reasonable and practicable in so far as social problems are concerned. He is aware of the implication of Allah's Prophet's directives. He is fully conversant with the significance and style of the Ahadith.

While explaining this point, Shah Wali Ullah also supports the above view, though his style is distinct from Maulana Kashmiri's. He says:

> *'Merely the opinion of the woman is not sufficient for the purpose of marriage It is only men who can solve difficult and knotty problems. Moreover, in the matters covering marriage the proposal by a woman is considered as arrogant and as an act of immodesty on her part. The intervention of a guardian is therefore, necessary to make a distinction between love-affair and marriage and to give due publicity to the proposed marriage. The woman, therefore, should consult the guardian, but the latter has no right to get her married to a person without her consent as the matter pertains exclusively to a woman. The benefits or loss occurring out of this marriage will have to be faced by her alone. So her consent must be sought.'*

Imam Nawawi, who belongs to the Shafii school of thought, is also of the view that the opinion of the woman has preference to the opinion of the guardian. He has written:

> *'The right of a woman has priority over the right of a guardian. If a guardian intends to marry a woman to a relative and she is not inclined, she cannot be pressurized. If she desires to marry with a relative and the guardian is not inclined, pressure will be exerted on the guardian. If he is adamant, the Qadi will get her*

married. This affirms the view that priority is to the right of a woman and this practice is in vogue.'

It is evident from what we have said above that in Islam a woman is not quite helpless in the matter of marriage but her consent must be obtained before the guardian arranges her marriage. If a woman refuses to marry a person, she should not at all be forced to do so. Peace and harmony, the foremost aims and objects of marriage cannot be achieved in the case of the unwilling marriage of a woman. The rules and regulations pertaining to divorce and Khula have been framed for this purpose.

It has been mentioned in "Masbut" that at the time of Nikah the consent of a woman must be sought. It is just possible that the woman may have some defect or disease due to which sexual intercourse is not possible or the woman may like another man. If she is married to a person whom she dislikes, she will never be able to live amicably with him.

After the woman, comes the question of the opinion of the man. Here too, the consent of the grown-up man, going to be married, must be sought. Since man is not helpless, this matter needs no detailed discussion, rather it is advisable that he should give due weight to the opinion of his elders and should not ignore them saying: 'This is my personal matter in which the elders have no right to intervene.' In the matter of marriage the views of experienced people and those who have deep human insight count much. It is an obvious fact that young men do not possess the wisdom and prudence of elderly people. In the former case sentiments and passions only play a part.

Now we come to the point as to what should be the criteria for the selection of a woman. According to the Shariah, the chastity and piety of a woman should be given top priority at the time of selection. A person may marry an ordinary woman or a rich and wealthy lady or a woman of high descent or one for the sake of her beauty, but her piety and moral character must always be kept in view. The Holy Prophet (peace and blessings of Allah be upon him) has observed: 'Marriage with a woman is contracted for the sake of four things: for her wealth, for her descent, for her beauty and for her piety, but you should succeed (marry), for piety.' (Bukhari)

A man chooses a woman for the sake of four things. Sometime he chooses for the sake of her wealth only. He thinks that if the woman possesses property or a grand building, he would lead a luxurious and comfortable life and would be relieved of a large number of worries. He does not care to ponder over the virtues of piety and chastity, in his haste. He is not aware that by marrying a rich woman, he would be deprived of the real pleasure and happiness of marriage, as in that case his wife would rule. He would not feel any pleasure in seeing the furniture and other household goods which have not been purchased by his hard earned income nor would he be glad to see his gaily dressed children after losing his respect and honour in the eyes of his wife. His status or position would be that of a manager or organizer, if his wife is of good behaviour. If, God forbids, the wife happens to be arrogant, she would annoy and taunt him at every moment. The children of that wife would also not pay due respect to their father. If the husband intends to admonish his wife for any mistake of hers, it would come to a fight. Under the above circumstances what pleasure and happiness would exist in his life? The Holy Prophet (peace and blessings of Allah be upon him) has observed: 'Do not marry women for the sake of their wealth. Just possible their wealth makes them arrogant.' (Ibn Majah)

Sometime a man chooses a woman of high descent even if she is deprived of any personal ability and virtues. If she is of high descent but lacks piety, she would be proud and arrogant and would not remain within limits. This kind of behaviour is almost intolerable for a man. It does not mean that one should not attach importance to the race and descent of a woman, but it should not be the only consideration. These things have no value if the woman has no personal ability and is not pious and chaste. Islam holds piety and chastity in high esteem and these virtues are far more important in the eyes of Islam than race and descent. The Holy Prophet (peace and blessings of Allah be upon him) said: 'A woman may be married for four reasons: for her property, her status, her beauty and her religion; so try to get who is religious.' (Sahih Muslim)

The other Ahadith also support this view. Once the Holy Prophet (peace and blessings of Allah be upon him) said: 'Wherever they may be and whosoever they may be, my followers are pious.'

According to some people, beauty is the only consideration for the selection of a woman. She must have appealing looks, attractive, wide eyes, fair complexion and a proportionate body. She should be of gay disposition and pert and coquettish. She must be aware of the etiquettes of the modern society and way of life.

But they do not take any trouble to think that the above qualities do not count much if she is lacking in ability and good manners. Mere beauty is not everything. If she is deprived of other virtues, the beauty would become an evil. It would make her proud, flirtatious and arrogant. She would become haughty and extravagant. Other people would try to allure her. The holy Prophet (peace and blessings of Allah be upon him) has said about this kind of beautiful woman: 'Do not marry women merely for their beauty. It is most probable that their beauty may prove disastrous.' (Ibn Majah)

The Holy Prophet (peace and blessings of Allah be upon him) has, therefore, made piety and chastity the real criteria for the selection of a woman. Wealth, beauty, race and descent of a woman are not the real virtues. The person going to be married must see the personal ability and intelligence of a woman. The Holy Prophet (peace and blessings of Allah be upon him) has said: 'Do not marry a woman merely for the sake of her beauty and wealth.'

In the matter of marriage, preference should be given to chastity and piety. A black but pious woman is better. The Holy Prophet (peace and blessings of Allah be upon him) has said: 'But marry women on the basis of religion and piety.' (Ibn Majah)

There is no denying the fact that a religious and pious lady is always solicitous for the welfare and comfort of her husband and discharges her household duties efficiently and carefully. Such a woman is not unduly proud. She takes the utmost care in bringing up and educating her children. She does not pick up quarrels with the neighbours, relatives and other people. The people rely on her and respect and honour her. She enhances the honour and prestige of her husband.

The Holy Prophet (peace and blessings of Allah be upon him) has observed: 'Whosoever achieves four things, is successful in this world and in the Hereafter: A heart which is grateful, a tongue which remains busy in Dhikr (commemorating the name of Allah) a body which shows patience, and a wife who abstains from sins and guards her chastity.'

Once the Holy Prophet (peace and blessings of Allah be upon him) said: 'Marry a woman who has excellent faith in Allah and who is helpful in making the life successful on the Day of Resurrection.'

Indifferent Attitude : Should the people adopt an indifferent attitude towards moral conduct and behaviour, devoting their all out attention to worldly pomp and show and exterior beauty, what would become of this world? A storm of evil and wickedness would rage and destroy the peace and harmony of this world. The respect and honour of everyone would be at stake. A large number of women could not get husbands and would be tempted to wickedness and debauchery as someone has rightly remarked: An idle brain is the devil's workshop. While explaining this fact the Holy Prophet (peace and blessings of Allah be upon him) has observed: 'Whenever a person whose moral conduct and behaviour pleases you, comes to you, get him married, otherwise there will be a widespread evil and wickedness on earth.! (Tirmidhi)

According to the Jurists, it is advised that the following principles should be observed while selecting a woman: 'It is better if the position of a woman is less in respect of her race and descent and wealth and property and influence, but she should be superior to the man in moral conduct, behaviour, personality and beauty.'

(Dur Mukhtar)

The following points should also be kept in view: The woman with whom a man is to marry should not be tall and weak and thin, nor should she be of short stature, ugly and of bad conduct. She should not be of advanced age. She should not be of easy virtue. (Shami)

In short, the woman with whom one is to marry should be suitable in every respect from the worldly point of view as well as from the religious point of view. Without this there can exist no mutual love and harmony between the husband and wife. As is evident from the Ahadith the woman should possess the following virtues:

- She should be religious and pious.
- She should share her husband's joys and sorrows and should be loyal and obedient.
- She should be chaste and honest and should manage the household affairs properly.
- She should be courteous, grateful and patient.
- She should pay attention to the needs of her children and should be kind to them and be healthy.
- She should love her husband and be a bearer of many offsprings.
- She should be of a pious and noble descent and educated.
- She should be virtuous and free from vices and evils.
- While living in this world, she should remember the life in the Hereafter.

SELECTION OF A HUSBAND

While selecting a husband, a woman should also keep in view the above criteria. This should enable her to lead a happy and cheerful life. The Jurists are of this view: A woman should have a husband who should be pious and broad-minded and of appealing manners, and should not marry a wicked person. (Dur Mukhtar)

Similarly, the father should also keep the above instructions in view at the time of giving the hand of his daughter. Nowadays the illiterate and avaricious generally keep in mind the wealth and status of a person and set little value on his personal ability, character and age. We must, therefore, raise a voice against this erroneous outlook and practice. The Jurists say: "The father should not marry his young daughter to an old and ugly man." (Dur Mukhtar)

It is the moral and religious duty of a guardian to see that there is not much difference in the age of the couple. The Holy Prophet (peace and blessings of Allah be upon him) had kept the age factor in view at the time of giving the hand of his daughter. Nasai has written a separate chapter on this subject: "Marriage of a woman with a man of equal age", and has narrated a Hadith on the authority of Hadrat Buraida (Allah be pleased with him):

Hadrat Abu Bakr and Hadrat Umar (Allah be pleased with them) sent messages of marriage for Hadrat Fatima (Allah be pleased with her). The Holy Prophet (peace and blessings of Allah be upon him) said: "She is lesser in age." Then Hadrat Ali (Allah be pleased with him) sent a message for marriage with her. He married her to Ali (Nasai).

The commentators of Ahadith have said that due regard must be given to age as it is an important factor and has many advantages. It is true that the Holy Prophet (peace and blessings of Allah be upon him) married Aishah (Allah be pleased with her) when she was of tender age, but this marriage had an extremely significant purpose. Everyone knows that this marriage proved to be a great blessing for the dissemination of Islamic knowledge and Hadrat Aishah's magnificent contribution in this respect can never be forgotten.

But it should not be construed from what we have said above that a man should not marry a beautiful woman. This is not our aim. What we want to impress upon the reader is that one should not be so deluded by the fair face that he overlooks the good qualities of a woman such as chastity, piety and moral conduct. If she lacks these qualities, her beauty is of no use.

A Hadith narrates an incident regarding a Companion of the Prophet (peace and blessings of Allah be upon him). He came to the Prophet (peace and blessings of Allah be upon him) and said: 'I have married an Ansari woman.' Thereupon the Holy Prophet (peace and blessings of Allah be upon him) observed: 'Have you satisfied yourself as Ansari women have something (defect) in their eyes?' In other words, we must first make proper investigation so that there may not remain any cause of complaint which may straiten the relations between the husband and the wife.

Marrying a Young Lady : An incident of Hadrat Jabir (Allah be pleased with him) has been narrated in a Hadith. He said to the Holy Prophet (peace and blessings of Allah be upon him): 'I have married only recently.' He asked: 'Virgin or a previously married (Thayyiba)?' He answered: 'A previously married woman.' Thereupon the Holy Prophet (peace and blessings of Allah be upon him) said: 'Why not with a virgin with whom you could sport and she could sport with you?'

In the Sahih the same words have been repeated, but with the following addition: 'She could amuse you and you could amuse her.' *(Muslim)*

He made mention of a virgin lady as she can be easily moulded and is more cooperating. She is contended with a little and is grateful and she loves her husband passionately. Moreover she is more fascinating. The Ahadith support the view that a virgin and beautiful lady has a joyful disposition and a sense of pleasure and amusement for her husband. The Holy Prophet (peace and blessings of Allah be upon him) said in another Hadith: 'You should marry virgin ladies as they are sweet in speech and bearer of more children and they feel contented with a little.' *(Mishkat)*

In the above Hadith special emphasis has been laid on marriage with a virgin. The reason for this emphasis is that a virgin lady is more beautiful, charming and buoyant. These virtues should also be kept in view at the time of marrying a lady.

Hadrat Alqama (Allah be pleased with him) reported: 'When I was walking with Abdullah at Mina, Uthman (Allah be pleased with him) happened to meet him. He stopped there and began to talk with him. Uthman (Allah be pleased with him) said to him: "Should we not marry you to a girl who may recall to you some of the past of your begone days?" *(Muslim)*

While commenting upon the above Hadith, Imam Nawawi says: 'It is preferable to marry a young lady as the purposes of marriage can be best achieved through it. She affords pleasure and her fragrance is sweet. She is more exciting and pleasing and beautiful to look at. She is buoyant and jovial, elegant in appearance and delicate in touching. A husband can easily mould her as he desires.'

Hafiz Ibn Qayyim has reported that the Holy Prophet (peace and blessings of Allah be upon him) used to exhort his followers to marry religious and beautiful ladies. *(Zad al-Maad)*

It is clear from what has been said above that there is no harm in marrying a beautiful woman, rather it is preferable; but beauty should not be the only consideration. Along with it due consideration should be given to good conduct and manners.

We must know that beauty does not mean only fair complexion, but the moral conduct of a woman should be spotless and she should be firm in her religious beliefs. Moreover, the criteria of judgement of feminine beauty differs with different people. It depends upon the tastes and aesthetic sense of a person. It is possible that a woman who is ugly in the eyes of other people may be liked by a particular person. Therefore, the likes and dislikes of other people cannot be the criteria for the judgement of beauty.

As a matter of fact, good conduct and behaviour and appealing manners add to beauty and grace. There are numerous instances where passion and wantonness have had the upper hand as compared to a woman's beauty and elegance. So it is not wise to sacrifice everything at the altar of beauty. If, however, one finds a woman who is beautiful and virtuous it is a great boon.

Islam has exhorted its followers to marry sweet and beautiful women, but has condemned immorality and debauchery and one should never even think of committing adultery.

Marrying a Widow

But this does not mean that it is not proper to marry widows. No doubt, in the Ahadith the people have been exhorted to marry virgins and there are solid reasons for it; that they can be easily moulded to the tastes and temperaments of men and that they love their husbands passionately and the husbands too have the same sentiments towards them. They are joyous and buoyant. Due to them men are saved from sins and wicked thoughts. But if a person has a wife or is advanced in age, it would be improper if he marries a young lady. An old man should marry a widow so that the husband and wife may live in peace and harmony.

The Holy Prophet (peace and blessings of Allah be upon him) whose life is a practical example for all mankind. A study of the history of the illustrious Caliphs and Companions reveals that a majority of them married widows. The Sahabiyyat also got married after the death of their husbands.

The above events bear out that if the marrying of widows were an abhorable act, no one would have married widows in the Prophet's or Caliphs' time. So it is not a bad thing to marry a widow, it is a good action and has its reward.

It is clear that it is permissible to cast a glance in a civilized manner within the limits of the Shariah so that there remains no doubt and suspicion in the mind of the person who is to marry. Moreover, this permission has been given so that he should not, after the marriage, give any remarks to his wife which are derogatory or taunting which would prevent the growth of sentiments of love and affection between the couple. It is, however, not necessary that a person going to be married should himself see the woman. Another person can also see her on his behalf. If he has confidence in a person it is better that he should see. It is permissible to gather any information regarding the wealth, property moral conduct, piety, chastity, race, descent, etc., of the proposed woman for his satisfaction.

This clear commandment of Allah's Messenger (peace and blessings of Allah be upon him) implies that it is preferable to cast a glance at a woman before marriage. It is mentioned in Tirmidhi that some scholars have drawn the conclusion on the authority of this Hadith that there is no harm in casting a glance at a woman before marriage provided that part of her body should not be seen which is unlawful to be seen. Imams Ahmad and Ishaq also hold this view. Imam Tirmidhi further writes that it means "so that lasting love could exist between the two."

It is evident from the above Ahadith that there is no harm in seeing the woman before marriage, rather it is preferable, whether the man sees himself, or appoints some reliable woman for this purpose. This would help to remove the doubts and suspicions in the mind and provide satisfaction as to the suitability of the selection. But the condition is that one must be sincere at heart and his aim should not be simply to annoy and create mischief.

It is an admitted fact that by casting a glance at the face, a man can judge a woman's shape and features. It reflects the elegance and ugliness of a woman. An intelligent person can gather much information about the woman from her face. It would not be out of place to say that the face is an index of the body and soul of a person. We have already mentioned the view of Maulana Thana Ullah Panipati that it is permissible to see the face and palms of a woman before marriage, and this view is also supported by the Ahadith. The Jurists have also added the words 'feet' to the above Hadith on the basis of Shariah.

Although there is difference of opinion among the scholars as to which portion and to what extent a woman's body could be seen; there is however, consensus of opinion on the point that the face and palms can been seen.

You will read in the next pages that the first glance is ,allowed, but a second glance should not be cast. It is not at all permissible for a man to meet and talk with a woman secretly. He can, however, see a woman, in case of need, in front of others. You will read more instructions on the subject. In view thereof it can be concluded that although Islam has permitted a man to see a woman, it has granted permission with certain limitations. One should not go further. One is allowed to cast a glance at a woman in her house, in her usual dress, but the glance should not be lewd and there should be no wickedness in the heart. In casting a glance the intention should be righteous, and the matter should be entrusted to Allah. *(Al-Uraf al-Shadhi)*

The main purpose of these laws is to lend stability and mutual love and cooperation between the couple and to prevent the occurrence of unpleasant happenings which make the lives miserable so that the full benefits of marriage may be derived.

Allama Rashid Raza of Egypt is speaking truly when he says that he has done much research work on the problems of women and on sexual relations of husband and wife and has read much ancient and modern literature, pamphlets and newspapers on the subject and has also written much on this topic. But despite this I do not believe in the wrong notion that the amicability of husband and wife depends upon premarital contacts and love-making between them.

Sometimes passionate love between husband and wife ceases after marriage. The basic principle to maintain amicable relations between husband and wife is that which was told by Hadrat Umar (Allah be pleased with him) to a woman who submitted an application to him saying: I do not love him from the core of my heart, that is, my heart is not affected by him. Thereupon, Hadrat Umar (Allah be pleased with him) observed: Do not tell this thing to your husband as there are many homes where sentiments of passionate love do not exist. The husband and wife ought to pay due regard to their noble descent, to the teachings of Islam and fulfil their duties and obligations which they owe to each other.

He further said: The husband and the wife should express more love than that they have in their hearts so that by and by it should find a place there and enable them to lead a pleasant and comfortable life.

Islam embodies all the important measures which are necessary to guard morality and establish a pious and healthy atmosphere. It has prohibited all things as might lead to evil and wickedness and the ruination of moral character.

Islam has allowed a boy and a girl to marry before he or she attains maturity. In other words, before the passionate age begins, so that they may not be led astray. The greatest advantage of this marriage is that they will never think of developing illicit and unlawful relations.

On attaining puberty, Islam exhorts its followers to marry without delay. It is the prime of youth, the passions run high and sexual urge is at its height. Although man has the capacity to think over the future and about his loss or gain, he is overwhelmed by passions and if the law does not impose restrictions on him, there is every chance of his being led astray. Addressing the young men, the Holy Prophet (peace and blessings of Allah be upon him) has said, 'O group of young men! He who is able to marry among you should marry.'
(Bukhari)

Youth starts when a person attains the age of puberty and it lasts upto the age of thirty-two and Nawawi has said that the more authentic view is that youth lasts from puberty to the age of thirty. Then begins middle age which is upto forty. Thereafter begins old age.
(Ibn Majah)

There is no age for grey hair. It differs with different people and depends upon their temperaments. What I want to say is that Islam has laid stress on the immediate marriage of a person upon attaining the age of maturity, so that he might not be led astray at that most passionate age.

During this period, the sons and daughters are usually under the care of their parents. They do not often possess the means to marry. Moreover, modesty and shyness stand in their way and they cannot convey their feelings and sentiments to their parents. Sometimes they succumb to evil temptations. Islam has, therefore, laid this responsibility (of getting the children married), upon the parents. The Holy Prophet (peace and blessings of Allah be upon him) has said: The person to whom a son is born should give him a good name and teach him ethics and when he attains maturity he should get him married. If he is mature and his father does not get him married, the responsibility of the sin committed by him will rest with his father. This Hadith was narrated by Baihaqi in Shab al-Iman. *(Mishkat)*

The above Hadith teaches us two lessons. Firstly, the parents should teach their children good moral conduct and tell them the righteous way of life so that they may fear Allah and abstain from sins and vices. Secondly, the parents should get their children married when they reach the age of maturity. They should not show any indifference or slackness in this matter as in the event of any sin committed by them due to the delay in marriage, the responsibility would devolve on the parents. The other Hadith pertaining to girls is given below:

> *The Holy Prophet (peace and blessings of Allah be upon him) observed: It has been written in the Torah that when a daughter attains the age of twelve and the person does not get her married and she commits any sin, the responsibility of that sin rests with him. This Hadith was narrated by Baihaqi in Shab al Iman.*

It is evident from the above Ahadith that when a son or a daughter attains the age of puberty, their marriage should be arranged immediately by the parents. The boy and the girl should give their consent and not try to put off the matter but the marriage should not be contracted without obtaining the prior approval of the children, an essential condition for a happy and stable home life.

Importance of Marriage

In order to emphasize the significance of marriage, it has been said that if the parents do not fulfil their duty and delay the matter, the responsibility for any moral lapse on the part of the boy or girl or both of them, would rest with the parents as well as the boy or girl who commits the evil deed, for whom there is severe punishment of Hell.

In contracting marriage, Islam aims at ensuring a happy and stable home life and where there should exist perfect harmony between husband and wife so that the relations between them may not grow strained with the passage of time. Due to this reason, the Shariah has stressed that the two strangers who are going to be wedded should profess the same religion and belief, and their way of life should bear similarity. The marriage of the believing men and women with unbelievers and polytheists has, therefore, been prohibited. While commenting upon the verse banning marriage with the polytheists, Maulana Mahmud al Hasan writes: The development of friendship and marital relations with the polytheists, men and women, cools down the sentiments of enmity and hatred towards polytheism and disbelief which may drag one into polytheism. There is the severe punishment of Hell-fire for such people, so marriage with them is strictly prohibited. Hadrat Shah Wali Allah gives the following comments: There is a lesson in the above verse. When the believers augment their friendships and relations with the infidels and polytheists and there is intimacy between them, resulting in intermarriages, it poses a serious hazard to Islam. The polytheistic creeds deliberately or inadvertently affect the minds.

Besides the above religious disadvantages, the worldly loss is that without religious concord there can be no real love and affection between a husband and a wife. The relations between them are bound to be embittered. By and by the gulf of differences between them is widened and the inevitable result thereof is that husband and wife do not remain loyal to each other and resort to evil and sinful lives, thus nullifying the very aim and objective of marriage.

Equality

In order to achieve mutual love and cooperation which is essential for a happy home life, equality in certain things is necessary. For instance, a pious woman should not be married to a wicked man, similarly it is forbidden to marry a wicked man to a pious lady.

It is evident that an adulterer or an adulteress is not equal to a pious woman or a pious man. There is a great difference between the two and there is little hope of their union.

Equality in wealth does not seem to be necessary. Only Imam Shafii believes in the equality of wealth. But experience has shown that wealth is not such a thing as stands in the way of sincere love and affection, rather it can lead to hatred and discord.

Some scholars believe in the equality of descent. Probably they have based their views on intellectual reasoning. It is a common experience that social difference among the various families give rise to many complications, but Ibn Hajar says that in so far as the religious aspect of this matter is concerned there is no authentic tradition stressing on the equality of descent. On the other hand, ample evidences and Ahadith exist which testify that during the Prophet's and the Caliphs' period, no importance was given to race and descent.

Imam Bukhari has narrated two such events in the chapter Al-Ikfa Fiddin from which it is evident that equality in descent was not considered as necessary. The first incident pertaining to Abu Hudaifa (Allah be pleased with him) a Companion of Badr. He married Hadrat Salim (Allah be pleased with him) a freed servant of a woman of Ansar, to his niece, Hind bint Walid (Allah be pleased with her) who was one of Muhajirat.

The other incident pertains to Dabaa bint Zubayr (Allah be pleased with her). She was married to Hadrat Miqdad (Allah be pleased with him) although Dabaa was a very high - ranking woman in the matter of her descent.

Hafiz Ibn Qayyim has written in detail on this subject and has proved that Islam has not laid any stress on descent and its strict observance is against the teachings and spirit of Islam. Allah has made tribes and clans as means of mutual relations and contracts.

Announcement of Marriage

The rules and regulations promulgated by Islam block all the avenues of sin and vice. We must try to adopt all the ways and means, remaining within the limits prescribed by Allah, to curb immorality and lewdness. Islam has, therefore, stressed the announcement of marriage. Secret or hidden marriage is forbidden in Islam as it involves many dangers. There is no room for flirtation, keeping of concubines or premarital sexual relations in Islam. In Islam the announcement of marriage is required to be made publicly and there is a clear distinction between secret and illicit relations and Islamic Nikah. The wisdom behind this is that one should never try to develop secret illicit relations.

If public announcement of marriage is not considered to be necessary, there would remain hardly any distinction between secret illegal love affairs and legal marriages and thus the way would be paved for illicit love relations, which are strictly forbidden in Islam. The real aim and subject of marriage, according to Islam, is spiritual elevation and the protection of piety and chastity and not mere gratification of sexual desire. The announcement of marriage is, therefore, necessary. The true significance of marriage has been explained in a miraculous style of the Holy Quran and emphasis has been laid on the announcement of marriage.

There is another way to give publicity to marriage and one cannot but wonder at this interesting and solemn function. It is appreciable in Islam that after spending a night with the wife, a man should give a marriage feast. The Ahadith lay special stress on it. The Holy Prophet (peace and blessings of Allah be upon him) himself arranged this feast at the time of marrying Hadrat Zainab bint Jahsh (Allah be pleased with her). He slaughtered a goat and served meat to his Companions in the marriage feast. When he married Hadrat Safiah (Allah be pleased with her) he got *Hees* prepared and served it to the guests. Hees is a kind of Arabian dish composed of dates, cheese and ghee. At the time of some marriages he could not, however, get anything and he arranged the marriage feast with two mud of barley.

He exhorted his Companions to give marriage feasts. Hadrat Abdur Rahman bin Auf (Allah be pleased with him) reported that the Holy Prophet (peace and blessings of Allah be upon him), said: Arrange the marriage feast even if with a single goat.

Some consider this feast as an incumbent duty, but the correct view is that the Holy Prophet (peace and blessings of Allah be upon him) recommended it or that it is his Sunnah. However, it is desirable that one should serve to the people whatever is easily available. It does not at all mean that one should borrow in order to make this arrangement.

The importance of the marriage feast can be judged from the above Ahadith. Apart from the expression of joy and happiness, another advantage of this feast is that the marriage receives due publicity and all doubts and suspicions about the marriage are removed. Another aim and object of the open announcement of marriage is to discourage illicit secret 'love affairs' and to guard chastity and morality which is possible only through a legal marriage.

Lawful Gratification of Sex

After marriage, Islam has imposed no restrictions on the husband and wife in gratifying their sexual desire in the natural course. There is no restriction of time. Sexual intercourse is permissible during the day and the night, during summer and winter and during spring and rains. No one is allowed to intervene in this matter.

Sexual intercourse is forbidden in the days of the month of Ramadan only, in which both husband and wife have been ordained to keep fast. During the fast, indulgence in sexual intercourse is prohibited in Islam. But no restriction is imposed on mutual conversation and things of other interest. This restriction is only during the period of fasting. After breaking the fast there is no ban on sexual intercourse except during the forbidden periods of which everyone is aware.

There are two occasions on which the woman remains naturally polluted. The first is during menstrual discharge, the maximum period of which extends to ten days and the minimum period of which extends to three days. The second occasion is during the discharge of blood at childbirth which continues for weeks together. Its maximum limit is forty days and there is no minimum limit for it. During these days of pollution, sexual intercourse is prohibited. As we have already said these are the days of pollution of a woman and there is a natural aversion for sexual intercourse. Moreover, there is every risk of contracting infectious diseases.

Besides the above periods there is no restriction on sexual intercourse in Islam. The women regain fresh vim and vigour after these days and their capability to conceive grows after the menstrual period. Apart from the above occasions, if there is no other reason of the Shariah, the husband and wife can have sexual intercourse at any time and Islam has granted them complete freedom in this respect.

Marriage: A Legal Bond

In marriage we find it to be that everlasting conduct which engulfs everything and by which all things become good and bear the required fruit for its kind.

Marriage is the natural tie between the pair (male and female) as the above quoted verse of the Holy Quran says: all things are created in pairs. It is more so true in everything in our dynamic world. You find this even in things like electricity: we have the positive and negative. Neither of the two will function satisfactorily alone without the help of the other.

We come to know that marriage is not for the sexual urge only as it could appear at the first instance to teenagers and their like. We cannot, deny this. Sexual desire exists, but it is just a small portion out of the secret that mere words fail to express the true feelings between the pair. It is more so true with the elderly people than with the younger ones. That top secret could be what was meant by the Holy Quran as rest and peace of mind, and love and mercy, mutual understanding, building up the home, as well as society in general. To quote, but a very simple example. When one of the pair is away from the other for one reason or another they both feel that there is something very important missing in their life.

The result of such a holy tie is not to bring up children and the satisfaction of sexual desire only, but consolation, quiet of mind, rest of the soul, love, mercy, mutual understanding, taking ones share in building up the society and the world at large and their advancement, etc.

No Monasticism

Islam encourages marriage. There is no monasticism in Islam. The following verse depicts this in a clear cut way:

> *"Then We caused our messenger to follow in their footsteps, and We caused Jesus, son of Mary, to follow, and gave him the Gospel, and placed compassion and mercy in the hearts of those who followed him. But monasticism they invented—We ordained it, not for them, only seeking Allah's pleasure, and they observed it not with right observance ..."* *(Quran, 57 27)*

The Messenger of, Allah deplored the idea of monasticism forthwith saying: No Monasticism in Islam.

The Prophet (may blessings and peace, of Allah be upon him) told a group of men who tried to do the following; One of them was saying prayers all night long without sleeping, the other used to fast all the time without eating and the third refrained from women, he never married. The Apostle of Allah (peace and blessings of Allah be upon him) told them what it meant: "I heard what you said I am much more pious than you are, but I fast and eat. I say prayers and sleep, and I marry. This is my Sunna (teaching). Anyone who does not follow it is not one of my followers (does not obey me).

The Messenger of Allah (peace and blessings of Allah be upon him) forbids his followers from marrying women solely for their social status or their wealth. There should be a stronger drive than rank and money. He is quoted to have said: "Do not marry women for the sake of their wealth, because wealth might make them haughty and proud."

He who marries a woman just because of her social status or her rank in society, Allah will not add anything more than deterioration and humiliation before the eyes of others. He urges the marriage of righteous women. He is quoted as saying : "If you find a pious woman, (bless your stars) you are lucky."

It is reported that a girl came to the Apostle of Allah complaining that her father forced her to marry a man without her consent. The Prophet (peace and blessings of Allah be upon him) gave her the choice between accepting the marriage or invalidating it. The girl responded: ."I accepted this marriage, but I wanted to let women know that .parents (fathers) have no right to force husbands on them." They must be given the choice of either accepting the marriage or vice versa.

Khaddam, Khansa's father forced her to marry a husband. She did not like the idea. Then she went to the Messenger of Allah (may Allah give him peace) who on his turn respected the girl's wish to marry a man of her approval, naturally the first marriage was made invalid.

It is also reported that the Prophet Muhammad (may blessings and, peace of Allah be upon him) said : "A widow (or a divorced one) is not to be married before her consent is sought." "No virgin girl is to marry without first consulting her, and her approval is her keeping silent."

A Muslim woman cannot be forced to marry without her approval. If she is forced to do so, then that marriage is invalidated.

Both husband and wife have equal rights and claims on one another, except for one thing or one responsibility (i.e., leadership). Islam regards leadership as a natural course in any collective life and it is more consistent with the nature of man.

Islam emphasized leadership in all human life. When more than one person say prayers; they are supposed to select a leader for prayers, who is called Imam.

Aqqaad says in his book, *al-Mar-'a fil Quran* (Woman in the Holy Quran): "..... We find in the nature of the sex physiological composition that one sex-desires while the other accepts. This is found in all animal species that have needs and have sexual relations from time to time.

"When there is a sexual urge from both the male and female; it is not the female that commences the wish and call, nor does she fight the rival of the same sex. This is not because of shyness or shame or because of religious obligations or morale. We find this habit even in male and female animals which know nothing of shame or morale. A female animal does not ask a male, one to have relations. She just draws his attention by passing in front of him, so as he might follow her, and get her at her own free will. A female animal generally waits the result of a quarrel between male rivals to win her."

Quran has the following rule about the family leadership :

> "*....And women shall have rights similar to the rights against them, according to what is equitable; but men have a degree of advantage over them. And Allah is Exalted in, Power, Wise." (Quran, 2: 228) (Abdullah).*

One might ask, "Is the husband, then, much superior than his wife, as he is given such an advantage before the law?"

Our answer is this, "Nothing of the sort, A man has been given a degree of advantage in maintenance and protection because of the natural differences between the two sexes. The sex that we all agree to be the fair and weaker sex shows by its name that it needs some sort of protection, especially in very tense situations. There should be no dictatorship on the part of the husband over the wife. There should be, counsel, understanding and mutual satisfaction in all matters pertaining to family decisions. 'If mutual understanding does not prevail in a Muslim family, then it is the innocent children who become poor victims of such a disintegrated family, and all the consequences of it fall on the society. Hence we have delinquents.'

Let us quote one example from the Holy Quran on the weaning of a child which will serve as a green light. This is more so after a divorce has taken place :

> *"Mothers shall suckle their children for two whole years; (that is) for those who wish to complete the suckling. The duty of feeding and clothing nursing mothers in a seemly manner is upon the father of the child. No one should be charged beyond his capacity. A mother should not be made to suffer because of her child, nor should he on whom the child is born be made to suffer because of his child, And on the father's heir is incumbent the like of that (which was incumbent on the father). If they desire to weàn the child by mutual consent and after consultation, it is no sin for them; and if ye wish to give your children out to nurse, it is no sin for you, provided that ye pay what is due for you in kindness, observe your duty to Allah, and know that Allah is seer of what you do."* *(Quran, 2 :.233)*

While discussing the status of women in Islam; at the coffee lounge after supper; with some of the fellow teachers from different parts of the world, who attended a. Refresher Course on the Teaching of English as a Foreign Language years ago; I remember someone to have put, the following before us :

> *"You must be kidding Eh! You pretend to treat women equally as you do with men; and just now you quoted a verse from, your book in which it was mentioned that a woman's share in inheritance is one half of the man's share, and you still want us to believe in your word. Forget it."*

This followed an uproar: "You can say that again, He is just fooling himself," "I can't agree with you more", etc.

I said, "I beseech you to be patient." After that our discussion was very hot it took us a nearly one hour when I asked them leave to go for Maghrib prayers.

The gist of our discussion from my side was: "It is generally agreed that a man spends one-third of his income on a woman; she, were a wife, mother, daughter or sister or on any other woman. That (a) and (b)-man (husband) is fully responsible for the full maintenance of wife and children. This responsibility is not reduced because the wife is either rich or has an access of any personal income.

On the other hand female is not overburdened with any claims or her possessions, so she is far more financially secure and well off. All her possessions before and after marriage remain hers and are not transferred to her husband. Islam does not ask her to spend a penny out of her income on marriage on her family while she is married. It is upon the husband, whether poor or rich, to maintain her. Islam does not forbid her from her sharing in family maintenance on her own freewill, especially if her means of income are much better than her husband's.

We learn from the above quoted verses that it is advisable for a man who divorces his wife not to ask for what he had given her as a dowry. What a lovely touch to some hard hearted men.

It is also quoted that he said that wives of a lot of people come to his wives complaining against their husbands beating them. He said, "... those husbands are not the beat of you."

It is permissible to flog a wife, as we shall see, but under certain circumstances beating a wife should be the last resort.

Divorce

Christianity waged war against Islam as to the problem of divorce. It used to criticize Islam as breaking the heavenly tie between husband and wife. Finally we see Christians accept the natural call and agree or rather recognize divorce as a social solution to many a family problem.

Western Europe is divided into three different ways of accepting divorce: (1) Nations agree with the idea of divorce but, without bodily separation; some such nations are: Sweden, Norway, Portugal, Romania, Switzerland, Germany and Russia. (1) Nations that accept bodily separation but not divorce. These countries are Spain and Italy. (1) Nations that accept both: divorce and bodily separation. They are France, Belgium, Great Britain, United States of America and some of Socialist States.

The reader might ask: What do you mean by separation?

It is like this: The husband and wife are separated for ever; while the female is still regarded by the society as his wife.

Each of the two has full right of doing, whatever he/she pleases without any interference from the other.

Islam does not only give the woman the right to decide on marriage, but also the right of divorce. In order to protect the family from rush divorce decisions under temporary emotional stress, especially if the partners are still young; certain steps and waiting periods must be observed. We shall discuss some such steps forthwith.

If the marriage contract states that the woman can, divorce her husband without resorting to court and file a case she may do so; otherwise she is asked to bring a good reason in asking why she has to divorce before the judge.

This is more so because a woman generally discharges two types of hormones monthly. These hormones affect her behaviour very much and they may even have an effect on her decisions.

It is reported that the Apostle of Allah (may blessings and peace of Allah be upon him) said something which meant: "What do those people who play with the limits of Allah think? You hear them say: "I have divorced my wife, or I have remarried her? Do they abuse the Book and I am still with you?"

He said this to people who misused the right of divorce.

Marriage is a sacred tie between the two sexes. It should never be misused. If there is an unsuccessful marriage, then they part from each other in accordance with the Shariah (Islamic Law) and not otherwise.

It was customary in Pre-Islamic Arabia that a husband would forswear his wife and decide not to live as husband and wife. He may leave her in such a state of suspense for indefinite period. Sometimes after much consultation he may decide to divorce her. This attitude was still in vogue in the early Islamic period. It was soon suppressed by Islam and reconciliation was recommended, but if both are still determined, then divorce is the only fair solution.

The wife is to stay after divorce for three months and ten days; and for four months ten days if she is a widow; this is called "Iddat" (legally prescribed period of waiting during which a woman may not remarry after for being widowed or divorced) before she can marry another husband whereas the husband, who divorced her, can marry at the same moment. This is so, because of the would be pregnancy. Generally if a woman is pregnant, it is known within the first hundred days of her pregnancy.

A very good step of divorce is shown in the following verse of the Quran:

> *"....so good women are the obedient, guarding in secret that which Allah hath guarded and for those whom ye fear rebellion, admonish them and banish them in bed apart, and scourge them. Then if they obey you, seek not a way against them. Lo! Allah is ever High, Exalted,, Great."*
> *(4: 34)*

The family life should be harmonious If anything goes wrong and there is any misunderstanding; four steps are to be taken to deal with such a situation: (1) verbal advice and admonition, (2) then the family relation is to be suspended, (3) after that slight physical correction (beating slightly) may be administered, and the fourth is a family council to settle the differences if there is any. No one is to lose his/her temper. There should be no nagging or sarcasm, they should speak to each other in other people's presence, nor should they remind each other of their forgotten faults of long ago because such faults have already been forgiven. They must always remember that Allah is always with them.

First the husband; who uses his reasoning more than his emotions; is asked to talk with her gently and explain to her that what she does angers Allah, and nobody can bear it when Allah is angry with anyone. He should find out the reasons of her rebellion and solve the problems if he can.

He is to go with his advice to her for some time. He is to deal with her very tactfully. He should never hurry and act angry with her. This fails, then the family relation (husband/ wife) is to be suspended. He is to banish her in bed apart. He is not to sleep with her in the same bed. He may be with her in the same room. If he can stay with her apart in the same room, that will be much better as a first step.

If he banishes her from bed apart, this will make her feel an infra dig. Feminism is the best and strongest weapon for any woman to attract a man, and make him follow her instructions. If a man banishes his wife, this act will pierce very deeply into the alter of her womanhood; thus the last stronghold of her's will have fallen. Then she might be in a position to listen to what, her husband tells her.

If she still resists, then he is to administer a slight physical correction. He is to scourge her. When he flogs her, he should remember that he is beating his own wife. He should not beat her When he is angry; whatever the cause of his anger could be. The flogging must never leave any marks on her. It should be slight and not very painful.

The Maxim

Spare the rod and spoil the child; stands true to the present time. Psychologists and educationists try to give different thoughts, ideas and arguments all discouraging scourging and beating. They have been trying this for the last thirty to fifty years. What are the results? Too many psychological and neurotic cases that need too many psychological clinics with scores of social workers and hundreds of psychologists and psycho-therapists. You see people being massaged, hypnotised or being given very good pieces of advice which the adviser himself will never practice, and the poor victims, confess under the pressure and torture of suggestion. And, worse still you find people indulge themselves into drugs, alcoholism, fornication, treachery, burglary, piracy, hypism, homosexuality and a hundred other evils that cost a society hundreds of billions of pounds trying to reduce such destructions.

Our daily life is full of reward and punishment. If we misuse our health we become sick and the like. So why for goodness sake do we discourage punishment at school at the same time we punish them when the same people do wrong elsewhere.

May I whisper to Muslim educationists? Islam tells us to teach our children till they are ten years of age. If, they do not follow what we have been telling them all these years, then we are to flog them.

Coming to our fourth point: family council to settle the differences or disputes, between a married couple.

The arbiters will know the facts and if they are all (arbiters and husband and wife) honest Allah will help them to effect a real reconciliation without any publicity or resorting to courts.

We have previously pointed out that man is much more rational than a woman. The, husband-wife relation is of a more emotional character, so Islam gave the man four different steps to deal with his rebellious wife, before taking the last weapon: Divorce.

A woman is much more emotional than a man, and as we have just discussed, the husband-wife relation is much more emotional than any other relationship between different people. So Islam has not much said about how should a wife deal with her rebellious husband. It left it to her (to deal with the situation). She knows very quickly; by her innate nature; the reasons of her husband's rebellion or ill-conduct and she has all those strong weapons at her disposal to deal with such a situation.

Let us cite a good example of how a wife notices the signs of ill conduct or rebellion from her husband.

Hadrat Sawda bint Zamla; one of the wives of the Apostle of Allah (peace be upon him) noticed that her husband (The Prophet) was not so much encouraged to remain with her. Thinking of the problem, she finally came to the conclusion, that it was because of her age. She was very old, or better still; the oldest of all his wives.

She decided on something very serious. She said to the Prophet something like this: "O! Messenger of Allah, I am too old to need a husband. I give my share and nights to Aishah, your youngest and beloved wife. What I want at this stage is to be among your wives in the Hereafter."

6

Islamic System of Divorce

The real purpose of marriage is that both husband and wife should be loyal to each other and lead a pious and chaste life; but sometimes the circumstances take such a turn that dissolution of marriage becomes a necessity.

We have already pointed out that before marriage both man and woman are allowed to make complete satisfaction as to the suitability of their marriage. If after proper investigation both are satisfied, the marriage should be held, otherwise not. This would ensure stability, love and cooperation between the couple. But sometimes the circumstances are such as defy the real purpose of marriage. Islam has framed some balanced rules and regulations to meet this situation. By acting upon them the risk to modesty and chastity can be averted and both husband and wife can lead a life of peace and comfort.

Apparently all the control seems to be in the hand of the husband and the wife is a helpless creature; but it is not so. A woman can go to a court of law in sudden difficulty and prosecute against her tyrant husband. The judge can deliver her from the clutches of her husband and resolve her problem.

It is not unusual that sometimes the husband lacks sufficient strength to gratify the sexual urge of his wife. In this case, if the woman desires separation and the husband is not willing to leave her, she can go to the court of law and bring a suit against her husband. The judge would issue a notice to her husband and make an investigation. If he is found impotent, the judge would order him to undergo a treatment for one year. If he becomes all right, so much the better. If, he remains defective, the judge would revoke their marriage.

Nevertheless, a wife can have a divorce from her impotent husband and can marry according to Shariah, with another man.

How can a woman have divorce from the husband whose sexual organ is cut off and is unable to gratify her sexual urge? She can get separation from her husband in the above manner except that she would not have to wait for even one year. On receipt of petition, the judge would investigate and decide the case in her favour.

The same rule which is applicable to an impotent husband also applies here. If any person by castration renders himself unfit for sexual intercourse, his woman is allowed to go to the court of law and submit a petition against him. The judge would institute an enquiry and give him one year for treatment. If he still remains unfit, the judge would order separation between them.

Although it is permissible to get divorce from the husband if she is afraid that she would not be able to keep Shariah, it is not otherwise permissible to ask for divorce. In Ahadith an incident of "Khula" has been narrated in detail. Habibah hint Sahl Ansari was married to Hadrat Thabit bin Qais bin Shams. At dawn Allah's Messenger (peace and blessings of Allah be upon him) went out for the morning prayer. When he arrived at the door of his house, he saw there a woman who had covered herself up and seemed to be rather frightened. Allah's Messenger (peace and blessings of Allah be upon him) questioned: Who are you? She answered: O Allah's Messenger! I am Habibah, the daughter of Sahl.

Allah's Messenger (peace and blessings of Allah be upon him) asked: What is the matter with you? She said: Neither am I with Thabit bin Qais nor is he with me, meaning thereby that they could not pull on with each other as husband and wife. Allah's Messenger (peace and blessings of Allah be upon him) heard her story and went to offer the prayer. When Hadrat Thabit bin Qais came to Allah's Messenger (peace and blessings of Allah be upon him) he said to him: Habibah Bint Sahl has told me what. Allah wills. She has also agreed to pay the dower money and return her husband's gift; take it. Thereupon Hadrat Thabit took the gift from his wife and their marriage was dissoluted.

It has been narrated in Bukhari that Hadrat Thabit's wife said to Allah's Messenger (peace and blessings of Allah be upon him): O Allah's Messenger! I do not accuse him of bad conduct or religion but I do not like joining infidelity and disbelief with Islam.

When Allah's Messenger (peace and blessings of Allah be upon him) heard this he said: Are you willing to return his garden? She gave her assent. He then said to Hadrat Thabit:

Accept the Garden and divorce her. *(Zad al-Maad)*

The above incident which has been narrated in Bukhari no doubt pertains to Hadrat Thabit's wife; but it was not Habibah, it was that of his second wife, Jamila bint Abi Salul. In Ibn Majah, this incident has been mentioned as pertaining to Jamila.

As a matter of fact, Hadrat Thabit bin Qais bin Shams was a short-statured, ugly and hot-tempered man and no woman could love him. According to some Ahadith, his wife used extremely harsh words against him.

Some other incidents of "Khula" have also been mentioned in Ahadith but we need not go into their details.

One of the critical times for a woman is when her husband is absent and his whereabouts are not known; whether he is alive or not. What should be done by the woman in such a case? We doubt this is a disputable point; but the verdict of the renowned scholars is that a woman should wait for her absent husband for four years. If his whereabouts are not known during these four years, their marriage would be dissoluted after the expiry of 'iddah for four months and ten days. She may marry according to her desire with any man in a legal manner after the expiry of this period. Imam Malik has mentioned the view of Hadrat Umar (Allah be pleased with him):

The woman whose husband is not traceable and his whereabouts are not known should wait for four years and then after the expiry of 'iddah for four months and ten days, she may re-marry. *(Muatta)*

Imam Malik also holds this view. The Hanifites have used verdicts basing their arguments on the above saying. In this connection the names of the writers of Jami al Ramuz, al-Dar al-Muntaqi and Dur Mukhtar along with the Indian scholars, Shah Wali Ullah, Muhaddith Dehlvi and Maulana Abdul Hye, deserve to be specially mentioned. They have supported the above view after giving convincing arguments.

Process of Divorce

The provision of divorce in Islam has a special purpose. If the relations of husband and wife become strained and the efforts to effect reconciliation between them fail so that it is not possible for them to pull on, the husband can divorce his wife.

Before we go into the detail of the rules and regulations of divorce in Islam, it is not out of place to mention here that provision for divorce also exists in other religions. The Jewish law of divorce is extremely flexible. The husband's desire to divorce is considered a sufficient plea to divorce the wife. If the husband wants to have a beautiful wife instead of the one he possesses he can divorce the former. Moreover, divorce can be given for minor defects and shortcomings; there is a defect in the eye, the arm-pit gives an odious smell, there is a limp in the leg or the woman is issueless. The divorce can also be given for defects in conduct and behaviour; if she is hot-tempered, talkative, foul mouthed, avaricious and of rough taste, greedy in eating, etc.

In the Jewish law of divorce men have been given great rights whereas sheer injustice has been done to women as they have been deprived of this right and they cannot demand divorce despite the defects and tyranny and oppression of their husbands.

There was no provision for divorce in the Christian law. Marriage was a permanent relation between the husband and wife; they could not be separated due to any reason. This strictness was based on Christ's teaching:

He whom God unites cannot be disunited. *(Bible)*

Christ's saying was wrongly interpreted by his followers as it implied a moral lesson that divorce should not be given without my genuine reason. It has been mentioned in the next lines:

A person who forsakes his wife, except on account of adultery, and marries a second woman commits sin.
(Bible)

It is evident from the above that divorce can be given if there is a necessity; but the Christian scholars think that this addition and alteration has been made afterwards and some other scholars are of the view that separation would be made between the husband and wife if they are guilty of adultery but the marriage contract will not be revoked. None of the two is allowed to re-marry. You will be surprised to know that among the Christians this practice was in vogue for centuries. Those who believed in divorce, lived solitary lives after divorce. Later on, the eastern churches recommended revocation of marriage in certain laws but the western churches refused to act upon this law. The Christians had to bear undescribable tortures due to this unjust and tyrannical law.

Reformation in Law

In the sixteenth century voice against this unjust law was raised; but it did not prove effective.

In England upto 1857, the court of law did no accept the laws of divorce unless the crimes of adultery and oppression were proved. Even if the crimes were proved, the law caused only separation between the husband and wife; but none of them was allowed to re-marry. Only the court could decide the cases of separation and any one, husband or wife, who desired to get divorce was legally bound to substantiate the charge of adultery against the other. Besides the charge of adultery, the woman had also to substantiate the charge of maltreatment or oppression by the husband. It is also surprising to note that the husband enjoyed legal right to receive fine from the friend of his wife having illicit relations with her as compensation money for playing with her modesty.

In the law of 1866, the court was given the right to make the husband responsible for bearing the expenses of food, lodging, etc., of his divorced wife; but in the law of 1907, the word 'guilty' was deleted and the court could now order the husband to pay the expenses of his wife despite complete separation between them.

In the law of 1898, it was decided that if a woman left her house and began to live separately due to the tyranny and oppression of her husband, the court could disallow the husband to go to his wife but it could demand subsistence for his wife. There was also a provision in this law that if the woman was guilty of adultery due to her husband's maltreatment or indifferent attitude and the husband demanded divorce, the court would reject the appeal of the husband.

In 1910, a Royal Commission was appointed to ponder over the matters concerning marriage, divorce etc., and submit their report. Besides other things, the Commission recommended: Keeping in view the causes and reasons of divorce, there should be no distinction between the husband and the wife, that is, the reasons due to which the husband can get divorce from his wife should also hold good in case the woman demands divorce.

In the law of 1923, it was added that if the husband was found guilty of adultery even once, the woman has the right to get divorce from him.

Thus, the reform now introduced was not only defective, the law itself was devoid of wisdom and prudence. The people did not accept it. In 1930 it was decided: We cannot allow a woman to marry when previous husband is alive. Briefly speaking, if the law of the Jews was liberal, the law of the Christians was stingy with the result that when it gave some relaxation for divorce, there was great rush in the number of divorces.

Once in the civil court of Spain, 294 marriages were revoked in one day. In 1844, when the new law of divorce was passed, 4000 divorces were taken. In 1900, the number of divorces reached 7,500 and in 1913, the number was 16,000 and in 1931 it was 21,000.

In 1922, in the city of Denwar, with each marriage there was also an incident of separation and one suit of divorce was brought in the court of law against two marriages. There was almost the same condition in all other cities of America. Arthur Garfield has written in a treatise: Out of seven marriages contracted forty years ago there occurred only one incident of divorce whereas the recent data shows that out of three marriages in the United Kingdom, one ends in divorce and this number is increasing day by day. When a court of England opened after vacation, four thousand divorce cases were instituted.

In the Days of Ignorance

Men in the Days of Ignorance gave a number of divorces to their wives and then re-established their marital relations. Thus, they tortured them for ages. Hadrat Aishah (Allah be pleased with her) reported that a husband could give as many divorces to his wife as he liked and resume marital relations within the fixed term ('iddah). A man generally gave more than one hundred divorces.

The results of this transgression were alarming. The extent to which it spoiled the moral conduct and behaviour of people can be read in other books. Millions of men and women lost their honour and chastity and had to bear unspeakable tortures due to unjust tyrannical laws of divorce.

In this all pervading darkness the resplendent sun of Islam rose and it gave to the humanity the most balanced and practicable laws of divorce. The oppressed and down-trodden humanity heaved a sigh of relief. The rights of both men and women were safeguarded and no one was deprived of his/her legal right.

Islam has strictly forbidden to use this right of divorce in haste as the matter pertains to two individuals and two families. Despite the fact that divorce is permissible in the Islamic Shariah in the case of extreme urgency, it is said to be one of the most detestable of all permitted things. Islam does not believe in giving divorce on trifling matters.

According to the Fuqaha (experts in Islamic jurisprudence), talaq (divorce) is not allowed except in the case of extreme urgency or when the marital relations of husband and wife are poisoned to such a degree as make peaceful home-life impossible for them or the hatred and enmity are aggravated to an intolerable extent or there exists a real danger to chastity and morality.

If the husband is impotent and lacks sufficient sexual strength to satisfy his wife or is castrated or his sexual organ is defective or cut off, in all such cases it becomes necessary to obtain divorce.

Man, however, reserves the right to divorce. It is an admitted fact that man is more wise, intelligent, farsighted, prudent and tolerant than woman due to the experience gained in the outside worid.

Moreover, he has to bear the major expenses of marriage and pay the dower money. He is also responsible to pay for food, lodging, etc., to women during 'Iddah. If he marries for the second time, he would have to incur all the expenses of marriage for the second time. Keeping in view the heavy responsibilities that lie on him and the large expenditure involved, it is not easy for him to divorce his wife.

A study of all the rules and regulations pertaining to divorce would further reveal that there remain only rare chances of divorce and this provision can be used only sparingly and under very exceptional circumstances.

In the Islamic Shariah the Ahsan (most laudible) way of divorce according to the Sunnah provides opportunity for reconciliation and resumption of conjugal relations, thus minimizing the chances of final separation. Although the divorce is confirmed on pronouncement of three divorces, the pronouncement of three divorces at one time is not considered to be an appreciable act, and is irregular.

A woman is not allowed to marry immediately after divorce. She should wait for the prescribed period. If she is a matured lady having menses, she must wait for three months. If she does not have menses or is an Aisa, (past child bearing) she should wait for three months. If she is pregnant, she should wait till delivery. This waiting for the prescribed period is to purify the womb. It is also necessary for the safety of the child. Moreover, it affords time to the man to reconsider all the pros and cons of the matter before the conjugal relations are resumed in the case of revocable divorce.

We do not want here to discuss all the rules and regulations pertaining to divorce. What we want to impress is that in Islam the law of divorce contains all such measures as are beneficial for the people or are helpful in protecting chastity and morality and saving the women from high-handedness, tyranny and oppression.

A statistical review of divorces has revealed that in the Islamic countries the number of divorces is only negligible which affirms the fact that Islamic law of divorce is full of blessing for the humanity.

Some people are of the view that only the courts should possess the right to decide the cases of divorce. But this view is not correct. It lacks sufficient prudence and farsightedness. To bring such cases to the court and prove the charges of adultery in the public is to spoil the lives of men and women. No one can deny the fact that after discussing such cases in the court, the chances of the marriage of women become rare. Islam detests slandering, back-biting and false allegations and their advertisement in public. A further probe into the matter would reveal that Islam has authorized the Qadi Oudge to revoke the marriage only when there is no harm to declare the allegation openly, for instance, when husband is impotent.

The Islamic law of divorce is beneficial for the humanity as a whole and is a means of protecting public chastity and morality.

If any husband accuses his grown up, pious, free Muslim wife of adultery and takes his case to the court, the Qadi Oudge would ask him, to bring four eye-witnesses in support of his allegation. If the husband fails to bring four witnesses, he would be required to take the vow in the name of Allah four times and say that he is right.

For the fifth time he should say that curse of Allah be upon him if he brings a false accusation against his wife. If the woman is innocent she would have to say four times: By Allah, my husband is telling a lie against me. For the fifth time she should say: Woe of Allah be upon me if my husband be right. This is called lian (invoking curse) in the Shariah.

After the proceedings of Wan according to the Shariah, the Qadi would order separation between them. It has been mentioned in the Holy Quran:

> *As for those who accuse their wives but have no witnesses except themselves; let the testimony of one of them be four testimonies (swearing) by Allah that he is of those who speak the truth; and yet a fifth, invoking the curse of Allah on him if he is of those who lie. And it shall avert the punishment from her if she bear witness before Allah four times that the thing he saith is indeed false. And a fifth (time) that the wrath of Allah be upon her if he speaketh truth.* (24:6-9)

The purpose behind the adoption of this method is that if the lives of both husband and wife are poisoned to a degree that it is not proper to legally bound them to live together as it would further aggravate the situation and turn their lives into a veritable hell, it is better to separate them.

The first incident of Wan occurred in the Holy Prophet's time, the detail of which is given in the Ahadith. Further details can be read in the books on Fiqh.

Islam has promulgated such rules and regulations for protection of modesty and chastity as are applicable to our daily routine life. Every responsible man must keep them in view. A slight lapse on the part of man and woman may result in spoiling their moral conduct and behaviour. Sexual instinct which has been ingrained in the human nature is so savage and uncontrollable that it bursts out at the slightest temptation and ruins the character. Moreover, the Devil has vowed to lead the man astray by all means. He is ever looking for an opportunity to allure him into evil and sin. Islam has therefore, enforced some measures to maintain modesty and chastity before and after marriage.

Shame and modesty are the virtues which save a man from going astray when he is prone to evil. Due to these pious sentiments of shame and modesty, people keep the private parts of their ladies hidden. Nudity is a means of excitement of sexual desire.

Many people of the world led a nude life and many tribes and nations of today go about naked. African countries are notorious for their nakedness. There is no concept of purdah in Europe. Their dresses are practically nude or half-nude. The western monthly and weekly journals print naked/half-naked photographs of women.

Nude pictures are being published in the name of art and health while morality and chastity is cast to the winds. How long man can resist this onslaught of temptation. This moral turpitude has not only ruined the character and moral of the people but also shattered their health. We give below an excerpt from the American Journal which we have taken from the book *Purdah* written by Maulana Maudoodi.

"There are three devilish powers whose triangle has overwhelmed the whole world. They are causing terrible havoc. Evil literature which is being published at an astonishing speed in an alarming large number, movies which not only excite the sexual passions but also give a practical lesson of love-making, moral degeneration of women which is reflected from their dress, their naked and half-naked bodies, their habit of smoking, and their freely mixing up with strangers. These three evils have become a fashion which would ultimately lead to the ruination of western civilization and culture. If proper restrictions were not imposed, our fate would not be different from that of Rome and the other nations who revelled in wine and woman which became the ultimate cause of their ruin."

An Essential Evil

As has been made clear in the previous chapter, Islam never regarded marriage as a sacrament indissoluble except under extraordinary conditions. In accordance with its view of marriage as a contract, it made provision for the separation of married couples if the terms of the contract were not observed by either party. Divorce is the necessary corollary of the freedom given to men and women to choose their partners.

The American authoress of *Male and Female* makes the sensible remark: 'With freedom to choose goes the right to change one's mind. If past mistakes are to be reparable in every other field of human relations, why should marriage be the one exception? If their choice of each other was what made marriage a real marriage, then once either makes another choice, its reality is gone. The spouse who, clings to such a marriage is committing one of the worst acts in the American list of sins, limiting the freedom of another person, exploiting and taking advantage of someone else's past dead impulse, freezing a past mistake into a present prison.'

The idea that there is something essentially and inherently immoral in divorce was bequeathed to the world by Christianity and Hinduism. Its impracticability has been proved beyond shadow of all doubt, so much so that there is now a swing in the reverse direction and the danger of frequent and easy separation of married couples threatens the stability of the home and the family.

According to the Roman Catholic doctrine, a consummated Christian marriage is a sacrament and must as such remain valid for ever. It represents the union between Christ and the Church, and is consequently as indissoluble as that union. It is also permanent according to the law of Nature, because only a permanent marriage can fulfil this object. And God made it so at the beginning of our race, when He decreed that a man shall leave his father and his mother and shall cleave to his wife, and they shall be one flesh. In spite of this doctrine, which never could work in practice, the Roman Catholic Church allowed separation of married couples under exceptional circumstances on the ground of the invalidity of marriage. Lord Bryce has pointed out in his book, *Studies in History and Jurisprudence*, that the rules covering these exceptional cases 'were so numerous and so intricate that it was easy, given a sufficient motive, whether political or pecuniary, to discover some ground for declaring almost any marriage invalid'. A man might secure a divorce by swearing that he was his wife's distant cousin, or had loved her sister in his youth, or had before his marriage stood god-father to one of her near spiritual kindred.

For a long time the doctrine of the Western Church was not accepted in full by the legislators. But since the days of Charlemagne, the canonical doctrine of the indissolubility of marriage has increasingly influenced the legislation of Western countries. It was only during the course of nineteenth and twentieth centuries that divorce was made legal in the Roman Catholic countries in the case of the Roman Catholic marriages. In the United States, South Carolina stands alone in granting no divorces whatsoever. It is the only Protestant community which nowadays holds marriage indissoluble.

The Roman Catholic doctrine of the indissolubility of marriage except by death was never accepted by Protestant reformers. They all agreed that adultery should be recognised as a ground for divorce, and most of them regarded malicious desertion a second ground for the dissolution of marriage. The views of the Protestant reformers influenced the course of legislation in various Protestant countries and laws were passed permitting divorce for a number of reasons. Apart from adultery and desertion, an attempt made by one of the couples on the life of the other is specified in the law of many countries as a legitimate ground for divorce. Ill-treatment of some kind has also been laid down in some countries as a sufficient reason for the dissolution of marriage. In the United States, divorce is obtainable for cruelty. The degree of cruelty necessary is usually actual and repeated violence endangering life, limb or health.

An extremely frequent ground of divorce is the condemnation of one of the parties to a certain punishment or his or her being convicted of a certain crime. In the United States, a husband who is able to support his wife but for a certain time neglects to do so may be divorced. Similarly, in some states divorce may be obtained on proof of the habitual drunkenness of either party for varying terms. In North Carolina, a husband may obtain a divorce if his wife has without good reason refused sexual intercourse to him for the space of twelve months.

Besides offences of some kind or other committed by either husband or wife and entitling the other party to demand a dissolution of the marriage, there are other circumstances recognised as grounds of divorce, which may or may not involve guilt in one of the parties, but in all cases are supposed to make marriage a burden for the other spouse. Impotence in the husband or the wife, existing at the time of the marriage and afterwards, but unknown to the other party, is recognised as a legitimate ground of divorce in some law books. In England it has long been a ground for pronouncing an otherwise valid marriage invalid; and in the United States also divorce is commonly granted for incurable physical incapacity, if the plaintiff was ignorant of the defendant's condition. Other grounds of divorce, according to many law books, are contagious, venereal and other diseases, and insanity which existed at the time of marriage or prior to it with knowledge of the other party, or insanity which has been pronounced incurable or gives no reasonable hope of recovery after three or sometimes five years' duration.

These are the most general grounds of divorce laid down in modern law books. English law is the only one in Europe that recognises none but sexual reason either for the dissolution or the annulment of marriage. The Majority Report of the Royal Commission of 1909 recommended that divorce should, in the future, be obtainable for the following reasons: adultery; wilful desertion for three years or upwards; cruelty; incurable insanity after five years' confinement; habitual drunkenness found to be incurable from the first order of separation; and imprisonment under commuted sentence of death.

Among Western countries, France has made divorce much easier. The 1792 Law of Divorce says that marriage is merely a civil contract, and that the facility in obtaining divorce is the natural consequence of the individual's right of freedom which is lost if engagements are made indissoluble. Divorce is granted on various grounds, among others, on the mutual desire of the two parties, and even at the wish of one party on the ground of incompatibility of temper subject only to a short period of delay and to the necessity of appearing before a family council who are to endeavour to bring about reconciliation.

In 1804, however, under the provisions of Napoleon's Code Civil des Francais, divorce was made more difficult. Mere incompatibility of temper is no longer recognised as sufficient cause for divorce. Marriage may still be dissolved on the ground of mutual consent, but on certain conditions only: the husband must be at least twenty-five years of age and the wife twenty-one; they must have been married at least for two years and not more than twenty-five years and the wife must not be over forty-five years of age; the parents or other living ascendants of both parties must give their approval; and the mutual and unwavering comment of the married couple must sufficiently prove that their 'common life is insupportable to them, and that there exists in reference to them a peremptory cause of divorce.'

The Soviet law goes even further than the French law in granting extreme facilities for divorce. It states that 'the ground for divorce may be either the mutual consent of the parties or the desire of one of them. If the union is not entered in the registry of books, man and woman part without formalities. If they have 'inscribed themselves,' all that they have to do is to 'write themselves out,' that is, record their separation in the books. The law steps in only when there are children and then not to hold the family together but to make provision for children.'

We thus find that the Western world which began with the doctrine of the indissolubility of marriage is now swinging to the other extreme by granting divorce on terms which can be regarded only as frivolous. Even in countries like England and America, where the divorce law is more stringent than in France and Soviet Russia, the number of divorces is increasing at an alarming rate. In the opinion of Dr. Westermarck, 'It is a mistake to believe that the fate of divorces is proportionate to the facility with which divorce may be obtained according to law.' Dr. Wilcox even maintains that 'the immediate, direct and measurable influence of legislation is 'subsidiary, unimportant, almost imperceptible'. With regard to the United States he remarks. It seems that the exceptionally great divorce rates in the United States are largely due to the laxity of procedure that has grown up there.

One wife alleges that her husband has never offered to take her "riding" (driving); another, that he does not come till ten o'clock at night, and when he does return he keeps the plaintiff awake talking. In England, according to the same writer, the removal of a legal obstacle has distinctly increased its frequency. Shortly after the Act was passed in 1925, which gave men and women equality as regards grounds for divorce, the divorce rate began to climb, and an estimate of this increase shows that between 1924 and 1930 an addition of about 35% per year was made to the residual divorces as a result of that Act.

We have already seen that Islam recognises the necessity for divorce in cases when marital relations have been poisoned to a degree which makes a peaceful home life impossible. But Islam does not believe in unlimited opportunities for divorce on frivolous and unimportant grounds, because any undue increase in the facilities of divorce would destroy the stability of family life. Therefore, while allowing divorce on genuine grounds, Islam has taken great care to introduce checks and balances designed to limit the use of- available facilities. Let us study in more detail the Islamic law on this point.

While permission has been given both to man and woman to obtain a release from the bond of marriage in cases of absolute necessity, the Prophet has made it clear that Islam does not regard it as desirable. A tradition of the Prophet states: 'The most repugnant of things made lawful in the sight of God is divorce.' Another tradition says: 'Marry but do not divorce, because God does not like men and women who relish variety in sexual pleasure.'

So far as men are concerned, they have been given liberty of divorce on certain conditions. First, as regards the dower they have bestowed on their wives, they are not permitted to withhold it or take back anything from it, if they decide upon divorce. Secondly, a divorce pronounced at a single sitting does not have the effect of final separation. It is laid down as a condition that a divorce, to take legal effect, must be pronounced three times at intervals of one month each.

There is some difference of opinion as to whether three pronouncements at a single sitting can have the effect of final separation. Most jurists hold that a divorce takes effect if it is pronounced three times even at a single sitting. But Imam Ahmad ibn Hanbal and Imam Ibn Taymiyyah reject this opinion and regard as one pronouncement three declarations of divorce delivered at a single sitting, so that separation does not come of at the end of three such declarations, but only when they are separated each by an interval of one month.

There are strong grounds for supporting the stand taken by Imam Ahmad and Imam Ibn Taymiyyah., In the first place it is obvious that the intention of law in prescribing three pronouncements of divorce separated by fixed intervals of time precedent to final separation was to leave open the opportunity of reconciliation. This intention is defeated by recognising three pronouncements delivered at a single sitting as having the effect of final separation. Secondly, there is evidence to show that the companions of the Prophet regarded this form of divorce as being morally reprehensible and involving the person responsible in a great religious sin. It is recorded that Umar, the Second Caliph, used to punish such persons who pronounced three divorces at a single sitting.

Ibn Abbas, another companion of the Prophet, was asked about a person who divorced his wife in a single sitting. He said: 'The man was guilty of disobedience to divine commands.' Ali is reported to have said: 'If the people faithfully observed the conditions of divorce, no one would feel sorry for the separation of his wife.' In the face of this strong evidence, it is strange that the majority of jurists should have recognised the legal validity of an act which has been universally condemned as being highly sinful and which obviously defeats the Law-giver's intention. The law-makers of modern Muslim communities should not be bound by the legal, decisions of old jurists but should boldly carry out the intention of the original Islamic law.

During the period of the first two pronouncements of divorce, the husband and the wife are required to live together as formerly, so that if the husband has acted hurriedly or in a fit of passion, he may revoke his pronouncement and normal relations may be restored.

Again, if the husband has sexual intercourse with his wife or indulges in the preliminaries of cohabitation, the pronouncement of divorce lapses automatically without express declaration on his part. But, if no such thing has happened and the two intervals of one month each have elapsed, normal relations cannot be restored except by re-marriage. If, however, the husband makes the third and final pronouncement after this period, marital relations are completely dissolved and the divorce is complete. If the husband repents after this and wishes to have his wife again, he cannot do so, except after his wife has been married to someone else and divorced by him too. This provision has been considered necessary in order that it may act as a deterrent for husbands who are prone to act rashly without considering the consequence of their action.

Another condition laid down for husbands intending to divorce their wives is that they should not pronounce the divorce during the period of their wive's menstruation. This condition has been deemed necessary because a woman is liable to become ill-tempered and easily irascible during the period of menstruation. This physical disability leads her sometimes to act and behave in, a manner which she disapproves herself on becoming clean. Another reason for this stipulation is that normal sexual relations between husband and wife are suspended for the time she undergoes her monthly course and sexual relations are commonly the basis of love and amity between husband and wife.

It is possible that a couple may resume their normal attitude to each other and forget their quarrels when their sexual relations are restored after the period of menstruation. There is a tradition that Abdullah b. Umar divorced his wife when she was having her monthly period. His father reported the matter to the Prophet who became very angry and ordered that Abdullah should revoke his divorce and wait until his wife is clean, after which he is free to do as he liked. Another tradition states that the Prophet told Ibn Umar to observe the following procedure in divorcing his wife.

'Ibn 'Umar,' said the Prophet, 'you adopted a wrong method. The right one is that you should wait for tuhr (period of cleanliness), then pronounce a divorce during one tuhr and another during the second. During the third tuhr you should decide finally either to retain your wife or to divorce her.'

So far we have given a brief account of the rights given to husband for securing release from the marriage bond and the conditions he is required to observe. Similar rights have been given by Islam to the female sex. There are two ways in which a woman is allowed to seek separation from her husband: first, through mutual agreement between the husband and the wife which is called Khula; secondly, through a judicial decree by filing a suit against the husband in a law-court. It will be seen that the wife is not at liberty, like the husband, to get herself released by an outright declaration of divorce. In case her husband refuses to release her from the marriage bond, she has to go to a court of law and obtain a decree in her favour.

This may seem to place her at a disadvantage in comparison with her husband and it may be asserted that this implies inequality of rights, as between husband and wife. Actually, the intervention of the State in the matter is a device for the fuller protection of her rights. Conditions all over the world, including even Western countries, are such that a woman is not altogether free to exercise her legal rights. The husband can, if he so desires, place many impediments in her way. If the State does not come to her help in order to safeguard her rights, the woman may find herself handicapped in many ways, despite all talks and preachings; of sex equality. It is, therefore, in her own interest to seek the support of authority in defending and exercising her rights. This was all the more necessary in the past when woman's social position exposed her to greater difficulties.

As in the case of divorce by the husband, the legal permission given to woman to seek and obtain separation through mutual agreement or the intervention of the court does not imply moral approval of the act. Islam has unreservedly condemned men and women who use their legal rights of divorce on any except legitimate grounds and in absolutely unbearable conditions. Thus a tradition of the Prophet states: 'God does not like men and women who seek variety of sexual experience! Again, 'God has showered curses on those men and women who make frequent use of divorce for the sake of sexual enjoyment! A third report says: The Prophet of God said: 'A woman who seeks divorce from her husband, without any excess on his part will be cursed by God and His angels.'

Yet another tradition says: 'Women who make a play of their divorce rights are hypocrites.' These warnings and moral exhortations are intended to discourage men and women from disturbing the stability of family life and resorting to separation except in cases of unavoidable necessity. Moral dissuasion apart, there is no dispute about a woman's legal right to seek separation from her husband. This she may do either by giving up a part or the whole of the dower given her by the husband or by offering an agreed sum of money to her husband in return for his consent to release her from the marriage bond. Thus, both men and women are required to undergo monetary sacrifice for securing their separation. This is likely to act as a deterrent in both cases. Should the husband refuse to part with his wife on any of these terms, it is open to the latter to seek the protection of law by filing a suit against him and obtaining a legal decree of separation.

Actual legal decisions by the Prophet of Islam show the spirit and principles which the law-courts should apply to cases brought by women against their husbands. The most famous case is that of Thabit b. Qais whose two wives sought divorce from him. One of them, Jamilah bint Abi Salul, disliked his features. She came to the Prophet of God and complained against him, saying: 'O Prophet, nothing can bring him together with me. I lifted my face covering to see him coming along with a few other men and I noticed that he is the blackest, the most short-statured and the ugliest of them.' Another report says: She said, 'By God, I don't dislike his morals or behaviour, but, I cannot stand his ugliness.' According to Ibn Majah, she is reported to have said: 'By God, if fear of God did not stand in my way, I would have spit him in his face.' According to the author of *Fath al-Bari*, Jamilah said: 'You see, O Prophet, how beautiful I am, but Thabit is an ugly person.' Bukhari reports that she said to the Prophet: 'I don't blame him for his morals or religion, but I am afraid Islam will lose its hold upon me if I am compelled to live with him.' After hearing her complaint, the Prophet said to her: 'Will you give him back the orchard he gave you?' She replied, 'Yes, and also more, if he wants.' The Prophet asked her not to give more and ordered Thabit to accept the orchard and divorce her.

Another wife of Thabit b. Qais, Habibah bint Sahil, according to a report from Imam Malik and Abu Daud, came to the Prophet early one morning. When the Prophet came out, he saw her standing before the door. On the Prophet's inquiring how she happened to be there, she replied: 'I and Thabit cannot pull together.' When Thabit came, the Prophet said to him: 'This is what your wife says about you, so leave her.' According to Ibn Majah: Habibah complained to the Prophet that Thabit had beaten her so badly as to break her bone in any case, the Prophet, on hearing both sides of the matter, ordered dissolution of the marriage.

During the time of Umar, the Second Caliph, a suit of divorce was brought to him. He advised the wife not to leave her husband and try to pull on with him. The woman refused to do so. Umar put her in a dirty room for three days. On the fourth day he asked her how she had fared. She said that she had real peace of mind only for those three days, whereupon Umar ordered dissolution of the marriage.

These three cases show that the mere fact of a woman becoming disgusted with her husband is sufficient ground for legal separation between them. In the case of Thabit b. Qais, the Prophet showed by his action that a woman's disapproval of her husband on physical grounds is a legitimate ground for a decree of separation in her favour. It is enough for the court to satisfy itself, that one of the partners has developed sufficient antipathy against the other to make reconciliation impossible. The court need not inquire into the detailed reasons of this antipathy, because a woman may dislike her husband on many grounds, some of which she may not like to state openly. There may also be reasons for disgust which may not seem valid to the court or any other arbiter, but which may be sufficient to spoil the marital relations of husband and wife. The court has no right to give its verdict on the point whether the reasons for dissatisfaction as expressed by the wife are valid. All it can do is to satisfy itself on the point whether the dissatisfaction is genuine or faked, whether it arises from causes which are temporary and may disappear or it is so deep-rooted as to preclude the possibility of happier relations being restored.

It is also inadvisable for the court to inquire whether a wife seeking divorce is doing so because she is sexually erotic and desires a variety of sexual pleasures or her aversion to her husband springs from genuine causes. The right of a man to divorce is not limited by the condition that he should not use it for satisfying his anarchic sexual desire. If this is so in the case of a man, it applies equally well to women who have got equal rights. Moreover, if a woman is really disposed to be sexually anarchic, the mere fact of being unable to obtain a divorce from a law-court will not prevent her from forming illicit unions, and in such a case the court, by refusing a decree of separation, will be supplying an incentive to illegitimate sexual activity, which is morally and socially more reprehensible than a frequency of divorces. The effect of a court decree in favour of separation is the same as that of the final divorce pronounced by the husband which dissolves the marriage finally and irrevocably. The couple cannot be remarried unless the woman marries another husband and gets a divorce.

As regards monetary sacrifices involved when a woman seeks divorce from her husband, it has already been stated that the husband cannot claim more than he has already given his wife as dower. If the separation comes of as a result of mutual agreement without the intervention of the court, the amount has to be settled between the two partners. But if the dispute is brought to the court, the latter can decide what portion of the dower should be returned by the wife, whether the full amount or half of it or one-fourth, etc. Many jurists agree that if separation takes place as a result of the ill-treatment of the husband or his excesses, and such charges are proved during the process of legal inquiry, the court can totally exempt the wife from repayment of the dower, or it can decide in favour of an amount less than that of the dower, according to the circumstances involved. Some jurists are also of the opinion that if the court is satisfied that the wife has no legitimate grounds for seeking separation and is merely the victim of anarchic sexual impulses it can order her to pay more than her dower.

Apart from cases of ill-treatment and genuine aversion of wife against the husband, Islam recognises other grounds of divorce also. These are: (1) option of puberty; (2) refusal to provide economic sustenance; (3) change of religion; (4) impotence; (5) infectious diseases in either partner; (6) wilful desertion; and (7) disappearance of husband.

The Quran has given some importance to the opinion of the guardians in the case of a woman's marriage, but it has not withheld from her the right of final acceptance or rejection. Actual legal decisions by the Holy Prophet show that while a woman is bound to consult her guardians, she is not under any obligation to abide by their advice. Abu Daud, Nasai, Ibn Majah and Imam Ahmad ibn Hanbal have reported a tradition from the Prophet stating that a girl complained to him saying that her father had given her in marriage against her will, whereupon the Prophet told her that she was at liberty to repudiate it. Nasai has given a report from Khansa' bint Khidhan that her father married her to a man whom she did not like. On hearing her complaint the Prophet gave her option to retain or repudiate the marriage.

Sunan Daraquod, another collection of traditions, contains a report from Jabir, one of the companions of the Prophet, stating that the Prophet ordered the dissolution of a marriage which was performed against the will of the wife. Nasai further gives a tradition from Aishah, the Prophet's wife, stating that a girl was married by her father against her will, whereupon she complained to the Prophet. The Prophet gave her liberty to repudiate the marriage. On hearing this, the girl declared: 'O Prophet, I accept the decision of my father. I wanted only to show to other women that their fathers' decision is not final.' Muslim, Nasai, Abu Daud and Muwatta also contain the following tradition: 'A woman previously married has a greater right than her guardians to decide her choice in marriage, while permission of a virgin should be sought in regard to her marriage.' Another report from Abu Hurairah says: 'No woman who has been married once should be remarried until she gives her permission; similarly, a virgin should not be married until she declares her consent.'

In the face of these traditions, the question arises: What is the position of minor girls married by their guardians or parents during their minority; are they free to repudiate their marriage on attaining puberty? Most of our old jurists give the option of puberty to the minor girls only in cases where they have been married by guardians other than their fathers or grandfathers. But if the marriage has been arranged by the father or the grandfather during the minority of the girl, they maintain, the girl is not at liberty to repudiate the marriage, except when it has been proved that the father or the grandfather is a man of loose character or that he is reputed to be a man of careless disposition. No precedent or authority has been quoted by the jurists for making an exception in favour of the father and the grandfather as distinguished from other guardians. Their opinion is obviously based on the presumption that the father and the grandfather, being the well-wishers of their family, cannot act against the real interest of the minor. This presumption for which no authority has ever been quoted from the Quran or the traditions of the Prophet is open to the following grave objections.

First, a very authentic tradition of the Prophet states that he gave away the daughter of Hamzah in marriage to Umar b. Abi Salama while she was still a minor and declared that after she reach reached puberty, she was at liberty to repudiate the marriage. Here the Prophet did not make any exception in favour of any guardian, nor did he specify it as a reason that because he was not the father or the grandfather of the girl, therefore she had the option of puberty. He made a general statement covering all cases. This shows that even a minor girl married by her father or grandfather has the option of puberty. Secondly, it does not stand to reason that a girl who has reached puberty should be given the right of final choice, but a minor girl should be refused the same right. If the presumption is that the father and the grandfather cannot act in disregard of the real interests of their lineal descendants, it should apply to both grown-up and minor girls. Thirdly, the presumption itself has a very frail basis.

There are innumerable cases where a father or a grandfather has not consulted the best interests of his descendants in deciding their future. Fourthly, even if the presumption be valid, it is quite possible that the husband of the minor girl may prove unworthy after he has grown up or he may develop habits and aptitudes ruinous to the health and happiness of his wife. For all these reasons the stand taken by the old jurists appears untenable and since the Muslims are not bound by the decisions of any person or persons except those of the Prophet, there is no reason why the Muslim law should not be amended in accordance with the spirit and principles made explicit by the Prophet in his own legal decisions.

In case a husband refuses to provide-economic sustenance to his wife, there are two courses open to the court. If the husband is able to make provision for her needs, but does not do so, the court can bring pressure to bear on him and force him to look after the needs of his wife. Should the husband still refuse, the court can issue a decree of separation and the marriage will be dissolved thereafter. In case the husband is absolutely, unable to provide for his wife, dissolution of the marriage should come about instantaneously, according to the school of Imam Ahmad ibn Hanbal. In the opinion of Imam Shafii, three days' time should be given to the husband, while Imam Malik would give him one or two months.

Conversion of either partner to any religion (other than Islam) leads automatically to the dissolution of the marriage, because Islam does not allow a Muslim woman to enter into marriage union with a non-Muslim. The only exception in this case is when a Muslim woman is converted to Christianity or Judaism. In such a case the husband can retain her in marriage because Islam allows Muslim males but not Muslim females to contract marriages with the members of the Jewish and Christian communities.

If the husband is impotent, the wife can obtain a decree of separation from the law-court. But in cases where the impotency is not constitutional and incurable, one year's time may be allowed to the husband for undergoing treatment. If he regains his potency during this period, the marriage cannot be dissolved. The medieval jurists have, however, laid down the following conditions which cannot stand rational scrutiny and do not agree with the spirit and intention of Islamic law: (1) That a decree for separation is eligible only if the wife was ignorant, prior to marriage, of the impotence of her prospective husband. (2) If the, wife was ignorant of the fact but consented to retain her marriage when she came to know of it, she cannot demand separation later on. (3) If the husband, after treatment, is able to have sexual intercourse even once, the wife loses the right to demand separation.

These conditions are very unfair and destroy the intention of the marriage and divorce laws, for the object of marriage in Islam is to provide a stable family life and to prevent the formation of illicit sexual unions. Both these objects are defeated if the conditions laid down by the older jurists are given legal sanction. If a woman foolishly commits herself to marry a man whom she knows to be impotent, it is just possible that she may repent her action somewhat later when she knows by experience what association with such a person means. It is a very heavy punishment to poison her whole life for a single act of misjudgment or folly. It is enough if she has to forgo her dower as a result of her separation.

The same is true of a woman who comes to know after the marriage that her husband is impotent but, out of sentiment or natural nobility of mind, consents to live with him. It is quite possible that later experience may render her disconsolate or she may be unable to bear a long period of sexual abstinence. If she is afraid that the continuation of marriage would expose her to sexual temptations which she may not be able to stand, she is perfectly justified in claiming separation. To refuse a legal decree on the ground that she had earlier consented to the continuation of marriage is to drive her to sin. But marriage is intended to safeguard men and women from sin and not to force them into situations where they find no alternative except to disregard their faith and conscience.

In regard to infectious diseases and other noxious ailments, there are three classes of opinions among the older jurists. One class of jurists holds that neither partner can demand separation on the ground of noxious or infectious disease in the other partner. Ali and Abdullah b. Masud among the companions of the Prophet, and Imam Abu Hanifah and Imam Abu Yusuf among the jurists, belong to this school of thought. The other school holds that in all diseases which prevent sexual intercourse between man and woman, such as lunacy, leprosy, venereal diseases, etc., either party has full right to demand separation.

This is the opinion of the Maliki school. Imam Shafii says that lunacy and leprosy entitle a husband or a wife to demand separation but not venereal and other diseases. Of these three schools, the opinion of the second school is more in accord with the spirit and principles of the Holy Quran. According to the Quran, the two essential factors in healthy marital relations are: the safeguarding of sex morality and the maintenance of love and compassion between husband and wife. Both these factors become non-existent in cases where the husband and wife develop antipathy against each other owing to physical causes. Where there is the slightest danger of either party failing into sexual aberration due to continuance of marriage, it is much more advisable to dissolve the marriage rather than expose the partner to the risk of sexual promiscuity.

In regard to the right of a wife to demand separation when her husband is missing or has disappeared, there is considerable difference of opinion among the religious scholars. The Quran as well as the traditions of the Prophet are silent on this matter. Among the companions of the Prophet, Umar, Uthman. Ibn

Umar and Ibn Abbas are of the opinion that the wife should be ordered to wait for a period of four years., Ali and Ibn Masud, on the other hand, hold the opinion that the wife should wait until the husband returns or the fact of his death is ascertained. Imam Abu Hanifah and Imam Shafii have expressed the same opinion.

Both these opinions seem to err on the side of caution and involve manifest wrong to the wife. They are also opposed to the principles of the Holy Quran. For example, in permitting conditional polygamy the Holy Quran has stated clearly: 'And you have not in your power to do justice between wives, even though you may covet it, but be not disinclined from one with total disinclination, so that you leave' her as it were, in a suspense' (iv. 129). Again, in enunciating the rules of conduct for the persons intending to divorce their wives, the Quran says: 'And when you divorce women and they reach their prescribed time, then either retain them in good fellowship or set them free with liberality, and do not retain them for injury so that you exceed the limits, and who ever does this is unjust to his own soul' (ii. 231). Further, in the case of husbands who swear not to go near their wives, the Quran says: For those who swear that they will not go in to their wives should wait for four months, meaning that such sexual abstinence should not last more than four months. If the husband does not break his oath after this period, the wife is entitled to ask for separation.

These three verses show that the Quran does not allow a husband to hold his wife in suspense for more than a limited period. How then is it permissible to keep a woman waiting not for months but for years, simply because no trace of her husband could be found? During the caliphate of Umar, there was a very striking incident which throws further light on the spirit in which such cases should be dealt with. It is said that while Umar was carrying out his nocturnal vigil, he heard a woman singing erotic verses in which she gave expression to the unbearable pain of separation from her husband and added: 'If there were no God, this bed would not be empty of a male partner.' Umar found, on making inquiries, that her husband was fighting on the war-front. He came home and asked his widowed daughter how long a woman could bear the pang of sexual abstinence.

After some hesitation she told him that six months was the maximum period. Umar at once ordered that no soldier should be sent on war for a period longer than six months. After six months of active service, every soldier should be given compulsory leave to return home. If it is recognised that a woman cannot forgo sexual enjoyment for a period of more than six months, why should it not be applied to cases of missing husbands? How can the wife be forced to wait for four years or for a longer period if such compulsion is likely to drive her into the quagmire of sin, and who is going to provide for her needs during all this period? Obviously the demands of elementary justice and the principles enunciated by the Holy Quran have been ignored in this respect. It is for these reasons, probably, that the jurists of all schools have adopted the rules laid down by Imam Malik which are more liberal and involve less hardship to the wives of missing husbands. According to Imam Malik, three situations may arise requiring separate decisions:

(1) If the missing husband has left no property wherewith the wife may provide for her needs, the court shall immediately order dissolution of the marriage and set the wife free for marriage with another man. The Shafii and Hanbali schools also agree to this rule as, in their opinion, failure to provide economic sustenance to the wife is itself a sufficient ground for the dissolution of the marriage.

(2) The husband has left property but the wife is so young that she cannot be expected to bear sexual abstinence without running the risk of sin. In this case the court can fix a period of one year or six months or even a smaller period, within which the wife will have to wait for the return of her husband, after which the marriage will be dissolved. In urgent cases the court may order instantaneous dissolution of marriage. It is not necessary for the court to force from the wife an express declaration of her inability to withstand sexual temptation. It is the duty of the court to come to a judgment on this point after studying the situation.

(3) The husband has left property and there is also no danger of the wife falling a prey to sexual temptation. In this case the following steps have been recommended:

If the missing husband was lost in a Muslim country or in another civilised country having diplomatic relations with Muslim countries, the wife will be asked to wait for four years and the Government will order a search to be made for the man.

If he was lost in a war, a full search should be made, after which the wife should be ordered to wait for one year.

If he was lost during a local civil commotion, a full search should be ordered after the completion of which the marriage will be dissolved without further waiting.

It would appear that even the Maliki law, which is followed now by all schools, leaves room for hardship. Six months is the reasonable maximum period for which the wife can wait. No further delay appears reasonable keeping in view the injunctions of the Holy Quran.

Opinions differ as to what would happen if the missing person is found after or without a search. Umar holds that if the husband returns before the wife is married to another person, the wife should belong to him, but if she is already married. The former husband loses all rights on her, even though her second marriage may remain unconsummated. Imam Malik has adopted this opinion. Ali, another companion of the Holy Prophet, however, was of opinion that the wife belongs to her first husband, whether she marries and has children or remains unmarried, If the marriage has been consummated, the wife is also entitled to her dower from the second husband. The Hanafi school has adopted the same rule.

According to Uthman, the Third Caliph, the returning husband will have the option to take back his wife or leave her and have his dower repaid to him. If he is willing to take back his dower or remit it to his former wife, the wife will be left with the second husband. Otherwise, she will be separated from her second husband and ordered to wait for a period of four months, after which she will become the wife of her first husband. Moreover, she would be entitled to receive her dower from the second husband.

The above is a general picture of the rights given to women by Islam for demanding separation from their husbands. As will be seen, Islam has maintained more or less absolute equality between man and woman in this regard. There is no doubt that man enjoys a greater degree of freedom in this respect, because he has no need to resort to a court of law. But we have also explained the circumstances which made this restriction necessary in the case of woman. In fact, there are so many ways open to a woman to secure her freedom from an unhappy marriage that if she fails on any one ground to obtain a decree in her favour, some other ground remains available to her and the court can hardly refuse a decree of separation to a wife who has determined to seek separation.

Major Problems

One of the objections raised against the Islamic Law of divorce is that in empowering man to divorce, Islam has been harsh and unjust to the woman. It depends entirely on the will even whims of man to divorce her and whenever he likes he can cut her off from himself on any trivial issue. Thus, the future of a woman becomes dark and she finds herself compelled to spend her days without any support.

The horrible picture of divorce presented, is firstly not to be found anywhere. Secondly, divorce is the only proper and reasonable solution to the many familial disputes and complications. It is an undesirable fact that at times it becomes impossible for man and woman to live together under the marriage tie and they are dead set on getting rid of each other. There can be many reasons for it. At times the temperaments are in total non-conformity and at heart they are not prepared to accept each other. At others their intellectual and educational levels are not the same and in spite of closeness a feeling of distance keeps them miles apart. In yet other situations the social and economic differences between them are so wide that the gulf cannot be bridged. They clearly appear even to the casual observer belonging to two different social strata—two definite classes alien to each other.

On some occasions such degrading moral weaknesses reveal themselves in either party that there is neither hope of reform nor can one put up with them as a sore in the side. In all such situations it is the demand of common sense that they should part quietly without much ado. If the society like that of Christianity, does not permit peaceful separation and they are compelled to go on living under the same conditions, the purposes for which they had come together under marriage-tie shall never be served. There are certain detriments associated with this state of affairs: Firstly, the woman shall become a burden to man and he is most likely to mete out the worst treatment, he can, to her. Secondly, after divorce woman can get a match suiting her temperament and other conditions, thus entering a better phase of life. By closing the door upon divorce this possibility will be eliminated. Thirdly, the domestic life of a conflicting pair at loggerheads under the same roof becomes hell for them both and their peace of mind departs. Fourthly, in a state of constant quarrel and tension the progeny cannot receive the attention it deserves. They shall grow up without any social and moral training and become the quarrelsome children of quibbling, quarrelling, intolerant parents.

Let us now take up the question who should be endowed with the right of divorce? There are three alternative answers to this query. The first option is that both should enjoy it. The second is that the husband should be so empowered. And the third option can be that the woman should have this right.

In the first instance, if both have the right of divorce, the plethora of divorces shall make family life uncertain and insecure. In the case of both exercising their right there will obviously be a much larger number of "casualties" than with only one armed with this weapon to sever relations. It is an admitted fact that a society with lesser number of divorces has a better and much more secure familial order. With frequent and free use of this right the organization gets disrupted. The West has vested it in both the parties with the result that the wedlock in the Western society has become a joke. Whichever of the parties concerned, whenever it likes can exercise his or her right of severance of conjugal relations and part. The frequency and number of divorces has shaken the foundations of the family and the society as a whole.

The second option is that adopted by Islam. It has vested this power in man for the reason that he enjoys a little more dignified position in the family. He is the supervisor of the family, maintainer of the wife and with that bears the heavy burden of the children's upkeep, education and training. Therefore, it is he who should decide whether it is possible to bear the burden of these responsibilities in collaboration with the wife or not? In the Quranic terminology "in his hands has been placed the power to tie the marriage knot (contract) or untie it." (Al-Quran 11 : 227). It would be harsh and unjust to compel him to go on maintaining a woman as the queen of the mini-realm, home, whom he does not like or whose cooperation has been denied to him.

It can hardly be asserted with conviction that armed with this weapon he will make use of it indiscreetly since it is he who will suffer in that case. He cannot demand return of the dower endowed upon her. If not already paid, he will have to pay it now after separation.

The ornaments and other gifts given to her, are her property and she will take it with her. And all that he spent on the occasion of marriage and on her while she was with him, he cannot claim. In case of a second marriage he will have to pay the would-be wife her dower, bear the expenses of marriage once again and undertake all the accompanying responsibilities. Moreover, he will be burdened with the upkeep of the children by the first wife (now divorced). Those objecting to man's right to divorce are living in an imaginary world, not one of hard facts. Perhaps they do not have time to give the issue a serious thought. But a person having all these problems before him, will have to think twice before divorcing one wife and bringing in another to embellish his house afresh. Rehabilitation after evacuation is not such an easy job !

Taking the third option in which woman will have the right to divorce, it is apparent that abuse of the right shall not be eliminated. If man through exercise of the right can harass woman, the possibility of its improper use at her hands and putting man in serious trouble by creating critical situations and factual calamities cannot be ruled out at all.

In bestowal of right upon her, there are some evils associated with it also :

1. It would be grave injustice to man to make him bear all the responsibilities of the woman (dower, gifts, maintenance and the like) and to grant the right of divorce to her.

2. Divorce is damaging to man entirely whereas the woman remains immune from any harm. If the right is granted to her, a morally irresponsible woman, whenever she chooses, she shall divorce the husband, and handing over children to him, she will take leave of him with the "booty" of her dower and jewelry and gifts in full triumph, and at the first chance coming her way, she will marry another man getting fresh dower and other paraphernalia.
3. It is an obvious fact that woman is much more sentimental than man and can any time under impulse of the moment sever relations with man. That will go a long way in mounting the ratio of divorce under normal conditions confronting the society with a new crisis.

The way suggested to wriggle out of this difficulty is that whichever party, husband or wife, who wished to loosen the bond and get freedom, should approach the competent court requesting separation. If it is satisfied that the reasons put forth are sufficient cause for it, it may legally separate them. And failing that their request be turned down.

The evil attendant upon it is that whichever of the couple is desirous of divorce, to satisfy the court not content with stating the factual shortcomings and excesses of the opposite party, will overstep to freely (with an easy conscience) charge him or her with false accusations. The rejoinder is sure to result to retaliation in a 'bigger way', which will bring them morally to a very low level in the sight of the society from which degradation, they can hardly recover. The family honour and prestige would have been dragged into mire leaving it, as the laughing stock for people.

Again, our courts in general are notorious for their lethargic pace in handling cases before them. They may take ages in administering justice to the couple that is "up in arms" and heaven only knows how they are going to put up with (suffer) each other under the same roof so long. The other aspect of this issue is that if the court decides against them refusing separation, they must remain tied together under severe compulsion of circumstances, making life most miserable, almost insufferable, for them, without even a distant future promise of pleasant time.

Moral Instructions

The way Islam shapes the mind and temperament of man and educates and trains him, divorce can hardly find room in his life and the lurking fear that merely for sexual enjoyment and gratification of abnormal lust he will go on divorcing women most carelessly is only a remote logical possibility. The moral instructions of Islam in this behalf, a faint idea thereof, is being given below:

> *According to Islam, man and woman through nikah do not come together for a brief span of "good times" but enter a life-long contract of the closest relationship and comradeship. This contract has been termed by the Quran a solemn covenant (Q. IV: 21). The person who seriously enters this trust does not easily commit breach of trust. Only one who does not realize its importance and makes such a serious agreement, can be guilty of playing this joke. The Prophet S.A.W. has declared joking (non-serious attitude) in the matter of nikah unwarranted (most improper), since it negates the seriousness which is the demand of this affair. Abu Hurairah R.A.A. reports the Prophet to have said: There are three things in which seriousness has its own reserved place, but even things said and done in joke shall be taken seriously (to be binding on him). And they are nikah, divorce and turning back upon it.*

Imam Khattabi says :

> *The Ulama have consensus on it that a major sane person's divorcing his wife is effective legally as divorce. If he, calling it a joke, wants to nullify this earlier pronouncement of his, it will not be accepted. Some of the Ulama are of the opinion that such a joke (in the serious matter of divorce) is just like playing and joking with the Quranic verses, since if it is condoned it will mean that a person after divorcing his wife or emancipating a slave can take back his earlier declaration saying that he was joking (not divorcing his wife or freeing a slave in real earnest). In this way there is every likelihood that divine injunctions may not be obeyed at*

all. Therefore, all that has been mentioned in this tradition, any statement made about them will make it binding on him to act on them, not willy-nilly but with determination.

Extremely Undesirable : Islam certainly allows divorce in need, but also pointed out that it is not a desirable act, rather, one of the most undesirable acts in the sight of Allah. Therefore, recourse to it should be had only when compelled by circumstances beyond control. Abdullah Ibn-e-Umar reports the Prophet S.A.W. to have said : In the sight of Allah, the Exalted, among the permitted things, the most undesirable is divorce.

Maharib bin Wasar R.A.A. reports the Prophet S.A.W. to have said : Allah has not permitted any thing more unwholesome than divorce.

A tradition with a similar import has been reported by Muaz. Although weak in authority but corroborates the two foregoing reports. The Prophet has been reported to have said : O Muaz ! Allah has not created anything more pleasing to Him than the emancipation of a slave. Similarly, he has not created anything more offensive than divorce.

On the one hand, it was impressed on the mind of man that divorce is a disagreeable act and on the other, instructed the woman not to make demands for divorce unnecessarily. Thauban R.A.A. reports the Prophet S.A.W. to have said : The woman who makes demands on man to divorce her without offering a compelling reason for it, even the fragrance emanating from heaven shall be denied to her (as unpermitted).

Collective life is not subservient to any individual. One has to sacrifice his will and personal opinion on any issue in the collective interest. In conjugal life too there are occasions when the opinion of the husband and wife conflict. However, it should not be allowed to develop into an issue of an erroneous notion of prestige with either party that they may jump up to a serious decision like separation. There are moments when sentiments and impulses of the moment overwhelm him and he fails to have the least consideration for any opinion other than his own and much greater interests are lost sight of. Islamic teaching in this behalf is that in view of the much wider expediency and important interests relating to the familial life, trifling errors of thought and judgment must be over-looked magnanimously and an attitude of love and benevolence should prevail. The Quran says :

> *Live with them on a footing of kindness and equity. If ye take a dislike to them, it may be that ye dislike a thing and Allah brings about through it a great deal good.*
> *—Al Quran IV:19*

Attempt at Reform : Even if the woman is lacking in obedience, is headstrong and not listening to reason, Islam does not allow decision on divorce. Man has been vested with discretionary powers so that he may try his best to improve the worsening situation through an agreeable blend of strictness and allowance (sufferance) so that the domestic affairs are amicably settled inside the sanctum (home) itself and not noised abroad. Divorce should not come for consideration in these petty domestic quarrels. Allah, the Exalted admonishes thus in the Quran:

> *As to the woman on whose part ye fear disloyalty and ill-treatment, admonish them (first), (next) refuse to share their beds, (and last) beat them (lightly) : But if they return to obedience, seek not against them means (of annoyment) : For Allah is Most High, Great (above you all).* *—Al Quran IV: 34*

To bring a woman, disobedient and headstrong, to terms and to reform, the Quran prescribed in the first stage to try to create in her fear of Allah's displeasure and the retribution of the Hereafter, drawing her attention to the mutual obligations and rights of husband and wife as well as the expediencies of the situation in the family perspective. All this can be achieved with tenderness and polite manners.

If the primary measure fails in bringing her round, the Quran goes a step further in stern handling and advises the husband to segregate her from the conjugal bed, meaning cessation of sex activities in various degrees. The companions of the Prophet and those following them or Tabieen, have given these different versions of this stern admonitory step. Let them share your bed but abstain from copulation. Even while sharing your bed, turn your face away from them, keeping mum, to demonstrate your displeasure. And the third and final stage is that you do not allow them to share the bed with you but sleep in a separate bed.

This is a psychological measure and a person can adopt it only in case he has sufficient control over his passion. However, if he is capable of that much self-control it is mostly to bring the woman to see reason and behave properly. Sex is a very headstrong passion and if man has a strong will-power of self-restraint, the woman cannot go far in keeping herself in check.

There may, however, be some whom this course of treatment may fail to cure. In such a situation man has been allowed to resort to corporal punishment also. Now, this measure appears rather too harsh and uncivil to adopt in dealing with the fair sex. But it has been allowed only after the first two have proved totally ineffective and the woman persists with her churlish behavior and disobedience. This is the last resort when nothing appears to avail. Secondly, the Prophet S.A.W. has forbidden hitting hard, not to cause a wound or disfigurement in any way and hitting the face is to be avoided at all costs. Abdullah Ibn-e-Abbas R.A.A. has made it only symbolic, advising to strike with a miswak (tooth stick). Qatadah R.A. and Hasan Basri R.A. advise against causing disability and a strike leaving a scar.

As against this corrective measure, if somebody beats up a woman like a barbarian, the Islamic law shall come to her rescue and duly punish the tyrant. Imam Nawawi says that even if a light corporal chastisement causes her death (it will be deemed murder by mistake) the husband (and his family) shall be liable to pay her blood-money, and the atonement for murder by mistake shall become due from the husband alone.

On the one hand Islam has repeatedly stressed it on man that he should be generous to woman, recognizing her rights and overlooking her mistakes, look to her redeeming features and reform her in the matter of her infirmities and shortcomings. On the other side it advised woman not to make frequent demands for divorce. If she notices carelessness and neglect on the part of the husband towards herself she should not only give up demands and insistence on her rights but should be prepared to forgo some of them. Instead of confrontation with the husband she should try to live in peace and amity with him as far as possible. In receiving some allowance from the wife the husband's pride is likely to be hurt. So if the wife makes some allowance in her demands on him, he should not feel slighted or insulted. Help in some way from the wife and his benefiting by it is in no way degrading to him.

Allah says:

> *If a wife fears cruelty on her husband's part there is no blame on them if they arrange an amicable settlement between themselves. And such settlement is best, even though men's souls are swayed by greed. But if ye do good and practice self-restraint, Allah is well acquainted with all that ye do.* —*Al Quran, IV: 128*

Hafiz Ibn Katheer says that if a woman fears that man is nursing hatred for her and showing signs of remoteness, she can forgo all the rights of her maintenance, his stay with her during the night, or reduce such days to a minimum. There is no harm in man's agreeing to such an offer and coming to be at peace with her. The wife can spend on her husband and he can accept her offer. The Quran says that their coming to terms of peace and amity is better than separation.

At times differences and conflicts arise out of mere trifles which develop gradually, becoming vehement, creating sort of remoteness and segregation between them. At this stage they are no more in a position that forgetting their quarrels and quibbles they can come to reconciliation by themselves. The Quran directed that in a situation where the principal parties concerned cannot remove their differences, their trustworthy seconds as arbiters, one of either side, should put their heads together and try to sort them out. If they undertake it with sincerity and good will, Allah's help will be there with their efforts and who knows the apparently irreconcilable affairs may somehow be resolved and peace may reign there once again :

> *If ye fear a breach between the twain, appoint two arbiters one from his family, and the other from hers, if they seek to set things right, Allah will cause their reconciliation. For Allah hath full knowledge, and is acquainted with all things.* —*Al Quran IV: 35*

Having failed in all attempts to join and keep joined, divorce presents itself as the only solution to the tangle. Islam took two initiatives by way of reform : In Arabia of the days of Jahiliyah or pre-Islamic period there was no such check on divorce and revocation. The person intending to harass his wife, divorced her, revoked before the expiry of the term, again divorced and revoked and continued with this nasty joke with her as long as he liked. In this way a woman with a husband and all, was compelled to do existence as a divorcee. The Quran put a ban on indefinite number of divorces and revocations declaring that one can divorce only twice and revocation is allowed with only these two.

> *A divorce is only permissible twice; after that, the parties should either hold together on equitable terms, or separate with kindness.* —*Al Quran 11 : 229*

Repeating it a third time shall deprive man of revocation and wife shall be separated from him automatically. A person could harass his wife benefiting by the right of even these three divorces, divorcing her for long terms. For example, divorcing and not revoking for a year or two and revoking later if he was so pleased. Similarly after divorcing a second time he used to keep her in suspense for a long time, neither meeting his obligations to her, nor separate her, and finally when fed up with her, he did divorce her a third time to throw her out at last on the dung hill. To render this mischief ineffective Islam fixed a short term within which man will have to decide about revocation or abstaining from it. This is called 'iddat' in Islamic terminology. Once it is over she is free from the bondage to marry again wherever she is pleased. The Quran directed that account must be maintained after divorcing. It is nothing to play with, divorcing and forgetting it:

> *O Prophet ! When ye do divorce women, divorce. them at their prescribed periods.* —*All Quran LXV : 1*

Divorce is possible after one has gone into the wife and before that stage also. In case of divorce after consummation her term of waiting shall be the period taken by three menstrual cycles. Allah says :

> *Divorced women shall wait concerning themselves for three monthly periods.* —*Al Quran II : 228*

This term is fixed for a young (menstruating) woman. Those not menstruating, past this age or in prepuberty stage or diseased, for them the period of waiting is three months. For a woman with a gravid uterus, the term is until she delivers her burden. Allah says :

> *Such of your women as have passed the age of monthly courses, for them the prescribed period, if ye have any doubts, is three months. For those who have no courses (it is the same). For those who are pregnant their period is until they deliver their burden.—Al Quran LXV : 4*

If divorced before being touched they have no period of waiting. Allah says :

> *Oye who believe! When ye marry believing women, and then divorce them before ye have touched them, no period of iddat have ye to count in respect of them. So give them a present and release them in a handsome manner. —Al Quran XXXIII : 49*

Islam has certainly permitted divorce but desires that it should not be exercised without giving it a serious thought. One should decide it sincerely and after due deliberation. It would be reasonably justified when there is no way out of the difficulties experienced by one or both the parties. To safeguard against carelessness in this matter, we will have to adopt the method prescribed in the traditions. We are guided here by two instructions.

Divorce during the period of monthly course of woman has been prohibited in a tradition of the Prophet. The reason is obvious. Although a normal physiological function, the woman is not her carefree, cheerful self during the period, and the husband is not so close to her as in normal days, a stern measure is most likely, for tempers in many cases are short.

All the six most authentic compilations of traditions known by the collective name of "Sihah" carry reports to the effect that when Abdullah Ibn-e-Umar R.A.A. divorced his wife during her period, he was ordered by the Prophet to revoke. He was directed to divorce her in a state of cleanliness without going unto her (so that pregnancy can be eliminated in counting , iddat'). The other thing stressed in the Hadith is that man should divorce his wife during the period of cleanliness without cohabitation. This should be a single pronouncement. This, if necessary, may be repeated after the period and also without intercourse. A third repetition under the same conditions and he is finished with her.

The protracted process of divorce mentioned in the Hadith has many aspects of wisdom and expediency. The first discretionary consideration is that the interval between the two periods is a guarantee against pregnancy. But cohabitation during this period can once again create a position of uncertainty and therefore, ban on intercourse if divorce is contemplated.

So many other complications would arise if she becomes pregnant under these conditions. The other psychological point is that when she is clean and approachable both are keen for sexual union and patch up their differences, if any, forgetting some and forgiving others. But once the passion is gratified, lack of lust and attraction towards her, her attitude of benevolence and indulgence may change. Hence the stress on abstinence.

This is rather a difficult job, a trial, long enough to tire the patience of man, and possible only in case of a firm resolution on separation. The Hanafite school of jurisprudence is of the opinion that divorcing a menstruating or pregnant woman, at intervals of one month is in keeping with the Sunnah of the Prophet S.A.W. Cohabitation is not barred in their case. But Imam Zaffer of the same school opines that in case of sexual union even with them he will have to wait for another month for divorce.

The woman not consummated may be divorced during her monthly course. The Sunnah does not make demands on divorcing her in a state of cleanliness. Imam Zaffer differs here too, saying that she should also be divorced during the period of cleanliness. The Quran has ordained that for the period of her iddat (waiting) she shall stay at the husband's house, barring cases of immodesty which make such stay unpleasant, even impossible.

Allah says:

And turn them not out of their houses, nor shall they (themselves) leave, except in case they are guilty of some open lewdness. —*Al Quran LXV : 1*

The underlying wisdom here is that living under the same roof man may be inclined to revise his decision and the woman to change her attitude, and who knows they may become indulgent to each other and become reconciled to live together as husband and wife after revocation. Acting on all these instructions together is likely to reduce possibilities of undue haste and heedlessness in divorce. And if even in spite of failure in the first and second stages divorce becomes imminent, man may yet have a chance to review his earlier decision and opt for revocation.

After divorcing once or twice before the expiry of the term the right of revocation can be exercised. If pronounced in unequivocal terms, revocation will take effect, there being unanimity on it. Imam Shafii says that revocation should be verbal. According to the Hanafite school, kissing, embracing and copulation also indicate it (in a practical form). Imam Shafii insists on witnesses to the pronouncement of revocation. But the Hanafites call it only desirable and preferable. Imam Malik too is of the same opinion.

After one or two pronouncements of divorce if man does not revoke within the specified period, parting of husband and wife becomes effective just after the expiry of the iddat. However, if man is desirous of their reunion and the wife too is willing, they can come together through nikah with a fresh mehr. But in case the wife does not consent to such a union, it cannot be thrust upon her. If a person divorces with a third and final pronouncement following the earlier two, their separation is Complete and remains disallowed unless the woman marries another man and gets divorced or widowed. Then alone she can enter wedlock with the former husband to whom she is now allowed.

Allah says :

So if a husband divorces his wife (irrevocably) he cannot, after that, remarry her until after she has married another husband and he has divorced her, in that case there is no blame on either of them if they reunite, provided they fee/ that they can keep the limits ordained by Allah. Such are the limits ordained by Allah, which He makes plain to those who know.

—*Al Quran 11 : 230*

This lengthy procedure makes reunion after three pronouncements of divorce a tedious job. Man's unsullied nature too abhors it. This rather severe check has been put on it so that the person intending to indulge in it heedlessly may have a chance to give it a serious thought before a hasty decision. Reunion may not always be possible even after adopting the prescribed course. At this stage a question arises here that if a person instead of divorcing in three intervals of cleanliness or once every month, pronounces all three in one breath as an outburst, shall he be entitled to the right of revocation or they shall be deemed irrevocable.

According to the generality of the jurists, three at a time make the divorce irrevocable and the person guilty of it shall stand deprived of his right of revoking as under the normal course. The jurists of the Ahl-e-Hadith school take it under the revocable category. Now this is a subject of debate between them and other groups of jurisprudence. However, there is a general consensus on it that this is a serious violation of the Prophet's Sunnah and highly undesirable. The Hanafite Fiqh has coined a term "The innovative divorce" since it is in direct contravention of the Sunnah. According to them the nice way to do so was to pronounce divorce only once and if the iddat passes off, at least there is a chance of reunion through nikah anew. They say that the companions of the Prophet S.A.W. never divorced more than once. (Those intending to make it final for separation can let the iddat pass and that is the end of the whole affair).

Three divorces in a single sitting are generally the outcome of momentary anger or any other disagreeable incident difficult to put up with. There is no cool calculated decision behind it. The erroneous and accidental step results in serious consequences, and the person concerned witnesses the ruination of his one time happy and peaceful home. His lamentation and grief cannot avail him aught. The remedy lies in the way of the Sunnah which is free from all complications. Divorce at times becomes inevitable. But the Islamic way is the safest way and must be taken to the ignorant masses as the remedy of this social evil. Its general adoption will also remove the objections levelled against the abominable practice.

KHULA

Some people would like the woman also to have the same right, of divorcing the husband which he enjoys. If she wants to get separation from the husband, there should be no restrictions on her and she may go her own way whenever she is pleased. According to them, "Islam has not been unjust to the woman with the right given to man of divorcing a woman, it has granted to her in turn the same right in the form of Khula". They take it for granted that if the woman returning to the husband the dower received by her, takes leave of him the act of Khula' is complete (and she is free). That means they believe Khula' to be the declaration of breaking the marriage tie or nikah on the part of the woman, no matter how the husband takes it (accepts or rejects it). This is a manifestation of their ignorance of the nature of Khula'. Here we would like to clarify its nature under the Islamic jurisprudence.

From the point of view of the Islamic Shariah through the agency of marriage tie or nikah the woman becomes the property of man (known technically as the proprietary right by virtue of nikah). Obviously enough this state of ownership can be used or be nullified only by man and the woman has nothing to do with it. Khula' only means that taking substance from the woman man may give up his ownership. In the well known Arabic compilation on lexicon, Qamus, it has been defined thus :

To nullify the ownership by virtue of nikah in return for the substance offered by the woman, no matter who pays it, she herself or someone else. Now taking up the opinions of the jurists Allamah Kamal-ud-din Babarti, after its lexicological definition has given its definition in the Islamic Shariah in these words: In the Islamic Shariah Khula' means to take the substance from the woman in return for ownership rights enjoyed by virtue of nikah, using the word Khula'.

Allamah Ibn-ul-Hummam says: To bring to an end the proprietary rights in return for something with the word Khula'.

About the word Khula' it has been said : Absolute use of Khula' will be taken to be divorce for something in return.

These are the expositions in the Hanafite Fiqh. In Maliki Fiqh too Khula' has been interpreted as divorce against something in return for it. Qadi Baizawi Shafi'i says : Apparently it is divorce since in separation the man has his say. In this way it becomes divorce for something in return. This makes evident enough that Khula' is also a form of divorce. It is a fact that Islam has endowed man only with the right to divorce and also exercise Khula'.

Not for Woman's Exploitation

One of the objections raised in this connection is that man in using his right of Khula' can exploit woman. If he wants to get rid of her, he would not divorce but tyrannize her so much that she may, at last, be compelled to pay him her substance for her speedy riddance. But this objection does not hold water since it is the firm principle of the Shariah that nobody can take any one else's substance by force. The woman's substance is her possession and property. If she gives it to her husband it will be permissible to him. But taken away from her by force against her will in the name of Khula' or on some other pretext, will be strictly forbidden to him. Allamah Ibn Jareer Tabri says : The husband's taking away the substance of his wife by force or to cause her grief and pain, so that she compulsively agrees to part with some of her substance as the return for her freedom from the bondage of the husband's ownership is strictly prohibited to him, be it silver weighing a grain of barley or more than that. Rather, he also goes on to say that if the man tries to snatch her property by wrongful means, she should try to evade him as much as she can. Succumbing to devilry without resistance will make her guilty.

Allamah Rasheed Raza Misri writes : To take something from the woman is permissible and in as much as, she gives it to him of her own free will and he on his part has not caused her grief or hurt for its possession.

Now let us take up the expositions of the jurists : The Hanafite Fiqh says that if the man compels the woman to accept Khula', divorce will be effective, but he will not be allowed the property of woman since the fair deal in this behalf is on the basis of mutual agreement and not under compulsion.

Durrul-Mukhtar says : If the husband compels the woman, the divorce shall be deemed to be in order without any part of her substance, since payment of anything from her property or nullification of her mehr is conditioned by her willingness.

The same thing has been said in Maliki Fiqh that if the woman were to sue him in a court of Law that she had to agree to Khula' since he was relaxing her, and she was being hurt in a way which justifies obtaining divorce, she can take back her substance given to the husband provided she produces evidence to prove his oppression and tyranny. For evidence it is enough to hear from the people living in the neighbourhood that they constantly heard that she was being tyrannized. If it is the case of an eye-witness two men would bear witness or else the woman would declare on oath her claim, with one man or two women to support it at the court. For eye-witnesses even one observation is deemed enough. Rather, it has been said that even if the man pronounces Khula' on condition that the woman would not furnish proof of his compulsion and tyranny, she can still come up with that proof after Khula'. However, divorce under Khula' is irrevocable.

Imam Shafi'i, Imam Ahmad and others regard such a Khula' false and ineffective. Ibn Qudamah, a Hanbalite writes that if somebody were to tyrannize his wife, beat her and deprive her of her maintenance as well as the night-stay with her, to compel her to consent to Khula', such a Khula' shall be deemed ineffective and her husband will have to return her property. The same is the opinion of Imam Shafii, Ishaq and Rahawaih and others.

Islam has introduced Khula' for the reason that if the man is guilty of excesses or the woman does not like him due to his irremediable faults, she may obtain her freedom in lieu of her property. It is not meant for the tyrannizing of woman at the hands of a despot of a husband. Where such a situation arises she can sue him in a court of law and the Islamic Law will come to her rescue.

Among the multiplicity of opinions on this issue, a section also demands that the powers of enforcing Khula' must be vested in the rulers so that in the presence of reasonable grounds for it, it may be pronounced through a competent court whe·eas in case of dissatisfaction with them due to their inadequacy it may be refused. This opinion was there among the ancestors also.

Hasan Basri R.A. says: Khula' can be pronounced only by one in the seat of authority and rule without which it cannot be permissible. Muhammad bin Sireen R.A. too has quoted it from 'the antiquity.' Later, Abu Ubaid too has adopted it. Their argument rests on the Quranic authority.

> *If ye (judges) do indeed fear that they would be unable to keep the limits ordained by Allah, there is no blame on either of them if she gives something for her freedom.*
> —*Al Quran 11 : 229*

At another place it has been said :

> *If ye fear a breach between them twain, appoint two arbiters, one from his family and the other from hers;*
> —*Al Quran IV: 35*

In these Quranic injunctions, apparently the husband and the wife have not been addressed but it is the rulers and the administrators that when they fear violation of the divine limits at the hands of the husband and the wife, they must come forward to bring them to terms or else affect Khula' between them.

But according to the general consensus of opinions on this issue among the jurists, intervention and decisions on the part of the government are not called for. Qadi Shuraih, Imam Malik, Imam Shafi'i, Imam Ahmad bin Hanbal, Ishaq bin Rahawaih and the Hanafites are one on this opinion. The following arguments have been put forth against the opinion of Hasan Basri R.A. and others :

> *This is an isolated opinion while the great majority is against it. Qatadah says that Hasan Basri has adopted it from the governor of Iraq of the Muawiyyah regime, Ibn Ziyad. According to Hafiz Ibn Hajar, Ziyad does not enjoy the status (in religious matters) that his opinion be accepted for pursuit.*

This opinion means that Khula' will be in order only in case there is tension and tangle between the husband and the wife, whereas it is not essential. Khula' may be allowed merely on the dissatisfaction and displeasure of the woman against her husband. We find in the reports that the wife of Thabit bin Qais R.A.A.

wanted to be separated from her husband due to the extreme disagreeableness of his. When she brought it to the notice of the Prophet S.A.W., he told her to return the date palm grove given to her by Thabit bin Qais R.A.A. as her mehr, ordering at the same time Thabit bin Qais to divorce her, after taking back that date palm grove. He did not ask him whether he too had any grievance against her.

Like divorce Khula' too is the right of man. Just as he can divorce his wife without the permission of the ruler, he can also exercise his right of Khula'. The right granted to him by Allah, he cannot be divested of it in favour of some one else. It would be wrong to do so. In a deal of Khula' man takes something in return for the release of woman. The ruler's permission is not required in such deals, return, sale or purchase.

The decision of the general consensus is also supported by the actions taken by Umar and Uthman R.A.A. Imam Bukhari says : 'Umar allowed Khula' without intervention of the authority and rule. Its details are to be found in the report of Abdullah bin Shahab Khaulani. He reports that during the Caliphate of 'Umar somebody had a deal of Khula' with his wife, he (Umar) allowed it as valid.

Rabi bint Muawwiz and her uncle came to Abdullah bin 'Umar Rabi' told him that during the Caliphate of Uthman R.A.A. she obtained her release from her husband, and when the Caliph Uthman R.A.A came to know about it, he raised no objection. Abdullah bin Umar R.A.A. too did not regard it improper, saying that the iddat for a mukhtaliah (separated by Khula') is the same as that for mutalliqah (divorced).

Urwah bin Zubayr says that some body arranged Khula's with his wife during the Caliphate of Uthman R.A.A., he allowed it as permitted. That makes it amply manifest that Khula' is a matter between the woman and the man and any intervention in it on the part of the government or inviting it to intervene at any stage would not be proper.

THE MAINTENANCE

One of the objections levelled against the Islamic Law of divorce is that man's mere pronouncement of the word 'divorce' throws the woman out of his house and she finds herself helpless, at the mercy of the society. This objection is very old and carries little weight. But it is repeated again and again as if it were a great challenge to the Islamic Shariah which has nothing to say in its support. Its hollowness has been made evident time and again. But those whose main objective is to hurl stones of objections only at the opponent, without ever listening to what he says, can never own their weakness and no explanation can satisfy them. They want that accepting their objections, the flaws in the law of the Shariah should be removed and thus it should be set right. According to them, the highest punishment that must be imposed on the person guilty of divorcing his wife is that he should be compelled to go on paying her maintenance charges life-long.

However, in case of her second marriage or her own employment and self-support the husband may be released from that imposition. The recent verdict of the Supreme Court, has in a way, declared this objection justified and has given legal sanction to the proposed demand of maintenance for the divorcee to be life long or her second marriage. So we feel obliged to take up this problem in some detail.

If a person were to demand that his economic responsibilities be transferred to an utter stranger will either take it to be a joke or that he has a cracked nut, because for such transfer of one man's burden to another, there must be some basis. There is no such basis to be found between two utter strangers. According to Islam one of the bases on which rest responsibilities is nikah. After entering the tie of wedlock the woman devotes her time to meet the wide-ranging demands of the conjugal life, applying her capabilities and energies to it. In return for this man undertakes the responsibility of her maintenance. The responsibility lasts so long as they are bound together by the marriage tie. Divorce snaps this tie and the man on his part is released from this economic cooperation.

A certain remoteness and alienation creep in between the two. If the divorce is irrevocable, the alienation is so vehement that it becomes easier for the woman to wed another man and for the man to wed another woman rather than reunion of these two persons estranged by divorce. In case they want to unite once again, it is the demand of the Islamic Shariah that before that woman should wed another man and he divorces her or dies. Without adopting this tedious course they cannot revert to their former relationship of husband and wife, their wishes notwithstanding. Where divorce generates such alienation and remoteness, taking them farther than utter strangers, who is to impose whose rights on whom and who is to undertake the responsibilities of whom?

It comes to divorce between husband and wife only when they are negligent in the matter of their responsibilities and do not recognize the rights on a mutual basis. When it comes to this there is hardly any cooperation and partisanship in the domestic life. Non-cooperation and conflict come to stay. But divorce is usually talked of as it is an excess, a tyranny on the part of the husband, and the woman has nothing to do with it. Whereas it cannot be ruled out that the woman might have created conditions, compelling man to divorce her. In spite of all that, imposing the maintenance of woman on man for the life time is a grave injustice to him, having no legal or moral justification.

After divorce and separation, the woman may not be prepared to cooperate with the man, likewise man naturally is desirous of throwing away the burden of his responsibilities relating to her. If even after divorce the economic responsibility of the women remains resting on him, abstaining from divorce could be more useful to him. Instead of divorcing and yet remaining burdened with woman's responsibilities, he would prepare to keep her suspended without divorce, depriving her of all her due rights. Some people take it for granted that a suspended woman can also demand her maintenance through legal action. But it has to be borne well in mind that it is not so easy to have one's rights relegated to him through legal procedure. The other consideration should be that man would like to escape from it and there are so many outlets for him. Thirdly, where does the wisdom lie in making divorce so difficult just by imposition of maintenance of the divorce that a person for, fear of payment of the upkeep of the wife may abstain from divorce, keeping her suspended. To perpetuate one mistake, committing another is not at all reasonable.

After divorce both man and woman are at liberty to choose another partner for themselves, thus filling this void created by divorce. But if even after divorcing her he has to bear the burden of the divorcee, the husband can hardly venture on a second experiment in matrimony. Compared with the total expenditure of the divorced woman and the new wife, he would rather think of and decide on a life of celibacy. This is most likely to make him morally corrupt and inclined to a career of dissoluteness.

There is an equal chance of the woman taking to the disagreeable and prohibited paths. If the woman is assured of her maintenance on a regular basis, even after divorce, she may be inclined to play the role of the naughty girl and vexing the husband off and on and prompted to get divorced. That is why we find that one of the promptings to divorce on a large scale is the wife's surety about the regular receipt of her maintenance from the husband all her life. Islam regards the tendency to divorce wrongful. It cannot support any rule or regulation which promotes this tendency in which every minor unpleasantness is sought to be removed through divorce.

There is another aspect also to it. Divorce alienates man and woman. Through continuance of maintenance, this estrangement is mitigated, wounds caused by separation gradually heal, meetings start becoming frequent with time, and display and declaration of familiarity and love are also on the increase. Since there is no bashfulness between them in the matter of sex relations, this recent familiarity and frequent meetings take a wrong direction. Maintaining a situation which is likely to lead to moral turpitude can never be condoned.

A rejoinder to this effect is possible that direct contact between them can be prevented by proper arrangement of intermediation. But in so far as they live in close neighbourhood this will be difficult to ensure. Very untoward consequences have been witnessed. So often they start living together as husband and wife as of old. And the society also is indulgent in this abominable affair. The demand of the temperament of the Islamic Shariah is that such conditions should never be created for any one that help and promote his advances towards dissoluteness, almost oblivious of his direction of approach. These are some of those social evils and complications that spring from declaration of the compulsive payment of the divorced woman's maintenance. It is not easy to overlook and carelessly brush them off as mere whims.

Some people earnestly desire that life-long maintenance of the divorcee could somehow be traced to the Quran. But the difficulty is that the Book of Allah is not at all prepared to even humour them on this issue. In case of divorce, problems of woman's dower, maintenance and iddat or waiting present themselves. The Quran and the traditions of the Prophet have definite injunctions in this regard. The only thing missing here is the incessant maintenance of the divorced woman. We have discussed mehr earlier in these pages. There are four different situations relating to payment of mehr :

- Mehr is fixed and consummation also a certainty, full amount of dower falls due to woman.
- Mehr is not fixed but the husband has gone unto her, entitling the woman to a dower rife in her family.
- Mehr fixed but no consummation. The dower due is just half of that payable after consummation.
- And in a case where there is neither fixation of mehr nor proper privacy (copulation), the woman will get mata' or some sort of parting gift from the husband.

The Iddat : Iddat (Idda) has been specified by the Quran.

In case of divorce after consummation iddat is the term of three periods. —Al Quran 11 : 228

It is only three months in all those cases where menses are absent either due to early age, prepuberty, or advancing senility or menopause. —Al Quran LXV: 4

And there is no iddat for a woman who has been divorced before consummation. —Al Quran XXXIII :49

Now taking up the problem of maintenance and lodging :

Divorce is of two types—revocable in which the husband has the right of revocation and irrevocable in which that right of the husband comes to an end. The laws relating to both are in brief like this : In case of revocable divorce, the jurists are unanimous on it that the woman is entitled to both her maintenance and lodging. They are one here also on the issue that when the woman is pregnant, she gets both board and lodge regardless of the nature of divorce-revocable or irrevocable. The Quran says :

And if they are pregnant then spend (your substance) on them until they deliver their burden.

—Al Quran LXV: 6

If the woman is not pregnant and the divorce is irrevocable Imam Ahmad, Daud Zahiri, and Abu Thaur with some others are of the opinion that neither her maintenance nor lodging is due from the husband. They take their cue from the report about Fatima bint Qais. She says: "My husband divorced me irrevocably. The Prophet S.A.W. pronounced on it, 'you are not entitled to maintenance from your husband now'." In another report the word 'lodging' accompanies 'maintenance'.

Imam Malik, Imam Shafi'i and some others are of the opinion that since the Quran has mentioned 'lodging for her' she will get it but no maintenance.

—(Al Quran LXV : 6)

Ibn Rushd, a Malikite, declares it (Maliki opinion) weak and vascilating. The Hanafite school appears to have a strong stand.

The Hanafite school and some other Ulama opine that irrespective of the nature of divorce the woman will get both the maintenance and lodging, their argument being that since the Quran has expressly mentioned lodging the maintenance naturally follows, being an accompaniment of (some body's stay). The Quran has made it binding on the husband to provide lodging for the term of the iddat, her support too naturally falls due on him; lodging makes maintenance inevitable. The diction of the Quranic verse supports the arguments :

Let the woman live (in iddat) in the same style as you live, according to your means : annoy them not so as to restrict them. *—Al Quran LXV: 6*

Jassas says that the words of the Quranic verse are general in nature covering both the revocable and the irrevocable. The words "according to your capacity" point to the fact that lodging in the property of the husband has been made compulsory. This naturally demands the right of maintenance also (equally) compulsory, since lodging is a part of maintenance. And over and above the instruction that "she should not be annoyed to restrict her," means that annoyance and restriction are just as much applicable to maintenance as they have been said about the problem of lodging.

The report about Fatima bint-e-Qais has been rejected on the plea that Umar R.A.A., the second rightly guided Caliph, did not accept it, saying :

> *"For the sake of a woman's statement we cannot abandon the Quran and the Sunnah of the Prophet S.A.W. Allah alone knows whether she remembers it (right) or has forgotten it, there is lodging as well as maintenance for the divorcee.*

That means according to Umar R.A.A., the Book of Allah and the Sunnah of the Prophet both allow lodging and maintenance both to the divorced woman.

It is evident now that on the basis of this authority that the maintenance and lodging of the divorcee is binding on the husband for the term of her iddat, but nothing after that.

The Mata : Those who try to prove the maintenance for the divorcee by the Quran argue with the support of the Quranic verse 11 : 241.

> *For divorced woman is a suitable gift. This is a duty on the righteous.* —*Al Quran II : 241*

It is argued from this verse that it makes payment of *mehr* and *mata'* compulsory. After divorce so long as she lives, she should get this mata' to subsist on. The Quran has mentioned mata' but not specified it, leaving it to popular usage. That means it can be made definite according to the custom of any particular age. According to these advocates, if this mata' is fixed in the form of maintenance for her life-term or until second marriage, it would be according to the dictates of the Quran and not in contravention of it. Its payment may be in a lump sum or in installments (according to the convenience of the parties) but pay he must. This quaint sense of mata' is neither supported by the Arabic lexicon nor the context of the Quran, nor the companions of the Prophet, their followers (*tabieen*) and the jurists of the Muslim Ummah take it to mean maintenance. To understand fully the sense of this word mata' or mutaah in which it has been used in the foregoing Quranic verse the following questions will have to be considered carefully: 1. What is mata'? 2. Is it moral or legal in nature? 3. If legal, is it so for every divorced woman in general or some particular ones?

Literally mata' means petty personal effects and also things serving some purpose only for a brief span of time. Zahri says : Mata' literally means something that can be utilised beneficially.

Imam Raghib says: To derive benefit for a short time is mata'.

He further goes on to say : Every thing from which benefit of any sort whatsoever can be derived is mata' or mutaah.

Imam Razi says: Mutaah and mata' is in fact something that serves and benefits but not for long (transient).

The word mata' has been used in the Quran to denote various utility articles—things of daily use in houses, for instance. The strangers have been directed to borrow the articles of daily use in the following manner:

> *And when ye ask (his ladies) for anything ye want, ask them from before a screen. —Al Quran XXXI 11: 53*

Metallic substances such as utensils and implements :

> *Even so from that (ore) which they heat in the fire to make ornaments or utensils therewith, there is a scum like wise. —Al Quran XIII : 17*

In Surah Yusuf (Q. XII : 79) it has been used for a bowl or a measure and at another place it has been used for the hunter's tackle and personal effects and in Surah Maidah (Q. V: 17) it has been used for water game. Similarly, among with these things of meagre importance, all those useful articles and substances supporting life, have been termed mata'. The Quran says :

> *"....On earth your dwelling place and your means of livelihood for a time. —Al Quran 11 : 36*

The entire world with all its paraphernalia, gold, jewels and articles of luxury and comfort, has been called mata'.

> *....(and also adornments of gold). But all this was nothing but enjoyment of the present life : The Hereafter in the right of thy Lord is for the Righteous.*
>
> *—Al Quran XLII : 35*

Here, compared with the life Here after, the worldly existence has been termed mata'. What is meant is that in keeping in view the life-eternal. Hereafter, and the bounties of the Benevolent Lord, this world and its riches and luxuries appear 'Mata'-e-Qaleel' (very little or almost nothing).

> *But the life of the world is but little comfort compared to the Hereafter.* *—Al Quran XIII :26*

At another place it has been said :

> *But little is the comfort, as compared with the Hereafter.*
>
> *—Al Quran IX: 38*

Now let us see what the mata' of divorce means? The Quran has ordained mata' of divorce as absolute without any conditions. It has not been specified what is meant by mata'. It evidently means that even if it is regarded compulsory, giving anything of any value whatsoever, after divorce, fulfills this demand.

The scholars who have laboriously investigated the true sense of the words used in the Quran and the traditions of the Prophet, do not for a moment take it to mean that maintenance is to be paid to the divorced wife life-long or she may be supported for a specified period even. According to them it means that she should be presented with some gift to please or console her in her grief. Imam Raghib who is a linguist of high standing where Quranic terminology is concerned, says about mata-e-Talaq : Whatever the husband confers on his divorced wife to be benefited by, is mata' or mutaah.

That means he regards the maintenance during the period of iddat mata' and does not consider her entitled to any other mata'. (The opinions of the jurists a little later).

An expert lexicologist of the diction of Hadith, Allamah Ibn Atheer, has given exposition of the term "mata'-e-Talaq" in these words: It is desirable for the person divorcing his wife that at the time of parting of ways he should give her some sort of gift.

Allamah Suyuti has prepared an abridged edition of Ibn Atheer's book on the lexicon of the Hadith. He says in it : Mata-at-Talaq is simply this that the woman be given something to console her in her grief.

The context in which the Quran has mentioned it also devotes the purpose behind it. It has said that:

> *The woman divorced before consummation shall be entitled to half her fixed dower, and the one with dower unfixed shall get only mataor a gift.*
>
> —*Al Quran 11 : 236-23*

Now, if the dower does not mean life-long maintenance, how can mata' come to mean life-long support of the divorcee? The word mata' cannot be taken to mean maintenance for a life-term for two reasons:

1. The Quran has specified that after divorce the maintenance and lodging of the woman shall be the liability of man for the term of the Iddat and there it ends. To make it binding on man after the expiry of the iddat for the life-time of the divorcee or her second marriage would be an addition to the divine injunction which is highly objectionable. The liability from which he has been declared free by Allah in view of so many considerations to over burden him once again with the same would be a wilful disregard of those considerations.
2. We have discussed earlier in detail that the responsibility of the wife's maintenance in return for her services to the household devoting her time and energy to run it efficiently, and after divorce since she is relieved of that duty and the man has no more claim over them she too cannot claim support any longer, not to say for the duration of her life or her second marriage.

Views of the Jurists

The jurists have tried to pronounce upon it according to the circumstances extant then. The Hanafite school recommends for the divorcee a change of clothes (usually a three piece suit) but left to the prevailing trends of the times. The standard and quality of cloth will depend on the husband's life-style and standard of living. Another group opines that the standard of life of both the husband and the wife shall be taken into consideration. The Hanafites, besides, have consensus on it that mata' cannot exceed half the 'mehr-mithl' since it is in lieu of it, and not less than five dirhams either, since according to the Hanafite school the minimum of dower is ten dirhams. If it is taken to be half of the dower in vogue, it can be more than the cost of a change of clothes.

In Malikite jurisprudence it has been said that after divorce whatever a person gives to his wife in keeping with his financial status is mutaah. Imam Shafi'i has specified mutaah thus : For a man of substance a servant and for a person of the middle class a change of clothes. The minimum that can be prescribed for it is thirty dirhams or something of that value. And the husband and the wife have the right to any agreement on more or less than that. More or less the same point has been made by the Hanafite school, that mutaah shall be that which man's status permits. The higher standard of it is a servant and the minimum is a change of clothes that can suffice her for her prayer (a three piece suit including a sheet). The husband can endow her with more than that at will and the woman can accept less than that if she is so pleased.

The Jurists have tried to fix mata' according to the then existing conditions and adjustments can be made under changed conditions in a particular age. The Quran and the Hadith have left mehr and nafqah (maintenance) unfixed, so has mutaah remained unspecified, depending on the conditions through the ages. The difference of opinions among the companions and the tabieen, Allamah Abu Bakr Jassas has opined on it : The quantum of Mutaah stated are the *ijtihadi* opinions of our ancestors. The opinion of one man was not questioned by another since he himself held a. different opinion of his own. That shows they were their own considered opinions (ijtihad). According to some jurists, the social and economic status of woman shall not be considered in fixation of mutaah since the Quran has declared that:

The moneyed shall endow mutaah according to their means and the poor according to their means.

—Al Quran II : 236

But the more agreeable opinion is that in apportioning mutaah consideration will be given to the status of both. Jassas says that sticking to maroof (pious popular opinion) has been stressed and over-looking the status of woman is against maroof. How can a lady of an affluent family be treated like a poor common woman in the endowment of mutaah? The foregoing discussion makes it amply evident that mutaah is the outfit gifted to a divorcee as a mark of sympathy and to console her in her grief. Trying to enlarge its scope and stretching it to life-long maintenance is an excess that cannot be expected of any serious and reasonable person.

Let us now take up the question whether mata' enjoys only a moral position or it is legal in nature. The point of view of Imam Malik on this issue is that it is agreeable to give the divorced woman something by way of gift. It is not a compulsory obligation. His argument rests on the Quranic words "This is a duty on the righteous," as the closing phrase of the verse. In the preceding verse 236, mutaah has been pointed out as piety and Ehsan in the closing words. We cannot declare it obligatory for one and all.

Among the tabieen Qadi Shuraih was also of the same opinion. It has been said in a report that a certain person divorced his wife after consummation. She filed a suit at the court of Qadi Shuraih claiming mutaah. The Qadi persuasively remarked during his talk to the husband that he should not deny himself the enviable position of joining the ranks of the righteous and the pious. However, he did not compel him to endow her with mutaah.

According to Imam Malik, the woman divorced before consummation but with dower fixed, shall get half the fixed dower but shall not be entitled to mutaah. It has also been reported as the opinion of Imam Malik that mutaah is obligatory, but his well-known opinion is that stated above.

The majority of the jurists have regarded mutaah as obligatory. Their argument is that the Quran has used the words; "matte-u-hunna" (bestow on them a suitable gift (Q. II : 241) which imperative form indicates that it is obligatory "For the divorced women" also indicates that it will be their property and therefore, they could demand it. That also proves its obligatory nature. The words "this is a duty on the righteous." (Q. II: 241) also suggest that it must be obligatory. To further stress it, it has been said, "is due from those who wish to do the right thing," (Q. II : 236).

Can it possibly mean that it is binding only on those who fear Allah and wish to do the right thing and not others? In response to this query Allamah Abu Bakr Jassas has proved with precepts from the Quran itself that it does not at all mean to eliminate those who are not righteous. It is there just to stress that people may be further persuaded to this righteous deed.

Now the question arises that if Mutaah is obligatory in nature, If it so for every divorced woman. Or that for some it is obligatory and for others it is not so. The Hanafite Fiqh has opined that mutaah is the due of that woman whose dower was not fixed and she got divorced before consummation. It is she for whom the Quran has ordained it (Q. 11 : 236). Other divorced women get their mehr and maintenance for the entire iddat term. The last mentioned are not entitled to it as a matter of obligatory duty. They may, however, get as a parting gift.

Imam Ahmad too is, of the same opinion.

Imam Shafii's says mutaah must go to all the divorced women save those with fixed mehr and divorced before consummation. The Quran is explicit about it that she will get half her fixed dower. (Q. II : 237). Among the companions Abdullah ibn Umar R.A.A. is reported to have the same opinion.

Saeed bin Zubayr, Abul Aliyah, Hasan Basri, and some others R.A., have said that every divorced woman must get mutaah as a matter of duty since (for the divorced woman is mutaah) is a Quranic injunction, which is general in nature, and there is no justification for any particularisation. The idea that only those divorced women will be endowed with mutaah whose dower had not been fixed is also erroneous since the dower of the Prophet's S.A.W. consorts was fixed and they had been consummated also, but in case of divorce the Quran ordained payment of mutaah to them. It says:

> *O Prophet ! Say to thy consorts that if it be that ye desire the life of this world and its glitter then come, I will provide for you enjoyment and set you free in a handsome manner.* —*Al Quran XXXIII :28*

This is said to be the opinion of Ali R.A.A., Imam Zahri, Ibrahim Nakhai, Ata bin Abi Ribah and Sufyan Thauri. This is also the opinion of Zahirites. Ibn Hazam Zahiri says that all types of divorced women are entitled to mutaah on a compulsory basis, whether the divorce is revocable or irrevocable, consummation or no consummation, mehr fixed or unfixed, since 'for the divorced woman there is mutaah according to the pious popular usage' is a general ordainment and it would be improper on our part to make it selective.

All these opinions are similar. Those who are in favour of making mutaah or parting gift to the divorced women obligatory, may favour this (immediately foregoing) opinion, but there are several evils in it. Firstly, the woman divorced before consummation, if her dower is fixed, shall get half of her fixed dower and mutaah, and in case of non-fixation of mehr, she shall get only mutaah, which appears to be sort of iniquity. Secondly, declaring mutaah compulsory would mean that like mehr and maintenance, it is also an undeniable right which she can claim legally. Undoubtedly, as stated above, the opinion of the Zahirities and some others is in support of it. The well-known commentator of the Quran, Ibn Jarir Tabri, has subscribed to it, and according to him mutaah like mehr is binding upon the divorcing husband and in case of non-payment, like mehr and other dues, the aggrieved party can sue for it in a court of law.

This opinion appears to be unsounded in view of the fact that the Islamic courts never pronounced such decisions. Imam Shabi says: By Allah! I never saw any one imprison for non-payment of mutaah. By Allah! If it had been obligatory, the Qadis would have put the defaulters behind the bars.

In the foregoing pages we discussed in detail the meaning of mata' and its legal position presenting the opinions of various jurists in this behalf, which make it amply manifest that it can not be proved on the authority of the Quran and Hadith that there is any responsibility of the support of the divorced wife on the husband, nor from the antiquity to posterity has any one expressed his opinion in its favour. It is a baseless idea that finds support nowhere.

ECONOMIC PROBLEMS

Lastly, let us take up the question of the economic responsibility of the divorced woman. This question is hurled at the Muslim community in such a way that after divorce the Muslim woman finds herself in such a difficult fix to which solution has to be found anyway. Then they put forth all sorts of suggestions, delving into the Quran for the support of their new tangled ideas where the problems of nikah and divorce have been presenting themselves for the last fourteen hundred years. Divorce is nothing new. There have been cases from the early period of Islam and problems relating to both young and old divorcees have been dealt with. The reasonable course that should have been adopted was to find out whether Islam has presented any solution to this problem. Rather they should have expected that like so many other problems it must have provided guidance here also. And overlooking all the considerations to think and make others believe that Islam has suggested no solution to this serious problem, the Muslim thinkers never cared to give a serious thought to it all this while, is an example of sheer ignorance.

According to Islam the relationship between the husband and wife gets snapped for good, and therefore, it has not at all associated the problem of the financial burden of the woman with the estranged husband but solved in other ways.

1. It is a baseless proposition that if a divorced woman does not receive her maintenance from the husband, there will be no way of providing her subsistence and she is most likely to starve. There are probably some other motives behind this idea rather than any sympathy for the woman. Or else it is a fact known to an ordinary student of Islamic Theology that under the Islamic Law there are various ways down which wealth flows to the woman, including inheritance, mehr, legacy and other sources. And the possibility of her coming into wealth from either of the

above mentioned sources, guaranteeing her subsistence satisfactorily can not be overlooked.

2. Earlier we have convincingly proved that though the woman is not under any compulsion to undertake any economic effort for her support, but there is no bar on her taking to a permitted source of earning her subsistence. She can seek employment, undertake agriculture and trade, partake in industry, in short, having a perfect right to undertake any economic endeavour, of course within the Islamic limits set for her here. Success in this field can enable her not only to support herself unaided but extend a helping hand to others in need.

3. Islam regards conjugal life for man essential. It has instructed the entire society to help the individuals in taking to conjugal life.

Marry those among you who are single and the virtuous ones among your slaves, male or female.

—Al Quran XXIV : 32

The word occurring in the Quranic verse above, is 'Ayama', the plural form of Ayyum, covering in its meaning both the unmarried man and woman. It also encompasses along with the virgins that have not yet found a suitor, those also without a husband due to divorce or widowhood. It is a fact that in the present age, the inclination of Muslims towards second marriage of the divorcee and the widow is at a low ebb. But Islam is in favour of giving it a fresh fillip and reasonably so. The Islamic teaching in this behalf is that if due to disharmony in temperament a husband and wife have parted ways or the death of one of them has closed the chapter of his or her conjugal life, a match should be found for their remarriage, since living alone permits corrupting influences on the morals and may blot characters. Acting on this teaching will itself solve the problem of the divorced and widowed women, since in conjugal life she becomes the liability of the husband. That is why we find during the course of Islamic history, so long as they adhered to this teaching, never did any problem of the support of the widow and the divorced woman confront the Muslim society. This is the best solution of this problem and it must be promoted.

4. If the divorced woman and likewise the widow fail to find suitors and have no means of support of their own, Islam has imposed the responsibility of their support on their families.

In this connection what should be kept in view is the principle that under the Islamic law the woman is never under compulsion to endeavour in the economic field for her livelihood. In the Islamic Fiqh it has been said: "To be a woman is enough for incapability, meaning thereby that for various reasons she lacks the capacity to earn her own bread. And that is why others have to shoulder that responsibility. The husband supports her under all circumstances. After divorce if she is not self-sufficient and her progeny is in a position to work and earn their bread, it becomes charged with her support. Here it would be in the fitness of things to make it evident that according to our jurists the maintenance of the parents includes all those facilities that have come for mention under the maintenance of wife.

The substances included in the maintenance of wife, that for the parents shall have all of them, namely board and lodge, so much so that the services of a servant have not been exempted.

If she does not get remarried after divorce and her children too are unable to undertake her support the burden of her maintenance shall be transferred to her parents and she will be treated as she was before marriage. The expositor of the famous book of Hanafite Fiqh, Hidayah, Allamah Ibn-ul-Hammam writes:

> *The maintenance and support of the daughters until such time as they get married, if they are lacking in substance, is the responsibility of the father. He cannot engage them in any work or service, even if they are able to undertake such jobs. If one of them gets divorced after the expiry of the term of iddat the responsibility of her maintenance will once again revert to the father.*

In the absence of father, whoever happens to be her closest mahram (eternally prohibited to her), such as uncle, brother and others (maternal uncle, maternal and paternal grand fathers) shall be held responsible for her support. If none of these relatives is there or is incapable of shouldering this responsibility, the Islamic state steps in to undertake her support. In the absence of an Islamic state the Muslim society should come forward to take her charge. The society of Indian Muslims desirous of solving the problem of such women can easily do so.

Those who go on raising objections for their own sake, jumping from one to the next, it appears they are totally ignorant of the 'Islamic Law of Maintenance'. We have shown just a glimpse of it here. They should try to acquaint themselves with its details.

7

WOMEN, POLYGAMY AND ISLAM

Much harsh and unthinking criticism has been levelled against Islam for having permitted polygamy. It is not realised that the Islamic permission for polygamy was and remains conditional. It arose out of the circumstance that Islam found itself engaged in an almost unending series of wars with its deadly foes. This naturally led to the progressive reduction of the male population. The problem of surplus women left in such circumstances could not be solved except by permitting men to marry more than one wife in order to provide for helpless women and save them from falling into the evil of prostitution. Moreover, in Arabia before the advent of Islam, polygamy was unlimited.

A man could marry as many women as he liked, there being no restriction as to the number of marriages he could contract. Islam could not have abolished such a deep-rooted custom with its far-reaching economic effects at a sudden stroke. Therefore, as in the case of slavery, it proceeded by gradual steps. First, it limited to four the number of wives a man could have. Then it laid down that a second or third marriage could not be resorted to unless the husband felt that he could do justice to all his wives in the matter of economic sustenance and general treatment

Christian writers who have condemned Islam on the score that it allowed polygamy forget that their own religion has nowhere expressly prohibited the institution of polygamy. Although the New Testament upholds the ideal of monogamy, it does not prohibit polygamy except in the case of a bishop or a deacon. It has been argued that it was not necessary for the first Christian teachers to condemn polygamy because it was rarely practised by the people amidst whom it was preached. But this is certainly not true of the Jews who permitted as well as practised polygamy at the beginning of the Christian era. Some of the Fathers accused Jewish Rabbis of polygamy, but no Council of the Church in the early centuries opposed polygamy, and no obstacle was put in the way of its practice by kings in the countries where it occurred. Polygamy was sometimes practised by Christian kings without the disapproval of the Church. Charlemagne had two wives and many concubines, and one of his laws seems to imply that the custom was not unknown even among the priests.

Even in the modern West there is a considerable number of thinkers and sociologists who recognise that polygamy is not an unmitigated evil and that in certain circumstances it may become desirable, even necessary. In England proposals were made in the seventeenth and eighteenth centuries to legalise polygamy as a means of restraining infanticide, adultery, prostitution and the evils of sexual relations outside marriage. According to Havelock Ellis, James Hinton declared that although monogamy be a good, nay even the only good, order, if of free choice, a law for it is another thing.

He says: 'We have arrived at it as a legal and universal form to carry it out in its entirety and so actually called into being more licentiousness than would be possible under an open polygamy. A forced monogamy is responsible for many of the evils of prostitution, and leads to hatred and quarrels, to intense jealousy in women, and to an insistence on the mere physical relationship which turns spontaneity and purity into corruption. The woman's natural jealousy is not at a man's loving another, but at his forsaking her.' Westermarck quoted a number of writers in his book, *The Future of Marriage in Western Civilization*, who advocate the legislation of polygamy on different grounds. He says:

> *Dr. Cope sees no objection to voluntary polygamy or polyandry being permitted, if agreed to by all the parties. Under ordinary circumstances, he says, very few persons would be willing to make such a contract, but there are some cases of hardship which such permission would remedy. Such, for instance, would be the case where the*

man or woman had become the victim of a chronic disease, or, where either party should be childless, and in other contingencies that can be imagined. For the most part, it adds, the best way to deal with polygamy is to let it alone. So also, according to Mr. Southern, the preference that most people give to monogamy is no reason why the state should enforce it. So far as other forms of marriage can be practised by mutual consent, and without detrimentally affecting children, the state hasn't the ghost of a right to veto them. Dr. Norman Haire, who maintains that legalised polygamy would offer many advantages to the majority of people, argues that if the children are supported by the state, there need be no limit to the number of legal mates. Professor Dunlop thinks it may well be that certain individuals cannot attain complete satisfaction in monogamy, but may reach a highly satisfying adaptation in polygamous marriage, and that the system of the future will leave individuals free to form whatever types of matrimonial alliances are most advantageous to them .... In France, Dr. Le Bon has predicted that European legislation in the future will recognize polygamy.... A return to polygamy, the natural relationship between the sexes, would remedy many evils: prostitution, venereal diseases, abortion, the misery of illegitimate children, the misfortune of millions of unmarried women, resulting from the disproportion between the sexes, adultery, and even jealousy, since the disregarded wife would find consolation in her cognizance of not being secretly deceived by her husband .... A radical champion of polygamy is Professor Christian von Ehrenfels, who regards it as necessary for the preservation of the Aryan race.

After quoting the above writers, Westermarck examines the grounds on which polygamy may be justified. In this connection he says:

If polygamy were permitted in modern civilization its actual prevalence would also be influenced by women's

> *feeling about it. It is said that if we reckon the age of marriage from twenty to fifty years, the disproportion between the sexes causes at least three or four per cent women to be, in normal circumstances, compelled to lead a single life in consequence of our obligatory monogamy.*

It is obvious that if what Dr. Westermarck says about the number of men and women of marriageable age is true, polygamy becomes a social necessity, provided it is on a restricted scale; in order to absorb surplus women into married life there is no doubt that if polygamy is resorted to by a very large number of men, it may ultimately lead to the problem of a surplus of unmarried men, as there may be many people who will not be able to find a mate for themselves. But there is really little danger of polygamy spreading on a very large scale or assuming uncontrollable proportions. As pointed out by Havelock Ellis in his *Psychology of Sex*:

> *Since the sexes are equal in number (with, at the start, a preponderance of males), the natural order in a civilized society cannot work out as two wives for every male, and in the societies which recognize polygamy, it is only practised by a small wealthy class. But it is incorrect to assert that in our civilization men (rare exceptions aside) ever desire two wives, whether in the same home or in separate homes; there are various considerations of different orders which make such an arrangement undesirable for the majority of men; while for a woman, to carry on two families, with separate fathers, is still more impracticable; she is necessarily monogamic.*

This conclusion is corroborated by Westermarck himself who says:

> *But this does not imply that if polygamy were legalized, any considerable number of men would indulge in it. It is a curious freak on the part of Bernard Shaw to say that as polygamy would enable the best men to monopolize all the women, a great many men would be condemned to celibacy. Apart from other reasons, economic considerations, fear of domestic troubles and*

the difficulty of finding a woman who would care to share her married life with a fellow-wife, would prevent men from taking advantage of the new right granted them. The experience gained from peoples who permit polygamy teaches us that generally only a small minority of the men practise it. In the Mohammedan world, for instance, the large majority of men live in monogamy. In Persia, according to Colonel Macgregor, only two per cent have a plurality of wives. Among the Mohammedans of India, according to a report, from the census of 1907, there are 1021 wives to every 1000 husbands, so that, even, if no husbands have more than two wives, all but 21 per thousand must be polygamous.

Among other reasons why polygamy may be legitimately resorted to by men, Dr. Westermarck mentions sexual abstinence during pregnancy. Some people regard sexual intercourse during pregnancy as injurious to the health of woman as well as her unborn child, and there are women who feel less desire for sexual course during pregnancy greatly preferring total abstinence. 'Of 81 married women,' says Westermarck, who answered Dr. Hamilton's questions on this subject, '28 stated that pregnancy did not affect their sex desire, 25 that they experienced increased, and 32 that they experienced decreased desire during one phase or another of at least one pregnancy.' Dr. Westermarck, however rejects it as a sufficient ground for a plurality of wives saying: 'But in no case does pregnancy, among ourselves, lead to general abstinence from conjugal intercourse, and however desirable it may be proved to be in certain cases and certain stages of pregnancy. I think such abstinences; ruled out as a cause of prospective polygamy. The same may be said of abstinence from childbirth.

Another ground on which polygamy may be justified, according to Dr. Westermarck, is the strong and innate polygamous instinct of man as contrasted with women who are generally monogamous by nature. 'The man's taste for variety in sex experience,' says Westermarck, 'is more intense than the woman's and this has led to the often repeated statement that he is instinctively polygamous. "Man," says Dr Robinson, "is a strongly polygamous or varietist animal.... To a greater percentage of men a strictly monogamous life is either irksome, painfully disagreeable or an utter impossibility." Michels writes: "We regard it as beyond doubt that there is no man, of whatever degree of virtue, who has not, at least in imagination or in dream life, possessed more women than one. Attention has been drawn to this fact by an unending series of writers, both of scientific treatises and of belletristic literature. . . . In the male, the stimuli capable of arousing sexual excitement (this term is not to be here understood in the grossly physical sense) are so extraordinarily manifold, so widely differentiated, that it is quite impossible for one single woman to possess them all. . . ." Dr. Miesel-Hess remarks that "in the male satiety ensues as soon as he has gained the goal of his desire.

He wishes to pass on in search for fresh sexual experiences, whereas the woman who has given herself up to a man clings to this person all the more firmly to him." According to Fore "woman is generally much more particular than man in giving her love: while the normal man is as a rule attracted to coitus by nearly every more or less young and healthy woman, this is by no means the case in the normal woman with regard to man. She is also much more constant than man from the sexual point of view.' and it is really possible for her to experience sexual desire for several men at once." George Hirth is of the same opinion. Of 324 female students at the University of Moscow, thirty-one thought it possible to love two men at the same time. Kisch says that "the young sexual conqueror is thinking of women, the sexually ripening women of the man;" and he attributes the predominantly monogamous character of woman's love to the commanding strength of its spiritual elements.

It is obvious that if man is by nature more strongly polygamous, the marriage law should not lose sight of this important fact and some provisions should be made for men in whom the sexual instinct is more than commonly strong; otherwise illegitimate sexual relations are likely to become more frequent. A social system which does not permit polygamy under any circumstances will be constantly threatened with disruptive tendencies owing to the frequency of sexual aberrations. The State may no doubt interfere by making polygamy conditional, as Islam has done, but it has no justification to stop it completely. Among other reasons for polygamy may be mentioned—barrenness, constant illness of the wife leading to prolonged sexual abstinence and sexual frigidity which makes some women dislike the act of coitus. Complete prohibition of polygamy under any one of these circumstances commonly drives men to adultery.

For various reasons, some of which have been explained above, Islam did not deem it expedient to abolish the institution of polygamy altogether. But it restricted polygamy and insisted that full justice should be done to all the wives, and if a man was afraid that he could not do justice in treatment and in the provision of economic sustenance, he should limit himself to only one wife. Thus, the Quran has stated: 'And if you fear that you cannot act equitably towards orphans, then marry such women as seem good to you, two, three and four, but if you fear that you may not do justice to them, then marry only one' (iv. 3). Explaining this passage Maulana Muhammad Ali writes in his translation of the Holy Quran:

> *This passage permits polygamy under certain circumstances: it does not enjoin it nor even permit it unconditionally. It may be noted here that the explanation of this passage as generally understood is based on a report contained in the Muslim, according to which Aishah understood this verse as meaning that if the guardian of orphan girls feared that by marrying them they would not be able to do justice to them, they should marry other women. This explanation, even if the report be taken to be authentic, requires the insertion into the passage of a number of words which the original does not contain, as the meaning is much more clear, and more in consonance with the context, without the addition of these words, the interpretation given below is preferable. It is admitted that this chapter was revealed to guide the Muslims under the conditions which followed the battle of Uhud, and the last portion of the last chapter deals with that battle. Now in that battle 70 men out of 700 Muslims had been slain, and this decimation*

had largely decreased the number of males, who, being the breadwinners, were the natural guardians and supporters of the females. The number was likely to suffer a still greater diminution in the battles which had yet to be fought, while the number of women would be increased by the addition of prisoners of war. Thus, many orphans would be left in the charge of widows, who would find it difficult to procure the necessary means of support. Hence in the first verse of this chapter the Muslims are enjoined to respect the ties of relationship, and as they' all came from a single ancestor breadth is introduced into the idea of relationship, inasmuch as they are told that they are all in fact related to each other. In the second verse the care of orphans is particularly enjoined. In the third verse we are told that if they could not do justice to the orphans, they might marry the widows, whose children would thus become their own children, and as the number of women was now much greater than the number of men, they were permitted to marry even two or three or four women. It would thus be clear that the permission to have more than one wife was given under the peculiar circumstances of the Muslim society then existing, and the Prophet's action in marrying widows, as well as the example of many of his companions, corroborates this statement. Marriage with orphan girls is also sanctioned in this passage, for there were the same difficulties in the case of orphan girls as in the case of widows, and the words are general.

It is clear from the above explanation that the permission given by the Quran for polygamy arose out of particular circumstances. Since these circumstances are likely to recur now and then in the life of the Muslim community and since there will always be individual cases where polygamy may become necessary in order to avoid more serious moral and social evils, it is not right to prohibit polygamy by legislation. But since the Quran has made it conditional on a just and equal treatment of the wives, it is open to the State to prescribe conditions under which polygamy will be allowable. For example, it may be laid down that polygamy will be allowed only if a person shows sufficient cause for it and satisfies the authorities that he will be able to bear the additional economic burden and will not thereby injure his health.

In the sight of Islam, polygamy is not an improper practice. Under certain restrictions it regards polygamy lawful and harmless. The objection raised against it is that human nature abhors it and demands a monogamous society. It is a great injustice to woman also that in the presence of one wife another may be brought as a rival to her-the co-wife as a life-long source of jealousy and heartburn. So to put an end to this iniquity many countries have put a legal ban on polygamy. In some other countries there is no such legal restriction on it but it is not looked upon approvingly either. Probably there are few countries in the world where it does not stand in disfavour morally and legally though not actually frowned upon.

To begin with, it would be in the fitness of things to point out that it is not proper to make only Islam the target of criticism with reference to polygamy. For, if it is a crime Islam is not alone in committing it. Most of the nations of the world practised it. It had the legal authority and moral sanctions of different religions and it was not regarded a crime or a sin. In the ascetic religions, however, not only polygamy but conjugal relations were despised: Christianity coming into its own had taken to asceticism (of the most rigorous type by way of exaggeration and fanaticism). In their misplaced enthusiasm they permitted a religious minded man even one wife with disapproval.

The Western society could not detach itself completely from the deep-set influence of world renouncing section of Christianity even during the period of its high-sounding claims of discarding religion and taking to agnosticism. It came to accept the concept of monogamy but found it hard to swallow the concept of polygamy (in spite of their claims of freethinking and secularism). The nations in bondage of the Western colonizers started supporting the issue as if they had for the first time come across this concept and their eyes were opened to the consciousness of woman's greatness.

Let us first look at it from man's point of view. Undoubtedly most men are content with one wife only. Still they alone can allege polygamy to be alien to the nature of man who have observed and studied that nature through the coloured glasses supplied by the West. It is an undeniable fact that man is naturally inclined to polygamy. Even if he remains contented with one wife, if the doors on polygamy were closed on him, it cannot be ruled out that he is free from any such tendency. Those with a strong sexual urge, if the doors of polygamy were closed on them, there is a great danger of their seeking gratification of that unusual urge by illicit means (outside wedlock). We have before us the experiment of the West with strict legally binding monogamy and its disastrous results. Rejecting polygamy it had to put up with fornication and illicit sex in all its other heinous forms. There in the West one man one wife may be the legal order in their society, but how many mistresses, stenos and secretaries and so called girl friends are associated with one man, he only knows. And they remain deprived of all those rights enjoyed by the legally wedded wife (even a co-wife).

Polygamy is not only a tendency of man but a need of his desire for sex is a natural urge. The highly sexed individuals and those whose passion is uncontrollable, one woman cannot meet their abnormally frequent demand of sexual gratification. For, she is prone to her period with its disability for several days every month, post-parturient bleeding disables and enfeebles her, when she is psychologically unfit for sexual union, advanced pregnancy and delivery being her other periods of disability. She regularly passes through these phases when her passions are at the lowest ebb. During these phases she is not her normal self and unable to respond positively to her husband's advances. The other aspect of it is that cohabitation during these periods is detrimental to the health of both of them, besides being abhorrent to human nature.

Sex during pregnancy is deleterious for the child's health also. And experience has shown that sentimentality in this matter on the part of the married couple adversely influences the moral build-up of the child born to them. Pregnancies, child births and breast feeding thoroughly shakes her physical health, her body reserves get depleted and early signs of senility overtake her much earlier than the husband who is not prone to any of his partner's debilitating phenomena. He finds himself much younger both in physique and spirits. For these reasons if a person is not contented with one wife and wishes to have another, he is in no way blameworthy. It would be unjust even cruel to condemn and, oppose him., He should, however, be compelled (through social pressure) to meet his obligations to both of them justly and neither should be neglected with impunity.

Now looking at the problem from the woman's point of view we discover that in some situations polygamy becomes beneficial to her, a blessing in disguise.

The desire for progeny in man is natural (said to be the manifestation of the suppressed desire for survival or immortality which somehow appears partially fulfilled through continuity of the family as well as partial projection of himself through progeny- his carbon copy). If somebody discovers that his wife is physically or psychologically barren and totally incapable of bearing children, he has two options open to him : he may retain the barren one and wed another, and the other course lies in divorcing the first and then taking another partner. Apparently barring rare cases of pride and self-aggrandisement the second alternative would be preferably acceptable to any right-thinking woman. The wife may be a chronic patient of some incurable malady or be disabled due to some serious disorder peculiar to her sex, would it not be beneficial to the disabled partner that the husband takes another while retaining his ailing life-partner. (Divorce without proper justification is woman's murder in cold blood and consigning her to the dung hill).

In all such situations it would be grave injustice, rather, height of cruelty to the first wife if the husband is compelled by the law of the land to divorce her before opting for another match. This compulsion becomes all the more abominable when she shows her willingness to go on living under the husband's protection and he too is reluctant to throw her out to fend for herself. Under certain circumstances polygamy becomes a necessity for the society itself -a dire need for that matter. Under normal conditions nature maintains the balance in the number of males and females born anywhere on earth. But when a country has suffered tremendous loss of life on the battle fronts, the male population is greatly reduced, particularly the younger men of marriageable age since it is they who largely become the gun-fodder, thus greatly distorting the balance and leaving the female population far in excess of the males. One solution of the catastrophic problem lies in leaving the young widows and spinsters to rot and go on suffering in silence, or take to the path of sin and create sexual anarchy and moral turpitude, their smouldering passions making them an easy prey to the lascivious and the dissolute. No healthy society worth the name can put up with this abominable state of affairs. (The European powers had to put up with it after both the world wars).

Man power plays an important role in the life of nations. It has a basic importance in the country's defence, industries, agriculture and other multifarious social services to promote the country's interests. Under certain peculiar conditions and in delicate situations their importance becomes manifold. Polygamy is also one of the ways of adding to the numerical strength. Women are overtaken by menopause at forty or thereabout, whereas men are fit at seventy or even later in exceptional cases.

That means man's second marriage, once his partner has become defunct, may start a fresh chain of births, thus adding to the man-power of the nation. That is why the nations standing in sore need of numerical strength have to relax their quaint policies of restrictions on polygamy (to the extent of making it a cognizable offence). They come down at times to compromise or even to encourage polygamy in the national interest. European countries like Germany, England, France and Sweden, in fact most of them barring Ireland, Greece and Italy and a few others, are once again confronted with the same confounding problem of lowered birth rate (about 1.2 per thousand in Germany and in England reduced to one third) — a grave danger signal for the very existence and well-being of any nation.

Some people may assert that if the male of the human species enjoys the privilege of polygamy, it would only be in the fitness of things that the right of the females be also recognized to polyandry — having more than one husband at a time. But even if she were thus "privileged" she would never have the temerity to be benefited by it, The custom of polyandry does exist in some uncivilized or semi-civilized tribes in India and else where too, but the cultured and civilized world has never accepted it. The civilized human society has rejected it once for all.

Woman's nature points to the fact that she can become the wife of only one husband at a time. Polyandry or multiplicity of partners in bed is abhorrent to her nature.

Woman bears the burden of familial responsibilities. She has taken upon herself the most onerous ones. It is she who undergoes the pangs of pregnancy, delivery and suckling the babe. She is so often obliged to discharge duties in the world outside. How can it be possible for her to submit herself to the sexual demands of several males. It would simply mean ruination of her health. The practice can also give rise to sexual and mental disorders. Experience has shown that women having extramarital relations (many at a time) are often victims of maladies pertaining to sex, and no more fit for life as respectable housewives.

Polyandry may also create a certain social problem. A healthy male given to polygamy may impregnate all his wives. And the issues one and all, shall be recognized as his. But a polyandrous woman having sex with all her husbands can conceive only through sexual union with one of them at a given time. And once she has conceived, intercourse with others is not going to contribute in this behalf at all. But the real and very ticklish problem arises when it comes to decide the paternity of the issue. Who is going to determine it and how? Maternity is a matter of certainty but not so the paternity-it is a matter of doubt (unless all avenues are closed on suspicions and uncertainties) ! All that can be said is that the child is (his or her) mother's son or daughter—a real stigma in respectable society, and a most disturbing and embarrassing situation for such indeterminate and unidentified progeny. Who is going to support, educate, and make him or her his heir or be himself that son's legatee? There are many other knotty questions, answers to which cannot be found in the existing familial system, headed by a male, recognized and accepted by the civilized world then as now. The system of polyandry can deleteriously affect the society also as we know it.

It is inherent in the nature of human male, however, immoral and corrupt himself, that he cannot for a moment put up with another male having anything to do with his wife. Several males having a common female as their partner in bed, must be deadly jealous, each one of all the rest. They become blood thirsty in establishing exclusive claim to her and the results of any conflict in getting sole possession of her may be very tragic indeed. Their tussle and constant fighting for her become unbearable for the woman herself and her peace of mind departs. It may be asserted that the same can be said of polygamy since each one of the co-wives is hell-bent on damaging the cause of all the rivals in her striving for the sole possession of the common husband and his exclusive love for and all the attention to her. This is undoubtedly true enough. But a woman's feelings in this behalf, compared with the jealousy of man are not so strong and the results too are not so serious and disturbing. May be one of the causes of this difference is that she regards polygamy justified and pardonable.

A woman is inherently more modest. This feeling is natural to her and emerging automatically from her. For all the sustained and laborious efforts of the immodest West, the agents of evil have so far been kept at bay by this strong sense in her. It could not be wiped out as in the West. It is due to this deterrent that she does not give laud expression to her passion for sexual gratification and openly invite the opposite sex for the satiation of her smouldering passions. This sense of concealment of her feelings has benefitted human society in a big way. She cannot go headlong with temerity to create anarchy in sex, totally oblivious of the consequences. Sex relations with more than one man badly injure or destroy this restraining factor of her character, and gradually she becomes totally devoid of any sense of modesty and chastity. Female of the human species once denuded of her sense of modesty and self-prestige due to chastity, society rushes headlong towards the abysmal depths of degradation as a result of sexual anarchy.

Not for Debauchery

Let us now consider the objection that polygamy is also a clever contrivance for debauchery. It provides man with total freedom to sexual gratification at will. That is why capitalists and feudal lords gathered around them hordes of women of their choice and spent their lives in the pleasant company of *huris* and fairies (in their self-made paradise). Islam in recognition of polygamy has supported and authenticated this very corrupt order (feudalism) and opened avenues for lasciviousness and debauchery, that a person may wed any woman whenever he likes and when he has reached the permitted number, four, he may divorce one of them and replace her by another beauty. He may even divorce all the four at once and bring in other fresh more elegant lot for his fairy-land.

This objection holds good in case of monogamy as well. Whoever desires can take leave of the old used one whenever another fresh and more charming damsel catches his eye and he takes a facy to her, he can adorn his luxury chamber again and again. But such an objection can be raised only by one who has closed his eyes to the very patent fact that a dissolute person is invariably the most irresponsible person. All that he cares for is his own pursuit of "good times." He does not like to burden himself with any responsibility. All those who opted for a life of dissoluteness took to unbridled sex. Not to say polygamy, they disapproved of the restrictions of married life. If at all they adopted it under social pressure, never met their obligations in this behalf. Under the Islamic way of life one is overburdened with responsibilities. Polygamy increases this burden many times over. So many responsibilities and restrictions have been imposed on him that without dire need he cannot think of more than one wife at a time.

Restrictions

The mode of thinking and temperament that Islam wants to create, if inculcated in the right spirit, man cannot for a moment tolerate a life of dissoluteness and debauchery. This is, however, irrelevant to our discussion here, and we are mentioning here some of the legal restrictions that Islam imposes in connection with polygamy. They will give an idea that Islam far from opening avenues on polygamy has actually created great barriers in its way. Before the advent of Islam polygamy was the common practice and Arabia in this regard was no exception. Some people wedded as many women as they were pleased, maintaining an entire harem at times and tyrannised them. Islam put a ban on more than four at a time. It recognizes and asserts to polygamy as a personal and social need but was never prepared to accept a situation where man needs more than four wives. It declares it improper and prohibited. Whoever exceeds the prescribed limits of four, Islam shall proceed legally against him. In this way it has put a ban on unlimited number of wives, more than four, then in vogue and prevented the practice for future.

Not an Injunction

Some people present polygamy as if Islam had ordained it and the Muslim, may or may not be observing its other injunctions, is compulsorily following this particular ordainment. One wife cannot meet his needs. He must always have four of them to embellish his bed chambers.

In this connection we would like to inform such disinformed people that the idea that all Muslims or at least a great majority of them practise polygamy is erroneous and totally baseless. Among millions of Muslims, there may be only a few having more than one wife. It is not just our guess work. Facts and figures on authentic surveys by some newspapers contradict it. On the one hand, they conclusively prove that some other people are much more involved in it compared to Muslims. The other misunderstood or deliberately mis-stated fact that Islam has ordained it is equally baseless. That is a matter of leave in case of dire need and not an injunction of the Islamic Shariah. By abstaining from it all his life a Muslim shall not be guilty of any sin of omission and lacking in piety or religiosity by any standard of judgement.

Thirdly, Islam has not encouraged polygamy. It did not persuade and instigate its followers in this behalf. Rather, it pointed out its intricacies so that they may give it serious thought before plunging into it. He should never adopt it as a means of satisfying his lust.

Fourthly, the idea that polygamy is a means of luxury and enjoyment alone. It can also be a means of sympathy and helpful attitude. Suppose a young girl remaining unmarried (not finding a suitor), or one getting widowed in prime of life with no one to support her, a person marrying her as his second wife out of sheer sympathy and compassion, can this act of his be termed condemnable or he regarded guilty of lustfulness?

Conditions and Controls

The person taking advantage of the leave granted to him by Islam and intending to wed another wife in the presence of the first, finds himself confronted by the following restrictions before acting on it: Financially he must be in a position that along with the first wife maintenance and residence of this second one is easily within his means. Some jurists are of the opinion that if she is not prepared to live with his first wife, he will have to provide a separate living space for her.

Physically he must be capable of properly maintaining conjugal relationship with both. The jurists have discussed in detail its legal aspect and also the interval between two performances of intercourse. Apart from this, one of the objectives of nikah is the protection of modesty and chastity. That is why many jurists have written that the interval between one sexual act and another should not exceed four months. This is supported by a decision of the period of Umar R.A.A., the second rightly guided Caliph.

Imam Ibn Taymiyyah says that a person should cohabit with his wife according to the common usage among nice well-behaved people. This is more important than her feeding arrangement. He goes on to add : According to some, copulation once in four months is binding on the husband. Some others have said that it depends on the desire of the woman and the sexual powers of man. And this appears to be reasonable.

Allamah ibn-e-Arabi Maliki says: If a person financially and physically is capable of meeting his obligations he may wed four women. In case of incapability he must rest contented with just as many as he can easily support and satisfy sexually.

That means a person incapable of meeting the challenges of polygamy must content himself with just one wife. Even if a person is financially and physically capable of a second marriage, he is bound to maintain the just balance between them in all matters where equality is possible in practical life, namely, the matter of maintenance, dress, residence and spending the night with them. Equity and justice are the real spirit in the Islamic order of mutual dealings. It has attached so much importance to justice in the matter that even if there is a lurking doubt about his maintaining the correct balance in his dealings with them, he has been directed to remain contented with only one wife.

The Quran says :

> *But if ye fear that you shall not be able to deal justly (with them) then only one.* —*Al Quran IV: 3*

Allamah Abu Bakr Jassas Hanafi says that if a person fears that he cannot deal justly with all the four wives he should come down to two, and if that too is not possible, he should keep only one. In traditions of the Prophet S.A.W. there is serious denunciation for failure of husbands in the matter of just dealings between the wives. Abu Hurairah R.A.A. reports the Prophet S.A.W. to have said : A person having two wives, failing to maintain balance of justice between them (leaning towards any one of them) shall come on Doomsday with half of his body reclining (to one side).

To maintain equality and just treatment with the wives in all those matter is lying within his power is binding on him. It is not, however, possible for him to love all of them equally. His heart may be inclined to one more than others. Similarly, sharing the bed and copulation with them all on the basis of equality is not practically possible. It depends so much on the desire (sex-urge) and preparedness (both mental and physical). It is among those things over which he has no control.

Hadrat Aishah R.A.A. reports:

> *The Prophet used to distribute things among his wives justly which could be divided easily. After that he used to say, "O Allah ! I have divided those things over which I have control. Those over which thou alone, heath control and do not lie in my power (love and other sentiments), in case of any discrepancy in these matters, do not hold me answerable."*

But it does not mean either that in the name of love and cordiality one should recline so much towards any one spouse that it may result in oppression and excesses towards others, and they, having a husband (legally and factually) may be pushed to one side to do existence as without one. The Quran explicitly interdicts it saying :

> *You are never able to do justice between wives even if it is your ardent desire : but turn not away (from a woman) altogether, so as to leave her (as it were) hanging (in the air).* —*Al Quran IV : 129*

Just as the second wife is entitled to all those rights and privileges enjoyed by the first wife, so shall the children of the latter have equal rights with those of the former wife. There shall be no discrimination between the progeny of the two legally. The responsibility of all these restrictions and conditions comes to the shoulders of the person benefiting from the leave granted by Islam to take to polygamy.

The fact is that according to the teachings of Islam it is not easy to have more than one wife. But under certain personal and social conditions granting leave as a last resort to polygamy is of greater utility than putting a complete ban on it. That is the reason why Islam permitted it conditionally.

Why Polygamy?

There are three suppositions as to the number of men to that of women in any given society from dawn of history to the present time: (1) The number of 'men equals to that of women. (2) The number of women surpasses that of men (3) The number of men is more than that of women.

The first case was during the oldest times, during the time of our father Adam and our mother Eve (Hawwa). It went on up to the time of Abil (Haabill) and Cain (Qaabill).

Adam had one wife: Eve, and each of his children did not have more than one wife. This was the beginning of monogamy, or better still the True Monogamy that was ever practised. In such a society where circumstances equated the number of both the sexes. There was an equal number of men and women. It was then, very difficult for a man to divorce his wife and marry another one. It was too risky to do something like that. He might have not been able to procure one. Women were very rare then.

The second supposition is that, there are more women than men at a certain period in a particular society, because of the standard of living they are in and the general cleanliness they have reached, or because of the calamities, that had befallen them, and in which men are much more exposed to and become easier victims than women generally are, especially in calamities of war, plague or famine. This generally applies to our present day society. Women as widows are left behind when men get killed in a war, hence it is essential to have more than one wife.

Going back to 25 years ago and raking up my brains, I recollect to have read something which meant: "It is of some supernatural wisdom that men are much more exposed to dangers than women are. Had a disaster befallen the world and lost three quarters of its men, then the befit solution could be to adopt and practise the Islamic Law, and marry four wives, so that the world could compensate what it had lost."

When a catastrophe falls on any society and it loses some of its male members, there normally become a lot of widows whose husbands have died because of it. Generally these widows have some children with them. It is very much difficult for an ordinary society to shoulder full responsibility over them. There should be some individual men who could maintain some of these women. Not only that, but also there is a stigma of unmarried women, who are badly in a need for the support of a man. There are many other problems which could be well done and treated had there been a religious tie between the man (supporter) and the woman (supported) i.e., marriage. This makes us recollect what German women were demanding for polygamy after the World War, II when many men died and there were a lot of widows, unmarried women and orphans. There were insufficient men to marry them. They were raising the slogans demanding for polygamy or lent husbands. The second supposition was and it still is the case with some of the North European countries (parts of Scandinavia), and it is also the case in Europe in general after the two World Wars. The loss in the World War I was 10 million and in the World War II it was more than 60 million.

The Last and Third Supposition: there are more men than women in a particular society at a given time. Could such a society practise polyandry? But, generally speaking, will a woman, who is a real lady, agree to be the wife of more than one husband simultaneously? Where is her honour, her prestige and respect? Who among those many a husband, is going to be the father of the child she begets?

It is sin in Islam to name a child after anyone else other than his natural father. Hence it forbade an adopted child to be called after the name of his adopter.

Secondly, if we go very deep and analyse the composition of both man and woman, we come to the conclusion that, they differ widely in their fertility. A woman can beget one child only in one year; while a man can have more than that number. This is true in all male living things: One, male date palm can pollinate tens of female date palms; one bull; by means of artificial insemination or through natural means; can inseminate tens of cows, etc. There is an uproar today with the people demanding equal rights for women as those for man.

Let us take very simple examples of the things that are agreed to be feminist, and are more or less done by women as part of their duty. Those things are cooking, embroidery, knitting, sewing, cosmetics, mourning, entertainment, joking, and laughter.

We find a male cook surpassing a female one in quick and good service, in quality of the food, in inventing new varieties or ways of cooking, etc.

In cosmetics, all the women who attend beauty parlours prefer their hair be done by male dressers rather than by female ones, because men have a better know-how of hair, thinning or eye pencilling. The same thing applies to the make ups taken by actors and actresses in theatre or stage.

Male singers and dancers have better performance than female ones. "Women generally prefer to have their dress made by male tailors and outfitters rather than by seamstresses."

So, why then, do we stop men to utilise their natural instincts of procreation telling them to practise polyandry. Man is a reasonable creature who can use his gifts by diverting the outlet of his energies. Personally, I do not remember to have heard of any society where there had been or have been more men than women. I would like to know. One might tend to think, that in the Gulf States there are less women than men, as the younger generation tend to go to Iran, India, Pakistan or Egypt and now to East Africa to find wives and get married there. It is not because of the shortage of women in this area, as there are people with up to four wives. Just in the village where I am writing these lines there are 80/100 houses and huts. I know ten people from the village with more than one wife each. The younger generation tend to marry abroad for some reasons: Dowry is too high in the area and many girls are, not well accomplished, and because of a change.

Even though, and regardless of whether there could be a society here, there are more men than women, there is a clear cut evidence that women generally get married, at a much earlier age than men do. Riding the chariot of history and going back to times immemorial we and the similar case. Just because girls got matured 2 to 6 years earlier before boys.

So in this case Islam would advise such a society where there are more men than women; to practise monogamy and young men who cannot, find wives for themselves are to observe fasting, because fasting, and not sublimation is the best remedy for sexual urges. Fasting should be in its true Islamic sense.

The Messenger of Allah is quoted as saying "O! ye young men, anyone of you who can afford marrying should got married. If some of you cannot afford marrying (for some reasons): then they should observe fasting...."

Fasting distracts the eyes from looking at the forbidden (the other sex) and protects the one who fasts from committing any illegal sexual intercourse.

Natural Differences : It is unanimously agreed that in every hundred adults, we got the ratio of at least 52 women to 48 men. Sometimes the number of women surpasses that of men. Suppose every man in such a society gets married to a woman. We still find four unmarried women out of hundred people. Multiply this population wise; we get an incredible number of unmarried women. The unmarried women form 4 per cent of the population. What is the society to do when it is on the horns of such dilemma? These unmarried women might get all the necessities of life and luxury that could be available then, but they miss one important thing: husband.

To a woman marriage is all her vocation in life, whether she is a doctor, teacher etc., no matter how excellent she is at her work yet her sub-conscious aim is that of having a family of her own shared by a good man, who is the father of her children. Mothers always think of their daughters being married to the best husbands possible.

Marriage means quiet of mind, rest, security, independent home, bringing up children and countless other things. That is why our present day life is full of young men who deceive naive girls by telling them that they are going to marry them. Our young girls take such words as a promise. They generally sacrifice the best thing that a girl could possess, honour and chastity, at the altar of the promised marriage. And when the young men get what they need they run away from those poor girls under many pretexts. This is one of the follies of Neo Jahilia. Oh ! those poor girls. They must be more precautions, as they say: Once bitten, twice shy.

Moreover, the period of fertility in men goes up to an average age of seventy, while in women it stops at the age of 45/50. There is a difference of at least twenty years of fertility in men which is not found in women. The Apostle of Allah urged Muslims to marry fertile women, so as to increase Muslim population, as it was suggested before. So polygamy provided very good opportunity to fertile men whose wives can no more give birth to children.

Furthermore, the wife could be sick (she could not satisfy her husband for one reason or another) or she might be sterile. If both of them go for a medical check up and the results show that only one of the couple is barren, while the other is fertile. They discuss their problem and come to a conclusion: either accepting their star as it is and live together without thinking of children or separation. It is too early, to depend on test-tube babies.

In such a case Islam has looked into the humanitarian side of the wife. Suppose she is barren and divorced. Then the possibilities of her being married by someone else after people knowing her case are almost nil. It will be much more logical if a rival is there, and she retains all her marital rights, rather than her being sacked to the streets. A wife is to answer to the call of her husband whenever he calls her to bed, even though she were fasting an optional (Nafl) fast. The only times Islam does not require her to answer to his call are when she is during her forty days of confinement after child bearing, during menstruation period and when she is observing a mandatory (fard) fast mostly.

Suppose a woman is married to a virile husband and she is either in her parturition or menstruation and husband calls her. He wants to see his wife several times daily. What is such a husband going to do? Is he to sleep with his wife under such condition or is he to commit adultery? Each of the two evils is worse than the other.

If we go very deep into the meaning of the Quranic verse that permits polygamy, we shall find something amazing. The same verse categorically restricts it: Let us read the verse thoroughly:

> *"....If ye fear ye shall not be able to deal justly with the orphans, marry women of your choice two, three or four; but if ye fear that ye shall not be able to deal justly with them, then marry only one, or a captive that your right hands possess, that will be more suitable to prevent you from doing injustice ...."* *(Quran 4: 3)*

One would ask, "Is there any connection between the treating of orphans and marrying several wives, as both are mentioned together?"

The answer is a positive Yes.

When Muslims were told before not to earn or spend the property of the orphans, they became much afraid of any other reprimand. They, then, refrained from doing injustice to the orphans and were very careful in their dealings with them, yet, they were not afraid of doing injustice to all or some of their wives.

There is another reason. We are told that Urwa bin Zubayr asked Hadrat Aishah bint Abu Bakr the true meaning of the verse. Hadrat Aishah said "O! cousin, an orphan girl would be brought up by her guardian who might be attracted by either her beauty or wealth. He would marry her and would not treat her justly. This verse forbids such a treatment." Generally if the guardian did not want to marry her, he might give one of his relative to marry her and it always happened without the girl's consent.

Man is required to deal justly with his wives in all matters within his limits, mainly in matters pertaining to maintenance in all its aspects. He is to divide the time he spends between his wives equally well, especially his nights. He is to buy them things, food and clothes of the same quality.

When the Prophet (peace be upon him) was on his death bed; he was carried to all his wives' rooms in turn. And when he was seriously ill, he asked all his wives to allow him to remain at Aishah for treatment. They all agreed and after a few days he left this moving world of ours.

Such a man who was dealing with his wives in such a way even on his death bed, yet he felt that there was something wrong, Love. He could not divide his love equally between them as it was something far beyond human control. He is quoted as saying "Allah! Almighty! This is my share to my wives in all what is under my control and ability. Forgive me O Lord and don't blame me on what You are in control, and I cannot control or do anything about it."

The Prophet's saying could be a true interpretation of the verse which some people misunderstand.

> *"Ye will not be able to deal equally between (your) wives however much ye wish (to do so). But turn not altogether away (from one) leaving her in suspense....."(Quran 4: 129)*

The gist of the verse is: deal with your wives justly, try your utmost and leave the rest to Allah.

Polygamy Already There

When Islam came into being polygamy was there in varying degrees in different parts of the universe in all the diversity of cultures as we have just seen. Polygamy was practised by the Jews, Christians, Buddhists, Brahmans, Pre-Islamic Arabs.

We cannot label Islam and say it created polygamy as some non-Muslims tend to say. Allah forbid. All that Islam did about polygamy was to organise it and restrict it to four wives under strict rule of justice.

Here I would like to point out one important thing. There were and still are and will be people who misuse what is given to them. In that case it is wrong to blame the authority or the giver, but we are to blame the person who misuses what he is given. There was a time when people used to enslave others and sell them. This state of affairs was the rule of the time, and it went on up to the nineteenth century of the Christian Era. This is completely contrary to the teachings of Islam.

POLYANDRY

In Islam a child must be called after the name of its natural father; and under polyandry it is very difficult to pin point the real father of the child, as there could be more than two husbands to the wife.

It also refutes the idea of polygyny under which a husband has marriage rights, over the younger sisters of his wife. To this Quran gives a full list of those one may not marry:

> *"Forbidden unto you are your mothers and, your daughters, and your sisters, and your fathers' sisters (aunts); and your mother's sisters, and your brothers' daughters and your sisters' daughters and your foster mothers and your foster sisters, and your mother-in-law, and your step-daughters who are under, your protection (born) of your women unto whom ye have gone in but if ye have not gone in unto them, then it is no sin for you to marry their daughters and the wives of your sons who (spring) from your own loins. And (it is forbidden unto you) that ye have two sisters together, except what has already happened (of that nature) in the past.,"* *(Quran 4: 23)*

It is forbidden in Islam to marry two sisters together because there could be misunderstanding between them, instead of mutual understanding and cooperation. But one I can marry, his former wife's sister provided he had divorced the first one and the Iddat is over or after her death.

No Mistress

Islam strictly opposes the idea of a man keeping a woman without first marrying her. It also forbids men to go to houses of pleasure, where they can easily contact with all sorts and kinds of people. Contagious diseases can easily spread in the community. A man who does these things loses prestige and respect in his family, contemporaries and the society as a whole. The offspring from such a mixture, that is out of wedlock becomes a burden to the society. They are generally unsettled and neurotic if they are lucky enough to survive, because usually their mothers get rid of them somehow to hide away from shame.

During school age a fatherless child is not only burden to society, but to himself as well; because he had hardly got full parental love (especially the paternal love). His situation is worse than that of another child of a separated family. The ultimate result could easily be a criminal, hitting back, as it were, against the society at large which had put a stigma on fatherless men and women. This is more so in the Eastern societies.

Natural Law

It is true to say that Allah has made and created us as individuals therefore people differ very much in their constitution. We find that some men are more virile than others; therefore they need more than one wife. Islam provides an excellent solution in allowing a man to marry up to a maximum of four wives, provided he gives them equal maintenance and deals with them, justly. Islam is the natural law. It is the human law, it goes side by side with his innate requirements. It corresponds with the dynamic wishes of different epochs.

From times immemorial to the present day our daily life depicts cases of certain people who are more virile than others. Their sexual urge is so strong that they have to find some means of satisfaction. They find difficulty if they cannot get satisfaction from their wives, at a time when the wives are under certain circumstances that stop them from satisfying their husbands.

Islam has arranged and solved this problem in the best form. It has given chance to those who are not satisfied with one wife to have more than one in the legal and legitimate way. It should not be misunderstood and thought that polygamy is for the sexually abnormal people only. No, it is not so. It is more than that. It solves many other problems as well.

One of the good things that polygamy does is to increase the Muslim population., where it is not as high as it is expected. Take for example: Libya, Syria, Sudan, Iran, Iraq, Saudi Arabia or Pakistan; where Allah has endowed the first with petroleum, the second with perpetual spring, the third with fertility of virgin land, the fourth with three rivers (Tigris, Euphrates and petroleum) the fifth with minerals and the sixth with cultivable land, so to speak, with enough rain, sunshine and fertile soils for food production for home use and export in exchange for other essentials needed. And in this way we could go a long way in helping FAO and other International Organisations that tell us that the world is going to starve if it does not take to birth control and family planning.

Muslim countries can learn a lot about agriculture from Arturo Tanco, the Philippines Secretary of Agriculture who master-minded and implemented his country's programmes which enabled his country which once was rice deficit country to build up enormous rice buffer stocks.

Philippine uses the most up-to-date weapons to fight Muslims; Moro National Liberation Front (MNLF) on one hand; and on the other uses the most up-to-date methods of agriculture to fight the poverty stricken country to one self-sufficient in food stuff. It may soon be having extra food for export.

It is said that the population of Egypt is 35 million and the ratio of Christians to Muslims was 1: 7. It is also reported that many a Muslim took into birth control for many reasons while Christians did not. Let us wait and see the results.

The following Hadith (Saying of the Prophet) bears witness of the aforementioned facts, viz., increase of Muslim population. The Hadith narrates: A man came to the Holy Prophet (peace be upon him) and told him: "O! Allah's Apostle, such and such a woman is very beautiful, but is infertile. Can I marry her?" Messenger of Allah responded, "No, don't marry her." This was repeated twice and with the same reply.

When the Prophet was asked for the third time, he answered. "No .... marry the fertile, the beloved, because I shall be proud before all the nations because of the biggest number of Muslims (my followers)."

The Messenger of Allah did not allow the man to marry the beautiful woman to stop those who get married just for the sake of sexual entertainment. It should not be taken that, Islam does not allow marrying sterile women. Far be it. It only encourages to get married to a pumpkin eater to increase the Muslim population.

Ad-Daar Qutny and At-Tabary quote from the Apostle as saying: "Marry and do not divorce, because Allah does not like men and women who get married to taste each other or who marry for sex (love) only."

People are to marry to preserve the human species and not for enjoyment only.

Birth Control

This is one of the major evils of the Neo Jahilia. The Pre-Islamic Arabs used to kill their children for fear of want. Infanticide was common in Arabia. Even now it is not unknown in some societies because of economic reasons. To this Quran says:

> *"Kill not your children for fear of want: We shall provide sustenance for them as well as for you. Verily the killing of them is a great sin.",* *(17: 31)*
>
> *"Lost are those who slay their children from folly, without knowledge, and forbid food which Allah hath provided for them, inventing (lies) against Allah. They have indeed gone astray and have no guidance."* *(6 :141)*
>
> *"Say: Come I will rehearse what Allah hath (really) prohibited you from .... kill not children on a plea of want;- We provide sustenance for you and for them ;- come not nigh to shameful deeds..."* *(6 :151)*

Islam has forbidden infanticide, anti as we have seen while discussing the status of Slavonic women, abortion was known long ago. But people did not like to use it too much because it endangers the women's life.

The Neo Jahilia not only encourages infanticide and abortion, but it has invented a fatal weapon birth control under the same pretext fear of want. The calamity of the twentieth century Muslims is that "when one pipes somewhere, all the Muslims dance." The average income has increased tenfold and the essentials of life have not increased so much. Why is there any fear of want, then? I see, it comes out of luxuries. We should not forget what role advertisements could play. And that is why you find some of the merchants are prepared to invest 80 per cent or more of the capital on advertisement and the remaining on the commodity. This is at least so in the initial stage. But we are not children, are we? So why, then, do we fall victims of suggestion?

May, I remind fellow Muslims, of the saying of the Prophet: When a man asked his advice on marrying a very beautiful sterile woman, and the Messenger's answer; No, do not marry barren women, marry pumpkin eaters. I shall be proud before all the other nations because of the large number of my followers. Let us consider the fertility of the Muslim land, their resources, the natural enemies that surround them, and compare with their population. Arabia; especially Gulf States; suffer from the lack of manpower because of its low population, you find hundreds of thousands of Sikhs, Gurkhas, Marathis, all working in the Gulf states. And yet, people practice birth control.

Origin of Family Planning

What we call today birth control, birth limitation or family planning, was engineered by the famous British economist Malthus some time in 1797, when he found that the population in Britain was increasing alarmingly. He thought that a time would come when there would be no sufficient place and food for such a big population. To stop the population expansion he advised his people to remain single. If they ever wanted to get married they should do so when they were advanced in age. They should try their level best to refrain sexual intercourse, lest they should get many children.

A hundred years later, in 1897, we hear Sir William Crooks; Chairman of the British Association, repeating in their words what Malthus had said,, saying the present means compared with the ever increasing world population will not be sufficient for more than thirty years from then.

They were right in a way, as the population explosion is a tremendous thing. Let us take British as an example. The population in Britain jumped from 12 millions in 1797 to 38 millions in 1897 and to 52 millions in 1977; and yet those present have better standards of living than their ancestors had. This took place regardless of all the necessary precautions taken. All contraceptives are available free from the National Health Service.

In France we come across Francis Palace, in the eighteenth century, advising people to use tablets and drugs to limit the birth rate. The aftermath of such steps was that France had to pay heavily during the two World Wars because of the shortage of population which affected France army. In 1975 France made all contraceptives available free for the public.

Europe learnt a very good lesson from the birth limitations. We see them then forming National Birth Rate; League of National Life, Marriage Loan, etc.

We hear one of the war Marshalle saying after the Worid War, "One of the main causes of our defeat in the war was we have Too Few Children."

We come across varieties of contraceptives. To name but a few, we hear of condom, pill, sterilization, intra urine device (ITD) and natural rhythm.

If you happen to ask the preachers and well-wishers of Family Planning and their itinerants they will say that voluntary sterilization has become more popular as it is regarded as the contraceptive phenomena of the seventies. In Japan condom is the most popular, while pill closely follows sterilization in the industrialised countries.

Sweden has removed all obstacles to sterilization, while Singapore legalised sterilization for consenting married couples. Indonesia mobilised village leaders to spread the programme.

Birth limitation was at full swing in India during the Emergency (from June, 1975 to March, 1977) when all democratic institutions were suspended. During that period Sanjay Gandhi, son of the Prime Minister Indira Gandhi, waged a war to implement sterilization. All the government servants were ordered to produce a certain number of cases for sterilization otherwise their salaries were withheld. There were no renewal of licences before the production of sterilization certificates. Any resistance was met by beating or firing. During the Emergency more than 10 million people were sterilized. Bruce Stokes gives us very good figures of the number of people who used contraceptives. He says that 75 million couples use sterilization around the world in contrast to — the pill 55 million, the condom 50 million, the intra urine device 15 million and other contraceptives 65 million. This brings us to 240 million people who use one type of birth control or another. One of the ills of contraceptives is that we have some deformed children who become a great burden to the society.

Ample Place and Resources

The preachers and well wishers of Family Planning claim that there is no room for all of us under the sun because of the population expansion and the means of livelihood are limited, forgetting that it is Allah who has the full control of all the things. Although people use a lot of contraceptives, yet more than seventy per cent of them fail as the pill generally becomes ineffective for one reason or, another. They are, then, forced to use abortion. Strange though; this is much more common with the people of the upper class in the society.

The Holy Quran tells us: "And there is not a thing, but its (source and) treasures (inexhaustible) are with Us; but We only send down thereof in due and ascertainable measures."

There is no problem regarding lack of room or place. Before us are Bahrain and Netherlands reclaiming, land. There are deserts and swarms and because of the highly advanced technology we can utilize all these sources that nature supplied us. A very good example that comes to my mind is the Amazon Basin that could accommodate the whole population of Europe which is one of the most densely populated part of the world, giving allowance to natural phenomena such as torrented rains, insaturated and high humidity.

Coming to food we see that only 10 per cent of the world cultivable land has been utilised for cultivation. Let us cultivate more land and make arrangements of interchange of commodity because the fertility of land differs from place to place.

Industrialization has urbanised people and made the farms in some parts to be deserted completely.

It is pointed out that people with limited income cannot meet the high standards of living and cannot give their children the best type of education they think would be suitable for them.

So far science has not been able to pin point which of the 220 millions or more spermatozoa will be able to penetrate into the egg cell or Ovum and which out of the 400,000 Ovarian is fully matured for fertilization.

As we all know that man inherits certain things from his ancestors. They, could go back down to his seventh grandparent. We cannot say for certain whether the child is going to be a boy or girl; a genius or a moron; an invalid or a healthy one. So why risk then, let us have as many children as Allah (or call it Nature if you want so) provide with; and give them the best education we can afford to. In that case we shall be doing a healthy thing, especially if the children are brought up with some sort of hardship. They say: vicissitudes are the salts of life. If we bring up our children with some kind of difficulty, they will be better world citizens on whom we could depend to solve many problem, as this will help them to paddle the canoe pleasantly through thick and thin with no delinquency before showing by our youth and neither complainers when grown up.

Bibliography

Abdullah, Muhammad : *Islamic Prayers,* Idara Ishaat-e-Diniyat Pvt. Ltd, New Delhi, 1999.

Ahmad, Ilyas : *Social Contract and the Islamic State,* Urdu Publishing House, Allahabad, 1940.

Ahmad, K. N. : *Muslim Law of Divorce,* Kitab Bhavan, New Delhi, 1988.

Ahmad, Khurshid : *Islam : its Meaning and Message,* Islamic Council of Europe, London, 1976.

Ahmad, Naseem : *Liberation of Muslim Women,* Gyan Books Pvt., Ltd., New Delhi, 2001.

Anwarullah : *The Islamic Law of Evidence,* Kitab Bhavan, New Delhi, 2000.

Arvind, Sharma : *Women in World Religion,* New York Press, New York, 1990.

Azmi, Majaz : *Muslim Wife,* Idara Ishaat-e-Diniyat Pvt. Ltd, New Delhi, 1991.

Baksh, S. K. : *Politics in Islam,* Kitab Bhavan, New Delhi, 2003.

Batty and Morgan : *War its Conduct and Legal Results,* Feroz Pub., Lahore, 2000.

Crone, Patricia : *Themes in Islamic History,* Cambridge University Press, New Delhi, 2000.

Dawud, Rahbar : *God of Justice,* Mac & Jac Pub., Leiden, 1960.

Engineer, Asghar Ali : *Islam : Women and Gender Justice,* Gyan Books Pvt. Ltd., New Delhi, 2001.

Gonda, J. : *History of Indian Literature,* University Press, Wiesbaden, 1973.

Hasan, S. Badrul : *Muslim Behaviour,* Kitab Bhavan, New Delhi, 1991.

Helminski : *Women of Sufism : a Hidden Treasure,* New Academic Publishers, New Delhi, 1990.

Hussain, M. Hadi : *Imam Abu Hanifah : Life and Work,* Kitab Bhavan, New Delhi, 2001.

Jotwani, Motilal : *Sufis of Sindh,* Publications Division, New Delhi, 1991.

Karnal, A. Faruqui : *Islam : Today and Tomorrow,* Deep & Deep Pub., New Delhi, 1989.

Mac, Closky : *Pacts for Peace,* New Century Pub., London, 1980.

Menon, M. Indu : *Status of Muslims Women in India,* Uppal Publishing House, New Delhi, 1993.

Mir, Valiuddin : *Love of God,* Amit Pub., Hyderabad, 1968.

Noorani, A.G. : *Islam and Jihad,* Manohar Publishers, New Delhi, 2002.

Rahim, Abdur : *Principles of Islamic Jurisprudence,* Kitab Bhavan, New Delhi, 1994.

Roberts, Robert : *The Social Laws of Islam,* Williams and Morgate, Ltd., London, 1925.

Sabiruddin : *Muslim Husband and Wife : Right and Duties,* Kitab Bhavan, New Delhi, 2000.

Shaikh, N. M. : *Women in Muslim Society,* Kitab Bhavan, New Delhi, 1991.

Sharma, S.R. : *Women's Education in Ancient and Muslim Period,* Discovery Publishing House, New Delhi, 1996.

Smith, M. : *Al-Ghazzali : the Mystic,* MacMillan & Co., London, 1944.

Stern, S.M. : *Fatimid Decrees,* Faber and Faber, London, 1964.

Ullah, M. : *Administration of Justice in Islam,* Kitab Bhavan, New Delhi, 1990.

Usmani, J.M. Tariq : *The Authority of Sunnah,* Kitab Bhavan, New Delhi, 1998.

Watt, M. : *Muslim Intellectual : a Study of al-Ghazzali,* Edinburgh University Press, Edinburgh, 1959.

Whitting, C.E.J. : *Al-Fakhri,* Oxford, London, 1947.

Wilfred, Seamen Blunt : *The Future of Islam,* Macmillan, London, 1991.

Zahid, Malik : *Subjects of Quran,* Kitab Bhavan, New Delhi, 1998.

Index

E

F

G

H

I

❑❑❑